JOE DARLING

Cricketer, Farmer, Politician and Family Man

Bernard Whimpress & Graeme Ryan

RYAN PUBLISHING

RYAN PUBLISHING

First published 2018 by Ryan Publishing
PO Box 7680,
Melbourne, 3004 Victoria,
Australia

Ph: 61 3 9505 6820
Fax: 61 3 9505 6821
Email: books@ryanpub.com Website: www.ryanpub.com

 A catalogue record for this book is available from the National Library of Australia

Title: Joe Darling: *Cricketer, Farmer, Politician and Family Man*

ISBN: 978 1 876498 75 7 (Paperback)
ISBN: 978 1 876498 69 6 (Hardback)
ISBN: 978 1 876498 93 1 (Leather Bound)
Notes: Includes references, index, appendixes, statistics and bibliography.

Copyright © Bernard Whimpress and Graeme Ryan

Apart from any fair dealing for the purposes of private study, research, criticism or review, as permitted under the Copyright Act, no part may be reproduced by any process without written permission. Inquiries should be addressed to the publisher.
Internal design by Luke Harris, Working Type Studio, Victoria, Australia. www.workingtype.com.au

Other Creators/Contributors: Graeme Ryan, editor.
　　　　　　　　　　　　　　　Terri Mackenzie, indexer.
　　　　　　　　　　　　　　　Moe Khin Thar, website.
COVER: Designed by Luke Harris, Clare Cannon and Graeme Ryan.

FRONT COVER:

Foreground

Joe Darling, c.1895

Background

Australian Team at Germantown CC, Philadelphia, USA. September 1896.

Thumbnails

Joe and WG Grace making their final appearance as opposing captains, Australians v South of England at Hastings, September 1905.

Darling House at 64 Fullarton Road, Norwood, purchased by John Darling jnr in 1886.

Family photograph taken at Florence Darling's wedding on 7 December 1904.

Scoreboard at the Adelaide Oval in 1893 showing Joe's 32 runs in the second innings against NSW.

BACK COVER

Background

Prince Alfred College, late 1880s, as it would have appeared when Joe was a student.

Thumbnails

Photograph by George Beldam of Joe practising at Lord's, 1905.

Election pamphlet when Joe stood for the last time in 1945.

Etching by J.C. Goodhart, c.1930. Giant Poppet Head, North Mine, Broken Hill.

John Darling & Son flour mill and grain silos at Albion, Victoria.

Clare Cannon is the founder of Cricket Without Borders which takes young women from Victoria around the world to play cricket and develop the game. She also sits on the Committee of the Melbourne Cricket Club and is a former Chair of the Women of the MCC. Away from sport, Clare runs Woomargama Station on the NSW/Victorian border. She has also sat on the boards of Earthwatch Australia, the Melbourne Community Foundation and the Council of St Catherine's School in Melbourne. Clare is married to Andrew and they have four children and two corgis.

Bernard Whimpress is a writer, editor, niche publisher and former curator of the Adelaide Oval Museum. The author of more than 30 books (mainly sports history), his best known cricket titles include *The Official MCC Story of the Ashes*, *The Greatest Ashes Battles* and, *Passport to Nowhere: Aborigines in Australian Cricket 1850-1939*. He published and edited the Australian cricket history journal *Baggy Green* between 1998 and 2010.

Since the early 1980s, Graeme Ryan has worked as writer, editor and publisher across many subject areas ranging from corporate finance, business and strategic planning to biographies and sport. In recent years his emphasis on sport has increased with the production of *Sport in Victoria: A History*, *Discovering Alex Russell* and *Stableford: A Life in Golf, Medicine and War*. These have been complemented by many other works for newspapers, magazines, television programs and the internet.

Artwork of Joe Darling, Empire's Cricketers by Chevalier Taylor which draws on the George Beldam photograph of 1905.

Foreword

It seems that the love of the 'Great Game' is passed down through the DNA. As I delved deeper into family photographs, I found many of the men in cricket whites and blazers—but just fleetingly. Sport was never seen as a serious or fitting profession. In the early years merchant, married woman and spinster featured heavily.

I always had a fascination for the man pictured in family photographs next to the legendary, larger than life, figure of WG Grace. My knowledge was a little sketchy: an extraordinary batting record as a schoolboy, the first six in Test cricket, a property in the midlands of Tasmania (enigmatically named Stonehenge) and 15 children!

I yearned to learn more.

My journey started in November 2017 in the library at the Bellerive Cricket Ground in Hobart. I was on a mission to find more about Joe and meet some of my Tasmanian relatives of whom I had met none. I must admit that I was disappointed when the librarian at Bellerive told me that the permanent Joe Darling exhibition had been taken down and he didn't know anything about relatives. Somewhat disconsolately, I was looking around the museum when the librarian returned.

"There is only one of you looking for Joe Darling relatives isn't there?" he asked.

"Yes," I replied.

"Well, there is a Joe Darling relative on the phone," he told me.

It transpired that Joe's grand daughter, Mary Burdon, had phoned the Bellerive Library at that moment to speak about donating a sporting trophy of Joe's. I had found my first relative!

Born into a staunch Congregational family, Joe was a man of principle, fairness and vision. His father, John, actively disapproved of Joe's pastime of playing cricket when he could have been working in the family wheat and farming business. John had to use some coercion to persuade Joe to leave cricket and did so by buying his son a rabbit infested farm in the midlands of Tasmania to earn a living. But the story does not end there.

As I searched deeper, I found more about Joe's cricketing life, his public life and his family life. I strongly felt that Joe's story needed to be told. Thus, it has been a great pleasure to commission Graeme Ryan and Bernard Whimpress to produce this biography of my great great uncle, Joe Darling.

Graeme has dug deep into family records and consulted genealogists to put together comprehensive family trees. Bernard has mused over old scorecards at Prince Alfred College and the Adelaide Oval. My husband, Andrew, has visited the CC Morris Cricket Library in Philadelphia to find photographs from when Joe and his team played there in 1896. Mary Burdon and David Darling, newly found relatives, gave much support and encouragement to the project as have other Darling relatives and family friends. Thank you to all who have so kindly supported this book. It has been a joyful project. I think Joe would approve!

Clare Cannon
September 2018

CONTENTS

Foreword v
Acknowledgements viii
Preface ix
    A Brief Portrait 1
    Young Joe 1870-87 3
    On The Land 1888-93 13
    Fledgling Player 1893-96 21
    First English Tour 1896 33
    Ascending The Peak 1896-99 41
    Second English Tour 1899 61
    New Directions 1899-1902 73
    Third English Tour 1902 85
    Second Interval And After 1903-05 97
    Fourth English Tour 1905 105
    Towards The Pavilion 1905-08 115
    End Of Play And Return 119
    Players 127
    Battles With The Board 137
    Beyond The Boundary 145
    Footballer 1885-95 157
    Pastoralist And Patriarch 165
    Politician 169
    Legend And Legacy 181
    Statistics 187
Appendix I: Family Trees 190
Appendix II: John Darling senior 207
Appendix III: John Darling junior 209
Appendix IV: Harold Darling 211
Appendix V: Gordon Darling 213
Appendix VI: David Darling 215
Appendix VI: Stonehenge 217
Appendix VII: Claremont House 221
Bibliography 227
Index 231

Acknowledgements

We are most thankful for Clare Cannon's inspiration to initiate this project and placing her trust in us to bring it to completion. She was a constant source of energy and encouragement. Also, to Luke Harris, our book designer and artistic adviser, who provided special expertise and patiently endured our many foibles and corrections.

Trove, the National Library of Australia's search engine, is the first point of call for many historical research projects. Much trawling was done through numerous references from newspapers nationwide to establish the building blocks for the narrative.

Of persons linked to institutions, Naomi Setchell and Tony Aldous at the Prince Alfred College archives provided access to Joe's school records, academic and sporting, which enlarged the picture of his life there; Mark Boucher from Pulteney Grammar School archive produced records of the enrolments of some of Joe's older brothers at the school; Sue Coppin of the University of Adelaide archives gave useful leads concerning his attendance at the Roseworthy Agricultural College.

Other significant providers were Melbourne Cricket Club librarians David Studham and Trevor Ruddell; Mariko Inagaki at the National Sports Museum; Gill McClelland at the Tasmanian Cricket Museum; Neil Robinson at the MCC Library, Lord's; Michael Fahey of Sports Memorabilia Australia.

Many current members of the Darling family generously contributed information about their relatives, children and grandchildren in mainland Australia. In Tasmania, Mary Burdon was very helpful. Others in Tasmania are Eliot McShane and Joel Van Sanden (current owners of Stonehenge and Claremont House respectively), historian Dianne Snowden and the eclectic Greg Ramsay.

Several sports historians provided important information, especially cricket historians Ray Webster in Melbourne, Rick Finlay in Hobart and Geoff Sando in Adelaide who are well respected for their depth of knowledge and attention to detail. Others supplied further details, and these include Robert Laidlaw regarding Joe's role in sport in Gawler, Reonaldo Cialini covering his career with the Norwood Football Club, Trevor Gyss for his football in both Adelaide and the country and John Lysikatos for his time at the Sturt Cricket Club.

Bernard Whimpress
Graeme Ryan
September 2018

Preface

As a South Australian historian, I have been interested in the major contributions to Australian cricket made by four giants of the game in the years before World War I. Hence, I have a written a short biography of fast bowler Ernie Jones; edited and annotated a memoir by Clem Hill; and written several articles, a couple of booklets on George Giffen. Yet, Joe Darling's story remained to be told.

I was thus delighted when Clare Cannon, Joe's great-great niece, decided to produce this book and publisher Graeme Ryan contacted me early this year to write this first major biography of Darling. It has presented some challenges, notably a short deadline, which certainly concentrated the mind. The exercise proved to be an excellent partnership with some division of labour.

At the outset I thought that I would concentrate on cricket and leave family affairs to Graeme. However, to know the cricketer it is necessary to know his roots and thus the background of his father John whose religious beliefs and business success would impinge on the formation of Joe's character. It required a boy of special character to bat for six hours and make a double-century in an intercollegiate cricket match.

My approach to writing about Joe's cricket was to cover all aspects including school, country, senior club cricket in Adelaide, for South Australia, Australia, and down the grades when in his fifties in Tasmania. Also, to provide the context for the career, it was necessary to examine his early life and education at Prince Alfred College and Roseworthy Agricultural College, his relocation to Burra and Mundoora, his football which fully occupied his winter seasons, and all before returning to the city to open a sports store as a young married man in 1893.

Past historians have passed over Joe's years in the country in his early twenties, yet his transformation from bush player to Test cricketer within two years was astonishing. Joe rapidly established himself in the Australian side, became a leader as captain of South Australian and Australian teams and as a state and national administrator. For these reasons his views on the governance of Australian cricket, the welfare of players, as well as their particular qualities as men and cricketers, were interesting and often forcibly expressed.

Joe's Test career encompassed the years from 1894 to 1905 with two major breaks as he established a major sheep grazing property at Stonehenge in Tasmania to ensure a secure future for himself and growing family. These matters are dealt with in later chapters along with his political career in the Tasmanian parliament and his long-term influence on Australian cricket.

Questions have often been raised of the relationship between Joe and other Australian Test-playing Darlings. Previous publications have sometimes stated that 1970s opening batsman Rick Darling is Joe's great-nephew but exhaustive research by historian Geoff Sando has concluded otherwise. Rick's great-great-grandfather (Robert Darling) is almost certainly a brother of Joe's father (John Darling). This would make Rick a first cousin three times removed from Joe. Further research by Sando has revealed that there is absolutely no evidence of any relationship between Joe and 1930s middle-order batsman Len Darling.

For fuller details of the wider Darling family history including genealogies and biographical details, however, it is necessary for me to hand over the baton to Graeme Ryan to elucidate on these matters.

Bernard Whimpress
Adelaide, September 2018

When Clare Cannon approached me to write and publish a biography of Joe Darling, I immediately thought of contacting Bernard Whimpress to come on board as co-author. Thankfully, he willingly agreed then set about the task with energy and enthusiasm. This revealed his passion for the subject, together with great skill based on knowledge and experience, which he committed to the writing of Joe's biography.

My role was to research the Darling family since the early 19th century in Scotland to the present day, assemble information and construct family trees. This turned out to be much more than I expected since, at first, family records were sketchy, incomplete and often inaccurate. However, as the task progressed, and with the help of many current family members, it started to take shape and the results of this work are included as appendixes in this book.

Since John Darling snr arrived in Adelaide in 1855 with his wife and two infant boys, the history of the family could readily be the subject of another book. Through the generations, many Darling men and women have made extraordinary contributions to Australia across a wide range of industries including farming and grazing, grain milling, shipping, mining, mineral processing, manufacturing and export trading. Also, they have contributed enormously in the areas of state politics, philanthropy, business management, sport, education and the arts.

Appendixes in this book include histories and descriptions of Joe's main properties in Tasmania, Stonehenge and Claremont House. Also, there are short biographies of four Darlings who became known as outstanding Australians because of their careers and what they gave to the nation. Many more could be added.

Graeme Ryan
Melbourne, September 2018

A BRIEF PORTRAIT

Joe Darling knew the measure of his own life.

While he had a major career as a pastoralist and in political life it is as a sportsman (mainly a cricketer) that he is chiefly remembered. As first points of call, this is conveyed by his son Douglas's entry on him in the *Australian Dictionary of Biography*, and even more so by Robert Bartlett's longer biographical sketch in *The Oxford Companion to Australian Cricket*.[1]

Youthful heroics and a mammoth score in an intercollegiate cricket match give way to farm work at the insistence of his father in country South Australia, a return to Adelaide where he opens a sporting goods firm, rapid promotion to the colonial and Test sides, a first English tour, a superlative batting series, accession to the Australian captaincy and a major leadership role on and off field are part of the progression.

Square jawed, square shouldered and heavily moustached the Darling batting stance, even as a young man, is a picture of strength and combativeness. In Bartlett's words:

> Darling, a confident and natural leader and a man of fine temperament was chosen Australian captain for the 1899 English tour … he believed in discipline, encouraging his players to work hard on their game, particularly their fielding. The ability to take sharp chances and save runs made the Australian side an effective unit. With astute field placing and excellent deployment of his bowlers, Darling maintained a tight rein. Although a tough and firm leader, he was well liked by his team, who appreciated his dry sense of humour and his warmth.[2]

Darling breaks from the game to establish a pastoral property in Tasmania but returns to captain part of an Ashes series at home in 1901-02 and lead two more tours to England in 1902 and 1905, playing a gigantic role in Australian cricket's early history.

Darling's 1902 team is regarded as one of the great Australian Test sides along with those led by Warwick Armstrong (1921), Don Bradman (1948) and Steve Waugh (2001) not because of the margin of the victory which was merely 2-1 but because of the high quality of their opponents.

---

1 DK Darling, 'Darling, Joseph (1870-1946)', *Australian Dictionary of Biography*, 1981, Vol.8, 1981, pp. 211-12; Robert Bartlett, 'Darling, Joseph' in Richard Cashman et al. (eds), *The Oxford Companion to Australian Cricket*, Oxford University Press, Melbourne, 1996, pp. 135-6.

2 Bartlett, 'Joseph Darling', *Oxford Companion*, p. 136.

Darling's role as captain was also critical because of his ability to deal with adversity as Australia responded to England's 376 in the first Test at Birmingham by being bowled out for its lowest score of 36 in the first innings and was only able to draw the game because of rain.

In some respects Darling had his critics for his selection in the 1905 team as he was seen as yesterday's man and merely a part-time cricketer but it has to be said that the spin of the coin had much to do with the overall results.

Let us now go back to his beginnings.

YOUNG JOE 1870-87

Anyone reading one of Adelaide's two morning newspapers, the *South Australian Register*, on 3 January 1871 would have reckoned it was a bad time to be alive:

> The year which closed with the last chime of twelve on Saturday night is not one upon which South Australia can look back with much satisfaction. It has been a painful year of trial and probation, or anxieties and painful cares, to some even of privation and want. Ushered in with an almost utter failure of our most important staple [wheat], and marked by unwonted depression in all our other producing interests, it leaves us a resulting legacy of diminished revenues, diminished population, and diminished capital, not, however, with diminished hopes for the future.

The article continued with reference to discipline 'stern and painful' but to confidence in 'the elasticity of our resources'. Looking back it reflected on the necessary replacement of a feeble colonial government and the opening of the Northern Extension Railway as one of the material signs of progress along with increasing returns from a number of gold mines. In closing it remarked that 1870 could not wholly be condemned as 'a year of unmixed trouble and depression' but that even in its worst period 'the cloud that overshadowed us was not without its silver lining'.[3] It is notable that sport was not mentioned among colonial activites and yet it would provide two important silver linings of the future. On 12 May 1870 the Port Adelaide Football Club was established and on 21 November 1870 Joseph Darling was born. One of Australia's greatest football clubs and one of Australia's greatest Test cricket captains thus arrived in the same year.

Joe's birth took place in Glen Osmond, a south-east hills suburb of Adelaide, the sixth son of John Darling and his wife Isabella, nee Ferguson who migrated from Edinburgh, Scotland on the *Achilles* in 1855 and prospered in South Australia after early setbacks. John Darling was a type founder and Isabella, the third daughter of James Ferguson, a printer, at the time of their marriage in 1850. Two of John's friends, Alexander Dowie and Joseph Ferguson (probably Isabella's brother and later an owner of the *South Australian Register*), emigrated in 1851 so the young couple decided to follow them.[4]

---

3 *South Australian Register* 3 January 1871, p. 9.
4 Darling family tree; *Observer* 15 April 1905, p. 35.

After brief employment in a general store and bakery John Darling set up as a contractor with a horse and cart and established his wife in a store adjacent to the Stag Inn in Rundle Street. When this failed to attract to sufficient custom they built a general store on Glen Osmond Road which Isabella managed and became profitable. John then joined Giles & Smith grain and flour merchants which he rose to manage for five years before transferring to RG Bowen's wheat and grain store. In 1867 he took over Bowen's and five years later changed the firm's name to John Darling & Son, taking his eldest son John into the business as a full partner aged 20. Together they quickly acquired interests in agricultural properties and flour mills, exported extensively to the eastern colonies and then internationally to the extent of establishing an office in London. Being known as the 'Grain King' he became the biggest shipper of wheat from Australia.

John Darling snr briefly held ministerial rank as Commissioner of Public Works around the time Joe was attending Prince Alfred College.

As a self-made man it was not surprising that John Darling should have sought to make a contribution to public life and he served for more than 20 years in both the House of Assembly and Legislative Council in the South Australian Parliament and briefly attained ministerial office as Commissioner of Public Works in the Downer Government. One of his early initiatives was to support a Bill for granting the lease of Adelaide Oval to the South Australian Cricketing Association. Of his political role it was said:

> He played a useful and an honourable part in the politics of the State, and he was remembered as a prudent, sagacious legislator. He held his opinions strongly, and was not swayed from his convictions by the desire for applause or popularity … He knew his mind, and did not waver, doing solid, conscientious work, supporting in particular the interests of the agriculturists, with whose requirements he made himself thoroughly conversant.[5]

John Darling was aged 39 and in the prime of his life when Joe was born. A member of the Independent and Baptist churches, he supported their missions and worked first as a deacon of the Hindmarsh Square Congregational Church before joining the Flinders Street Baptist Church in 1865. With the latter church he served as a Sunday school superintendent, and apart from the two years when he lived in Melbourne, or was overseas on business was an active member as a lay preacher and serving on committees. He was also regarded as a 'generous though unostentatious philanthropist' and helped found the City Mission Hall in Light Square towards which he gave £500.[6]

---

[5] *Advertiser* 11 April 1905, p. 4; See also HT Burgess (ed.) *The Cyclopedia of South Australia*, Cyclopedia Co., Adelaide, 1907, p. 211; JJ Pascoe (ed.) *History of Adelaide and its vicinity*, Hussey & Gillingham, Adelaide, 1901, p. 416-7.

[6] http://adb.anu.edu.au/biography/darling-john-3368; John Darling obituary, *Observer* 15 April 1905, p. 35; Pascoe, *Adelaide and vicinity*, p. 416.

John's Darling's religion came as part of his cultural baggage to his new country. In the 19th century, 'Independent' largely meant Congregationalism, a theological position between Presbyterianism and the radical Protestantism of the Baptists and Quakers. It emphasised the right and responsibility of each properly organised congregation to determine its own affairs, decide their church's form of worship, confessional statements and choose their own officers. The two foundational tenets of Congregationalism were *sola scriptura*, a doctrine which stressed the infallible authority of the *Bible* alone, and the 'priesthood of believers' which meant that every believer was a priest and there was no need for intermediaries. Baptists (like Congregationalists) regarded the local congregation of gathered believers as the best visible representation of Christ's people on earth. The Baptist requirement of free personal decision as a prerequisite of membership in the congregation, however, led to the restriction of baptism to believers. Both Congregationalists and Baptists opposed state established religion.[7]

A pious man, John Darling had a strong social conscience as can be seen in his efforts towards education for the poor and concern for the plight of unmarried mothers.

The foundation stone for a school was laid in November 1870 and inauguration of the school 'for the unsectarian education of the children of the poor' was reported in February 1871. Two years earlier an enlightened citizen had suggested that good, cheap instruction, both religious and secular, was not available for the families of poor labourers and artisans and that the evangelical churches 'with large and commodious rooms lying virtually unoccupied during week days' should provide this. Joe Darling's family was not poor but his father John was a member of a management committee of the Norwood Baptist Church which heeded this challenge and established such education in the newly-erected church hall on The Parade.[8]

In 1879, when he was a Member of Parliament, and Joe was eight years old, he penned a poem, to the *South Australian Register*:[9]

A PLEA FOR A FOUNDLING HOSPITAL

Out in the lamp-lit street,
    With the babe of shame at her breast,
A wild-eyed woman with hurrying feet,
    Walked on with a strange unrest;
On, past passage and lane,
    On, past terrace and square,
Her white face wet with the falling rain,
    And the wind in her loosened hair.

---

7 http://en.wikipedia.org/wiki/Congregational_church; www.britannica.com/topic/Congregationalism; www.britannica.com/topic/Baptists

8 Geoffrey Manning, *A Colonial Experience*, chapter 24.

9 *South Australian Register* 26 August 1879, p. 5

Behind her a father's curse
>	A curse and a close-shut door;
Madness at work in her soul, or worse;
>	And — God knows what! Before,
Not in the whole world wide
>	One friend to whom to turn
Not one to counsel and help and guide,
>	But plenty to scorn and spurn.

Only a servant girl
>	There are dozens to fill her place;
And virtue coldly its lip will curl
>	At the story of her disgrace.
'Twas no one's fault but her own'
>	Whether true or false that be,
Shall the punishment fall on the girl alone,
>	And the sin of the man go free?

On! with her lips apart,
>	With a long and a shuddering sob,
Is it strange that this fallen creature's heart
>	For her child of shame should throb?
'Tis the only love now left
>	Yet the thought her soul alarms
That 'twere better she were by death bereft
>	Of the burden in her arms.

She stops and in anguish wild
>	With many a pitiful tear,
She stoops, and lovingly lays her child,
>	Asleep, on a doorstop near.
One look — what a look, alas!
>	And she flies, with a broken prayer
That some good, kind woman may pass,
>	And find her baby there.

Later a bulwark of the Caledonian Society and chief of that body from 1892 to 1894, it is likely that some of John Darling's religion was modified by colonial experience. Yet it was also a root of his social improvement and business success and certain of these values would be passed on to Joe although with some resistance along the way.

School days

In South Australia, a colony founded as a 'paradise of dissent', there was frequent religious rivalry exacerbated by the promotion of the Church of England Collegiate School of St Peter (more generally known as St Peter's College) in 1847 with the only opposition being the opening of the South Australian High School which became the Adelaide Educational Institution in 1852, a secular establishment supported by Independents and Wesleyan Methodists.[10]

John Darling, however, was obviously a pragmatic man regarding education because his three eldest sons John, Robert (born 1854) and James (born 1857) all attended the Anglican Pulteney Grammar School which was co-educational in its early years.[11]

Early plans for a Wesleyan school foundered but revived in 1866 when among the features of its prospectus were that while it would be headed by Wesleyans it would not be sectarian, and its course of studies would offer sound commercial education along with the classics and mathematics.[12] An absolute boon for the institution was that Prince Alfred, Duke of Edinburgh, laid the foundation stone for the college on 5 November 1867, the first time a member of the royal family had done so for dissenters from the Church of England, and added prestige came from him giving his name to the school.[13]

For Prince Alfred College the classroom was the centre of education in the early years and under third headmaster Frederic Chapple mind and morals were disciplined by the will. Chapple also supported examinations as an external measuring stick with able boys rising to the top, hard work bringing success, and tryers exhorted to try again. This method bore fruit in the 1880s in particular as Princes became the leading school in the colony in Matriculation examinations and the award of university scholarships.[14]

These achievements might well have impressed John Darling. Games were not overvalued although their influence grew as Chapple, a Muscular Christian, was as adept as a cricketer and tennis player as he was in the science laboratory. Chapple's role in developing sports in school life was significant and intercollegiate contests with St Peter's in both cricket and football began in 1878 and quickly became a focus of interest for boys.[15]

Joe Darling' elementary education is unknown and he certainly did not follow John, Robert and James to Pulteney.[16] It is possible that he was a pupil at the Norwood Model School which

---

10 Ron Gibbs, *A History of Prince Alfred College*, Prince Alfred College, 1984, Adelaide, p. 14.
11 Personal communication with Mark Boucher, Pulteney Grammar School Archives, 5 July 2018. John attended the school from 1862 to 1865, Robert was enrolled in 1864, and James was a student from 1868 to 1871.
12 Gibbs, *Prince Alfred College*, p. 26.
13 Gibbs, *Prince Alfred College*, p. 5.
14 Gibbs, *Prince Alfred College*, pp. 70-1, 75, 90.
15 Gibbs, *Prince Alfred College*, pp. 79-80, 118-19.
16 Personal communication, Mark Boucher, 5 July 2018.

Prince Alfred College with the added Waterhouse Wing, 1878-81, as it would have appeared when Joe Darling was a student. Image courtesy State Library South Australia.

opened at the corner of Beulah Road and Osmond Terrace, Norwood in September 1877 but unfortunately student registration records for boys are missing until 1885.[17]

Joe Darling was the fourth of his brothers to attend Princes. John and Robert, were aged 17 and 15 when the school opened in 1869 and thus missed out but James, George and Charles preceded him. James was a student for three years from 1871 to 1873 from the ages of 13 to 16 but George (born 1864) and Charles (born 1867) perhaps enjoyed their entire education there. George was aged 10 to 18 for his years from October 1874 to March 1883 and Charles was seven when he began in January 1875 and 16 when he left in December 1883. Joe's younger brother, Frank (born 1875) also attended the school later.[18]

Joe was enrolled at the school from 1884 to 1887 from the ages of 13 to 17 and his schoolwork began well. In the third term of form Three (a rough equivalent of today's Year Nine) in 1884 he finished second in a class of 32 but his interest in both cricket and football began to prevail. A member of the first eleven all four years he was merely a boy in his first season when

---

17 Confirmed by a visit to State Records on 19 June 2018 to examine GRS/12046 Admission registers – Norwood Primary School 1877 to present.

18 Darling brothers enrolment records supplied by Prince Alfred College co-archivist Tony Aldous by email 13 June 2018.

he was described in the *Prince Alfred College Chronicle* as a 'sure, certain and steady' and 'the most patient player in the eleven'. It might have been said that he was flattering to deceive after opening the batting and being bowled for 1 in the annual intercollegiate match against St Peter's College which was drawn.[19] However, by the end of the 1884-85 summer he had become more aggressive and scores of 59 for the School against the Fifth Form and 50 for the Day Scholars against the Boarders presaged a brilliant career ahead.[20]

Prince Alfred's 1885 cricket team for the intercollegiate match against St Peter's College in which Joe scored 252 runs. (Standing from left): ASJ Fry (captain with bat), EW Castine (with ball), F Chapple (headmaster), P Heath, J Darling (with bat) (Seated from left): P Hill, FM Wilkinson, RH Fawcett, J Goodfellow (coach), GC Braund, DG Evan (umpire), AE Cook (vice-captain with pads), HW Rischbieth. PAC Archives

The college first elevens and football first eighteens regularly engaged in matches against adult teams as well as St Peter's and Whinham colleges, and Glenelg Grammar School. Over his schooldays the eleven thus played games against such clubs as University, Imperials, Austral, Styggians (made up of masters of various colleges), wandering clubs (Wanderers, Incogniti), works-based sides (Telegraph, General Post Office, Unity, Insurance Offices) as well as country town and suburban teams (Mt Barker, Coromandel Valley, Gawler Union, Somerton, Kent Town, Avenues and Glenelg).

Darling began the 1885-86 cricket season with an innings of 35 against Somerton and followed that with scores of 56, 97 and 14 against Imperials, Wanderers and Whinham College, before his mammoth innings of 252 runs in his second intercollegiate game, the highest individual innings then recorded in South Australia. Achieved the day before his fifteenth birthday it came out of a total of 500 and he gave just one chance in six hours at the crease. Opening the batting Darling

---

19 *Prince Alfred College Chronicle*, Vol. 1 No. 3, 24 November 1884, pp. 11, 21-2.
20 *PAC Chronicle*, 1. 4, 24 February 1885, p. 15.

lost his partner early, but then shared a huge partnership with his team captain, 20 year-old ministerial student ASJ Fry, who made a hard-hitting 125. In reaching 195 at the end of the first day's play, Darling had the bowling completely under control and his off-side hitting was a feature of his innings. He was more subdued on the second day but his defence remained resolute and Princes boys shouted until they were hoarse and rushed on to the field when he was finally dismissed. Seizing their hero they then carried him in triumph to the dressing room.[21] Many years later he told his son Douglas that when he completed his innings both hands were covered in blood blisters because in those days bats did not have rubber grips on the handles.[22] Mind was disciplined by force of will on the sports field.

Darling's feat was enough to place him in the College pantheon of heroes and at the end of the same summer he was included in a team styled Fifteen of Australia (but really a South Australian Fourteen plus Harry Trott) which met the Australian Eleven in 1886 at Adelaide Oval. This must have been enormously exciting for a boy, not only playing against the Australian players but sharing a dressing room with South Australian first-class players, and young Victorian all-rounder Trott who, along with Jack Lyons, would make big names in the future. What turned out to be a four day game began in front of a fine attendance made larger on Friday 19 March by colonial government offices being closed at 1 o'clock and Prince Alfred College boys being granted a half-holiday to see Darling perform.[23] In fact, he did not get an opportunity at the crease until the third day when, batting at number ten, he applied himself for an hour against a Test attack of George Giffen, George Palmer, Tom Garrett and Edwin Evans in scoring 16 runs in a manner which brought praise and marked him as a future champion.[24]

In his last two years at school he won a number of silver medals given by Chapple for scoring fifty runs in first eleven matches and particularly in the 1886-87 season when his batting average was 65 and perhaps again in 1887-88 when it was 69. An irony of Darling's big score was that Princes did not have time to dismiss St Peter's College and thus the game was drawn. In the next two years, as captain of the eleven, he made smaller but significant contributions of 54 and 75 in narrow wins on each occasion, an early indication that he was a team-oriented player.[25]

Darling was also making a name as a footballer, playing in the school first eighteen in his last two years. As vice-captain in the intercollegiate match against St Peter's in 1887 he was described as 'kicking and marking well and a tower of strength in the following division'.[26] Like the cricketers, the footballers played matches against other

---

21 *South Australian Register* 20 November 1885, p. 6; 21 November 1885, p. 7; *South Australian Advertiser* 21 November 1885, p. 7.
22 DK Darling, *Test Tussles On and Off the Field*, DK Darling, Hobart, 1970, p. 3.
23 *Observer* 20 March 1886, p. 19.
24 *Observer* 27 March 1886, pp. 18-19.
25 *PAC Chronicle* 2.12 10 February 1887, p. 3; 3.16 20 February 1888, pp. 11-12.
26 *PAC Chronicle* 3.14 22 July 1887, p. 12.

Illustration of Darling House at 64 Kent Terrace (now Fullarton Road), purchased by John Darling jnr in 1886 and where Joe may have lived briefly while attending Prince Alfred College. The building is still standing and has recently been used for offices by the Adelaide Fringe.

schools (Whinham College, Glenelg Grammar School) as well as such men's teams as University, Ariels, South Adelaide, Medindie, Semaphore and Glenelg In the same year he played football for the Adelaide Football Club which won the South Australian Football Association premiership and while still a teenager turned out for the Norwood Football Club.[27] There is more detailed discussion of his senior football later in this book.

It appears, though, that John Darling was concerned that his son (and the school) were putting more emphasis on the body than the mind.[28] A particular weakness in Geography regarding drawing maps was apparently overcome, however, as a result of a deal struck with a fellow student. The other student would draw the maps but omit the printing and in return was given one of Darling's cricket medals, a scheme which it was claimed resulted in improved school reports.[29] In fact examination of archival records at the school reveals the reasons for John Darling considering that a good education was going to waste.

Over his four years Joe Darling was examined in Latin, French, Arithmetic, Algebra, Euclidian

---

27 Darling, *Test Tussles*, p. 3.
28 Gibbs, *Prince Alfred College*, p. 122.
29 Darling, *Test Tussles*, p. 4; Gibbs, *Prince Alfred College*, p. 122.

Geometry, Grammar, Spelling, Reading, History, Geography, Science, Essay writing, Copying, Book-keeping and Map making and there is no doubt that his academic work deteriorated. In the final term of 1884 (perhaps coinciding with cricket) he dropped from second to 13th place. The following year in Lower Fourth he showed a similar fall away from 10th in third term to 23rd out of 31 at the end of the year. His school work lifted in the Upper Fourth at the start of 1886, enabling him to top the class[30] but fell away dramatically in Lower and Upper Fifth forms. Even dropping both Latin and French did not save him as he ended bottom of his classes of 34 and 31 students in his final terms of 1887.[31]

Aside from Joe, Charles and Frank also appeared in Princes' sporting teams. Aged 16 in his final year, Charles starred in the intercollegiate win over St Peter's in 1883 taking 6 for 60 from 20 overs as Saints were dismissed for 169 and then was undefeated with 19 runs out of 6-187.[32] And Frank played in both the first eleven and first eighteen in intercollegiate matches. In 1890 at 15, he opened the batting, making scores of just 3 and 9 in Princes' eight wicket defeat; and in 1892 whe as described as 'playing back on the right wing, good kick and mark, should play the ball more' and was a member of Princes' team which defeated St Peter's four goals to two.[33]

At the time of his enrolment Joe's address was given as King William Street. However, a couple of sources indicate that John snr lived for a time in Melbourne during the 1880s while establishing a main office of John Darling & Son and so for a time at least Joe and Frank might have lived with their elder brother John jnr and his family in the imposing two storey bluestone mansion at 64 Kent Terrace (now Fullarton Road), Norwood which later became known as Darling House and remained in the family until 1929.[34] Built in 1883 it was purchased by John jnr three years later but may well have been occupied by the extended family as John snr died there in 1905.

---

30 *PAC Chronicle* 2.9 22 April 1886, p. 22.

31 PAC Examinations 1884-87 passim.

32 *St Peter's School Magazine* 1.1 June 1884, p. 4.

33 *St Peter's School Magazine* 3.4 December 1890, p. 52; 3.10 30 June 1892, p. 127; *PAC Chronicle* 4.33 17 June 1892, p. 112; 4.34 20 September 1892, p. 125.

34 'John Darling', *Australian Dictionary of Biography* Vol. 4, 1972; *Observer* 15 April 1905, p. 35; *Kensington and Norwood Heritage Review* Vol. 3 F-K, p. 179.

ON THE LAND 1888-93

In the early years of colonial settlement the South Australian Government sold Crown Lands only for cash. Pastoralists leased vast runs, but small farmers found it difficult to support a family growing crops on 80 acre sections. The *Waste Lands Amendment Act* 1869 introduced by Premier Henry Strangways enabled Crown Lands to be purchased for cash or credit with a deposit of 20 per cent and the balance to be paid after four years. Selectors were unable to purchase more than a square mile (640 acres), had to be more than 21 years of age and reside on their land. Agricultural areas were opened up in the Mid-North, Yorke Peninsula and South East with a minimum price of £1 per acre.

There was an immediate incentive for farmers to buy land and new counties and hundreds (approximately 100 square miles) were surveyed across the colony. Within three years a million acres were sold, most on credit, and on easier terms, the deposit lowered, the credit liberalised and the residence clause allowing a selector to place his son, son-in-law, male relative or servant on his land. John Darling and his sons took advantage of the Act.[1]

The County of Daly (consisting of Yorke Peninsula and the adjacent Mid-North) was proclaimed in 1862 and the Hundred of Mundoora (near Port Broughton) was proclaimed in 1874 and surveyed in 1877.[2] John Darling selected 563 acres on section 478 at £1 an acre on 20 November 1877 and funded superior land of 603 acres for his second son, Robert, on adjacent section 477 for £2412 on the same date. Ten days later a further 37 acres on section 468 was purchased by Robert and two years later, eldest son John jnr bought 489 acres at £1 an acre on nearby section 481. Fifth son, Charles, would acquire a selection in 1889 from a previous selector who had suffered personal hardship.[3]

In a book written for the Mundoora Centenary History, the pioneers were seen as having made an adventurous decision to purchase the land as clearing had to be done by axe before it could be ploughed with a one furrow plough pulled by two horses. After harrowing the seed was sown by hand and ploughed into the ground. Harvesting was performed by a stripper and chaff and grain put through a hand-operated winnower and placed into four bushel bags. Small houses

---

1 Maureen Leadbeater, 'Credit Selection of Land, South Australia', www.familyhistorysa.org/sahistory/land.htm.
2 www.familyhistorysa.org/sahistory/hundreds.html
3 Maureen Leadbeater, 'South Australian Land Purchases by Credit Selection 1869 to 1890' www.familyhistorysa.org/sahistory/landselectors.html

were constructed of mud and plaster daub and building them was a formidable task with limited tools. Water supply was precarious so dams and large underground tanks had to be built.[4] There was much work to be done.

On leaving school Darling played for the Avenue Cricket Club in the Metropolitan Cricket Association. The Avenues were an eastern suburbs team made up predominantly of young men who had recently left St Peter's and Prince Alfred colleges and he began impressively with an innings of 108 in February 1888.[5] It is not known what Joe Darling did for the remainder of that year although it is likely that he might have gone to work on one of the family properties or been employed in various enterprises of John Darling & Son.

Roseworthy College

In 1889, however, he was sent by his father to study at Roseworthy Agricultural College, 50 kilometres north of Adelaide, where he was enrolled for seven months between May and Christmas.[6] At the time there were 33 students of whom six graduated.[7] Examination papers from the preceding year indicate that among the subjects studied were Book-keeping, Natural Philosophy, Geology, Veterinary Science, Live Stock and Dairying, Agriculture, Practical Agriculture, Botany, Chemistry, and Surveying and Mensuration. It is not known whether he took some or all of these.[8]

Darling was aged 18 when he attended Roseworthy which, although it had only been established in 1883, was esteemed by some as a place of training for farming when it was described as the noblest profession in the world. College principal Professor William Lowrie remarked that when a student first arrived he was full of promise and willing to take his coat off; after three months he steadied and his coat was seldom removed; and during his last three months he believed he knew all, criticised farm practices and became an authority. He then returned to his father and told him he had learnt everything. Lowrie hoped that such a father would realise the young man was not proficient and return him to the college so that he could become more sensible in his second year. At the time the college was not fully recognised by men on the land but it was hoped that it would give students not only knowledge but practical knowledge so that they could become apostles of agriculture and horticulture for the future.[9] There is no record of Joe Darling's state of mind at the time nor whether he was regarded as a know-all.

In his brief time there he turned out for the college cricket team at the start of the 1889-90 season in three matches, once for Gawler and once for the Gawler Association but without success,

---

4 Kym Kelly, *Mundoora Centenary 1874-1974*, Mundoora Centenary Committee, 1974, pp. 2-3.
5 *PAC Chronicle* 3.16 20 February 1888, p. 13.
6 Roseworthy Agricultural College Student Register
7 *Roseworthy Agricultural College Annual Report 1891*
8 Roseworthy Agricultural College Examination Papers
9 Gawler *Bunyip* 20 December 1889, p. 2.

*Roseworthy Agricultural College in 1885 four years before Joe Darling attended.
University of Adelaide Archives.*

gathering just 57 runs in six completed innings. In his first match for the college against Prince Albert he made 26 not out of 42 in the first innings and 2 in the second; and 3 out of a team total of 47 against Gawler in his second game. A fortnight later he played for Gawler against Unions but was dismissed for 1 and this was followed by an innings of 8 for the association against Semaphore. In his final match for Roseworthy he scored 16 and 1 but at least made a notable contribution with the ball by capturing six wickets.[10]

After leaving the college in January 1890, Darling returned to cricket with the Avenues where he revealed his class and showed he was a cut above that competition. In the six games remaining

---

10 *Bunyip* 11 October 1889, p. 4; 25 October 1889, p. 4; 8 November 1889, p. 4; 15 November 1889, p. 4; 6 December 1889, p. 4; 13 December 1889, p. 4.

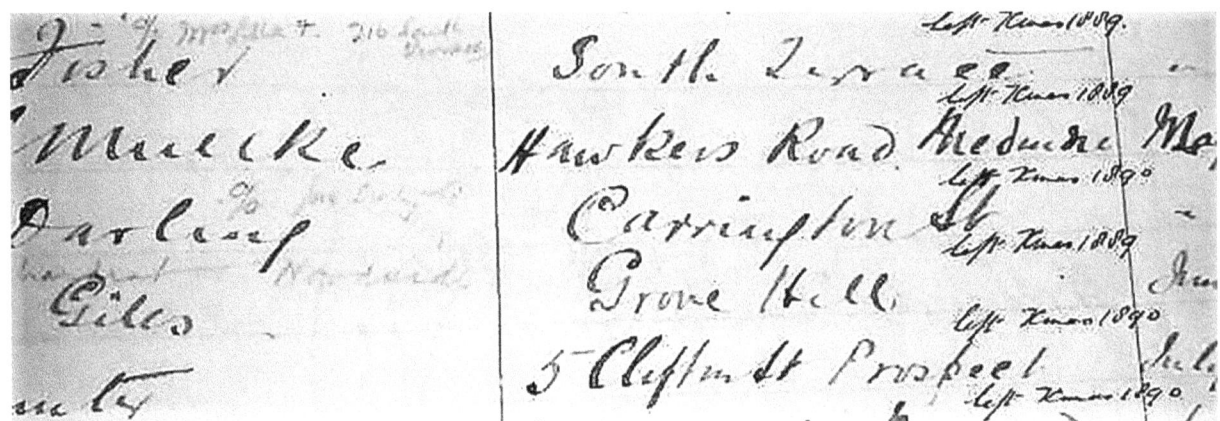
Roseworthy student register showing Darling's departure from the college.

for the season, Darling returned scores of 79 not out, 46 (run out), 32 not out, 57 not out, 56 not out and 17 absent against Adelaide Young Men, Kent Town, Prospect, Middlesex, South Suburban and South United respectively, for an average of 287. There were also some curious anomalies. In the second match against bottom side Kent Town his score of 46 on the first day came amid rapid scoring which saw the Avenues reach 6-254. Including 1 nine, 2 sevens, 4 sixes and 6 fives it would indicate a lot of sloppy fielding as only fives were awarded for hits over the boundary. In his match against Prospect he was left stranded on the second Saturday when the opposition failed to turn up and the match was forfeited. And in the final match against South United he was absent because he was required to do business in Burra.[11]

Burra

Darling carried his bat with 53 not out of Burra's 101 and easy win over Clare who scored 47 in each innings on the Burra Oval on Good Friday. Described as playing beautiful cricket with his strokes being 'clean and hard' the match was remarkable for a member of the opposing team named Hagger also carrying his bat for 15 not out in Clare's second innings.[12]

Joe played two innings for senior association club North Adelaide at the beginning of the 1890-91 season for scores of 61 and 0. At age 20 he was invited to join South Australia's eastern

Burra around the time Joe Darling was living there in the early 1890s.

---

11 *Observer* 1 Febuary 1890, p. 18; *Chronicle* 29 March 1890, p. 14; 5 April 1890, p. 15.
12 *Burra Record* 11 April 1890, p. 2.

colonies tour with a game starting on New Year's Day against Victoria. However his father, who was in the flour milling business and at the time disapproved of his interest in sport, appointed him to manage wheat farms in the country.[13] Certainly Darling was playing little organised sport as even major centres like Burra and Clare had difficulty raising even a handful of cricket and football matches each season.

Mundoora

The next mention of Darling appears to be for Port Broughton against the Barunga Braves on 25 February 1891 at the seaside town and a colourful report in the *Northern Argus* conveyed the rough match conditions.

The wicket was so poor that if 'a phrenologist [was] alluding to it he would say it had the bump of bouncing strongly developed'. After the Braves won the toss and put their opponents in to bat they soon had captured five wickets for 2 runs, including Darling, described as 'the hero of hundreds'. Fortunately there was time for a second innings and he then 'electrified the western backwoodsmen by driving and cutting lightning-like streaks to the chains, and depositing eagle-like soars amid the wild woods that brought down the sandhill on which an interested and excited audience were perched, till bowled by a wild shooter for 43'.[14]

Darling's other main cricket for 1891 included two more of these matches between Port Broughton and the Braves, the first an away game and the second (in which he captained the Ports) at home. In neither of these were there any heroics as the Braves won both games, the first narrowly by 47 runs to 41 and the second comfortably by a 45 run margin. The matches were contested at a strange time of year on 29 July and 1 September and the second game was virtually decided by the first ball of the Port's innings.[15] When Darling faced the Braves' lion (S Thoday): 'Silence reigned supreme as the bowler prepared to fire the first ball, but when that ball broke through the defence there was

> Loud rounds of applause,
> And dropping of jaws,
> Mid blanks and haw haws.

and the raking fire was continued to until they were out for 25 runs'.[16]

It is difficult to ascertain how much sport Joe is playing at this time because he fails to turn out for Port Broughton in any of their cricket matches in 1892 or at least those which are reported in the *Northern Argus*. He appears once for Mundoora against Redhill at Mundoora's ground on 4

---

13 *Observer* 3 January 1891, p. 19.
14 *Northern Argus* 10 March 1891, p. 3.
15 *Northern Argus* 7 August 1891, p. 2; 11 September 1891, p. 3.
16 *Northern Argus* 11 September 1891, p. 3.

March 1893. After Redhill has posted a total of 185 he opens the batting with his younger brother Frank and makes 42 of Mundoora's 6-83 in reply.[17] However, he misses Mundoora's victory by 80 runs over Port Broughton a month later in which Frank Darling top scores with 44 runs.[18]

In March 1893 he was briefly at the centre of a controversy when he took legal action in the Redhill Court seeking £400 (the equivalent of four year's wages for a working man) in damages for slander against Thomas Watt, wheat buyer of Mundoora.

The case was heard before the Local Court on 22 March before stipendiary magistrate AJ Edmunds and two justices of the peace and was reported as follows:

DARLING v WATT

The slander complained of was 'Joe Darling stole 46 bags of wheat at night-time and nothing was done to him. If it had been anyone else he would have got in for it.' Messrs Colton and Johns appeared for the plaintiff and Mr Badger with Mr Durston for the defendant.

GEORGE ANDREW, Mundoora, wheat buyer — On January 27 last, at Mundoora, outside the blacksmith's shop the defendant said, '46 bags of wheat have been stolen from D. Touchell by some one and the party that received the wheat, knowing it to be stolen, is as bad as the party who stole it.' He understood Joe Darling was referred to. Cross examined — He was Darling's wheat buyer. The defendant bought wheat for Dunn & Co. Don't remember saying to defendant 'You had better say who took the wheat.' The defendant replied, 'I can't say who took the wheat, as it was taken in the night.'

O. PALMER, shearer, gave similar evidence.

ROBERT MOORE, Port Broughton, labourer, said on January 27 last was at Port Broughton and heard defendant say to Grandsden and Mildren he was 'not quite so well as Mr Joe Darling who stole 46 bags of wheat at night-time from Mr Dan Touchell and nothing was done to him. Had it been you or me we would have got into trouble over it.' After this he was riding with defendant in his buggy when he said, 'If he had stolen the wheat he ought to get seven years for it.'

ALBERT GRANDSDEN corroborated Moore.

THOMAS WATT, the defendant, said he never injured plaintiff by word or deed. Touchell told him his wheat was stolen and desired him to write a letter to Andrews cautioning him not to buy the wheat. He did write that letter and Touchell signed it. At Port Broughton he said to Mildren and Grandsden, 'The wheat was gone right enough, Touchell said it was stolen.' The question was asked, 'Who took it?' Replied, 'It's not for me to say, only I have been told.' Did not say Joe Darling stole the wheat.

H. MILDREN did not remember much of the conversation at Port Broughton, but Darling's name was not mentioned in connection with the wheat.

---

17 *Northern Argus* 10 March 1893, p. 2.
18 *Northern Argus* 14 April 1893, p. 2.

J. ARMOUR had a conversation with Moore, who told him he never heard the defendant say anything about Darling stealing the wheat.

Verdict for the plaintiff, 5s.

Because of conflicting evidence the court decision made the award to Darling which meant that his name was cleared but the damages of five shillings were a far reduced recompense.[19]

On 3 May 1893 he married Alice Minna Blanche Francis at Mundoora. Alice's family were farmers and presumably gave consent to the union.

The young couple returned to Adelaide where he opened his own sports store in Rundle Street near Gawler Place with financial support from his father and with Alfred 'Topsy' Waldron as a notable employee. Waldron, best known as multiple premiership winning captain for the Norwood Football Club, as well as captaining South Australia, was also a useful cricketer who represented the colony on two occasions and so was a bigger sporting name than Darling's at that time. The store boasted an excellent stock of cricketware and equipment for other games. A feature of the business was repairing bats and balls with the practical Waldron, undertaking such tasks.[20] During his years in the country, Darling gained in strength on an already stocky fame and was ready for action. Interstate cricket selection quickly followed.

Alfred 'Topsy' Waldron, sporting star employed by Joe Darling in his sports store.

---

19 *Northern Argus* 31 March 1893, p. 3.
20 Darling, *Test Tussles*, p. 4; *Observer* 23 September 1893, p. 19.

FLEDGLING PLAYER 1893-96

The start of the 1893-94 cricket season saw Joe Darling resume with North Adelaide and score 103 in a minor match against Kent Town, and 0 (on a sticky wicket), 67 and 28 not out against Norwood, Adelaide and Port Adelaide in association matches.[1]

He was then chosen for his first-class debut for South Australia in the opening Sheffield Shield match against New South Wales at Adelaide Oval in mid-December and batting at number eight was run out for 5 and lbw for 32 in the home side's 237 run win. The visitors were weakened by the unavailability of William Murdoch, Charles Turner, Harry Moses and Arthur Coningham but even so fielded a strong side. When rain softened the pitch on the first morning, only Jack Lyons and George Giffen were able to counter the NSW attack as they were dismissed for 106 in a little over two hours play. The local players hit back, however, with express bowler Ernie Jones delivering fiery spells in taking 5 for 50 so the eastern colony's lead was reduced to 12.

Lyons and Giffen then took the initiative in SA's second innings. With Lyons in typically hard-hitting fashion, and George with his long occupation of the crease, fashioned the first double-century in the competition in around six and half hours batting. Another feature of SA's second innings of 483 was that every player, except for number eleven batsman Jones, reached double-figures and thus assisted George to build a match-winning score. With Darling he shared a partnership of 52 for the seventh wicket and a remarkable photograph of the old white scoreboard located at the south-eastern end of the ground was taken by Terrence McGann at the end of the third day's play when the South Australians had been dismissed and the board was being reassembled.[2]

Aside from his ability with the bat, the newcomer was welcomed into the side for another reason as a story from Jack Reedman is told in Elliott Monfries' book, *Not Test Cricket*:

> Joe Darling was an even more powerful man than he looked and those who can remember the fine physique of Ernie Jones, the South Australian fast bowler, will probably imagine that Jones was the stronger man of the two but he was not as strong as Joe.

---

1 *Observer* 14 October 1893, p.20; 21 October 1893, p.20; 11 November 1893, p.21; 25 November 1893, p.18.
2 Bernard Whimpress, *Adelaide Oval Scoreboards*, WHIM Press, Adelaide, 2017, pp.4-5.

A record of Joe Darling's first appearance in first-class cricket in December 1893 was recorded on this white scoreboard at the southern end of Adelaide Oval and captured by photographer Terrance McGann. Joe's second innings of 32 might have been dwarfed by George Giffen's 205 but it helped South Australia to a 237 run win over New South Wales.

When Jones came into the South Australian team and had found his legs, so to speak, he was very keen after a bath to wrestle with the other chaps in the 'altogether'.

Ernie was a big powerful chap and had been a Broken Hill miner and as he was top dog in the wrestling business and the fun was all his way until Joe Darling came into the team. Upon Ernie turning his gentle attention to Joe he found himself and his team-mate waltzing around the room for some time each struggling to get the right grasp on the other, until finally the originator of this particular form of after-cricket pastime found himself sliding on his back into the corner where the showers were located. That cured Ernie of his wrestling habit and after that, peace always reigned in the dressing room.

Jones made his South Australian debut only a year before Darling and a new player will often seek ways to fit in and be accepted by the group. He might be a prankster or (like Jones) parade his muscle. By putting the fast bowler on his behind, Darling would have won early respect which carried into the future.

Darling made his first tour of the eastern colonies in January and, promoted to number five, top-scored in South Australia's first innings against Victoria at the Melbourne Cricket Ground with 63 not out and a duck in a match won by 74 runs, but missed out twice in his first visit to the Sydney Cricket Ground with scores of 4 and 1 in an innings defeat. He performed well in the final home 58 run victory over Victoria in March with innings of 87 and 24, thus playing an important role in South Australia's first Sheffield Shield win. Overall he finished seventh in the Australian batting aggregates and fourth in the South Australian averages with 216 runs at 30.85. In association matches he recorded his first century (106) against Port Adelaide in February and finished the season with 294 runs at 42.00.[3]

South Australia's Sheffield Shield winning team 1893-94. From left back row: AH Jarvis, WF Giffen, F Jarvis, E Jones, JC Reedman, GT Parkin. Front row: J Darling, H Haldane, G Giffen, H Blinman, JJ Lyons.

The design of the Sheffield Shield had not been completed when Victoria won it at the end of the first season in 1892-93 so the first actual Shield was not presented until the half-time interval of an Australian Rules Football match between Norwood and Port Adelaide at Adelaide Oval on 14 July 1894. It was a wintry day and heavy rain over the Friday and Saturday virtually rendered the ground unfit for playing football so that less than 2000 people attended the fourth contest between the sides for the season. The cricket trophy was handed to Sir Edwin Smith, one of the SACA vice-presidents, to be its custodian but in a lengthy press report in the *Advertiser* no mention was made of any cricketers attending the event. For his part though Darling was

---

3 *Observer* 5 May 1894, p. 14.

present at the ground as a Norwood half-back flanker, and a member of a team whose colours were lowered by seven goals to five.[4]

Test Debut 1894-95

The big excitement of the 1894-95 season was the visit of Andrew Stoddart's English side to contest a Test series even if the concept of the Ashes had not yet firmed in either the minds of the players or followers of the game. It was an opportunity for Darling to make his mark in the higher reaches of the sport.

Darling had no club form behind him when he stepped out at number six for South Australia against the Englishmen to join his captain George Giffen late on 10 November at 4-103 chasing the tourists huge total of 477. In an innings which changed the game and accelerated his career he reached 33 at stumps on Saturday before progressing on Monday to a score of 117, his first century in big cricket, as well as adding a record fifth-wicket partnership of 173 with Giffen.

The weekday crowd of 8000 was exceptional and the erection of a smoking pavilion north of the members' stand was appreciated as it relieved the crush of Saturday. Darling gave a fine exhibition of batting, scoring from strokes all round the wicket, timing the ball nicely as well as using force when required.[5] Considering that this was his first essay against English bowling, and that it was a high-class attack consisting of pace men Tom Richardson, William Lockwood and William Brockwell backed by left-arm orthodox spinners Bobby Peel and Johnny Briggs, his success was remarkable. Darling wasn't quite man of the match, despite being undefeated with 37 in the second innings, as Giffen scored 64 and 58 not out as well as obtaining match figures of 11 wickets for 224 runs in the colony's first win over an English eleven. However Darling's performance, and especially ending the game by lifting Peel onto the asphalt cycling track, gave him a strong claim to a place in the Australian side for the Test matches.[6] His prospects were underlined three weeks later when he made 46 at number three in SA's ten wicket win in the opening Sheffield Shield match against Victoria.[7]

George Giffen had long been the lion of South Australian cricket and he was never more of a lion than for Australia as well than in the 1894-95 season. In the days leading up to the opening Test match in Sydney he was also an Australian selector with Jack Blackham (Victoria) and Charles Turner (New South Wales), and made no secret of the fact that he wanted five of his colony's representatives in the side. South Australian claims were based on their Sheffield Shield success the previous summer and their wins over Stoddart's team and Victoria in the weeks just past. Giffen's preference also revealed that in the Australian Test team regional allegiances were

---

4 *Advertiser 16 July 1894, p. 6; Observer 21 July 1894, p. 19.*

5 *Advertiser 13 November 1894, p. 7.*

6 *South Australian Register 13 November 1894, p. 6; Ray Webster, First-Class Cricket in Australia Vol. 1 1850-51 to 1941-42, Ray Webster, Melbourne, 1991, p. 189.*

7 Webster, *First-Class Cricket*, p. 192.

still as strong as nationalist spirit despite the momentum towards Federation. While Giffen carried the day with the selection of himself, Jack Lyons and Darling, Jack Reedman and Ernie Jones making their debuts, the team (as others in the past) did not practise together as a unit. Two days before the Test, three of the Victorians — Harry Trott, Charles McLeod and Harry Graham — and the South Australians practised in the morning, while New South Welshmen Turner, Frank Iredale and Syd Gregory did so with Trott and Graham in the afternoon. Skipper Blackham did not practise at all in what proved to be his final match. The hard-working Graham was seeking to impress, but to no avail. He had made 107 on his Test debut at Lord's in 1893 but ended up as twelfth man in this match.[8]

Recently turned 24, Darling would not have realised that his first appearance would be in one of the most famous matches in all 141 years of Test cricket history although at a personal level it began in the worst possible way. Play began at the Sydney Cricket Ground twelve minutes after noon on 14 December when the burly Lyons and Trott opened against fast bowler Richardson and left-arm spinner Peel. That was regarded as an ideal way of operating although had the fast man Lockwood been employed the match might have opened and concluded differently. As it turned out Richardson put the Australian innings in a whirl in the first twenty minutes. The 'Surrey Catapult' got a delivery to glance Lyons' leg stump when had made just one run and he then removed Trott's off peg at 2-21. Darling now joined Giffen at the crease and the situation was ripe for the re-enactment of their Adelaide Oval heroics five weeks earlier. Not so. This time Darling did not disturb the scorers as he departed first ball to a yorker which crashed into his middle and off stumps, his only consolation could have been that this was the performance of a truly great fast bowler at the top of his game. It would be a long time before he would bat again.[9]

For most of the first day Giffen put down roots, first in a 171 run partnership with Iredale for the fourth wicket, followed by 139 with Gregory before departing for 161, his only Test match century. The following day Gregory topped that with a scintillating 201 in just over four hours as he and Blackham (74) also achieved their highest Test scores, added a long-standing ninth wicket partnership of 154, and saw Australia to an astonishing score of 586 from 172.3 six ball overs delivered in a fraction over seven hours. It wasn't just the batsmen who rattled along but it was a game which would take some strange twists and turns.[10]

Joe Darling sketch which appeared in the Adelaide satirical paper Quiz and Lantern in 1894. The '117' refers to an innings by Darling in the opening game of Andrew Stoddart's English team's tour of 1894-95. Darling's first century in big cricket, it propelled him into the Australian Test team a month later.

---

8 Bernard Whimpress and Nigel Hart, *Test Eleven: Great Ashes Battles*, Wakefield Press, Adelaide, 1994, pp. 27-8.
9 Whimpress and Hart, *Test Eleven*, pp. 30-1.
10 Webster, *First-Class Cricket*, p. 194.

Perhaps the strangest was off-field and occurred (as Darling noted) when the Australian fielding side adjourned for lunch:

> One can well imagine our surprise when on entering the dining room—in those days the players dined with the delegates and hosts of their friends, 'dead heads' who had been invited to lunch, not at the expense of the delegates, but as part of the expenses of the match—when three of us were unable to obtain seats, and had to wait until such time as these hangers-on had finished. Our time was limited to three-quarters of an hour for lunch, during which time we had to have a wash, eat our dinner, and have a few minutes rest before taking the field again. It was not until the players took a stand and demanded a room be set aside entirely for the two teams to dine in that these so-called legislators for the benefit of Australian cricket gave way, and ever since then a room has been set aside in Melbourne and Sydney for the players to dine exclusively.[11]

Syd Gregory who scored 201 at Sydney in 1994 in the same innings in which Joe opened his Test career with a duck.

England's reply ended with a respectable tally of 325 at twelve minutes to six on the third day but had to follow on as the rule was then compulsory and the 261 run deficit was much greater than the 120 run margin required. As the time for the changeover for the innings was a quarter of an hour play thus ended for the day. Australia's most grievous misfortune was that Blackham cracked the top joint of his thumb so badly in taking a ball from Lyons that he was forced to surrender the gloves to McLeod. Not only did he not keep wickets again in the match but it signalled the end of his first-class career which came at the end of the following month when he reinjured the same finger in a Sheffield Shield match.

Giffen took over the captaincy as England batted throughout the fourth day to reach 4-268 and well into the fifth to post 437 runs. When Australia began its second innings at 4 o'clock it faced the relatively easy task of 177 runs to win. After Lyons departed for a brisk 25 and Trott for a circumspect 8 the Australian score was 2-45 and Darling now had the opportunity to prove himself in Test cricket when he joined Giffen. Having quickly escaped his pair and being dropped by Stoddart he chanced his arm to the extent that in the last hour the batsmen scored at a run a minute to reach 2-113 at stumps. With Darling on 44 and Giffen 30 just 64 runs were required with eight wickets in hand. The result must then have seemed a formality.[12]

The only trouble was that it rained during the night and a look at the pitch justified Australian fears. A famous story tells of Giffen, having slept soundly, greeting Blackham cheerily at breakfast only to be met by a man with a forlorn expression. Blackham was often regarded as a pessimist

---

11 Darling, *Test Tussles*, p. 39.
12 Whimpress and Hart, *Test Eleven*, pp. 38-42.

but on this occasion curator Ned Gregory (father of Syd) agreed with him that the batting side would be beaten. The pavilion end was soft but the other end was hard and dry as Darling and Giffen opened confidently with Peel bowling to the difficult end. Darling lifted the spirits of the small crowd when he raised Peel over the fence for five but in trying to repeat the stroke was caught on the long-on boundary for 53 at 3-130. Forty-seven runs were needed but after Giffen departed Gregory with 16 was the only batsman to offer resistance as Peel and Briggs ran through the side for 166 to give England victory by 10 runs.

Darling was not to know that in over 2300 Test matches this would be the first of only three — all involving Australia — in which a side following on won the match. Darling's solace was that he had top scored in the second innings. Unlike fellow South Australians Jones and Reedman who were immediately dropped, and Lyons who lost his place after the second Test (but returned for the fifth), he along with Giffen remained throughout the series, and would never be dropped throughout his 11 year career. In the coming games, Darling's contributions were solid: 32 and 5 in Melbourne, 10 and 3 on his home turf in Adelaide, 31 in the second match in Sydney, and a final double of 74 and 50 in Melbourne for 258 runs at 28.66.

According to his son Douglas, Darling considered his best innings were his 32 and 31 in the second and fourth matches, both played on sticky wickets. What he would have liked about his 31 was that it transformed the game on the first day. Entering the field to partner Harry Graham on a rain-damaged SCG wicket with Australia in a perilous position at 6-51 he immediately struck Peel to long-on for four and then drove him for two. Then he spanked Briggs to the fence, and lifted the next ball not only over the fence at long-on but over the heads of the crowd, landing the ball in the middle of a tennis court — a magnificent drive. Darling's confidence brought his partner to life and Graham drove grandly through the off-side field and then repeated the stroke. As the batsmen began to score fast, onlookers breathed more freely. In the end he played a full toss on to his stumps from Richardson at 7-119 but with batting conditions improving a scintillating stand of 112 in 65 minutes that followed between Graham and Albert Trott enabled Australia to reach 284 when at one point three figures seemed scarcely credible. The total certainly proved beyond reach for the Englishmen who, after a deluge on the second day, succumbed on the third by losing 17 wickets in three hours to level the series.[13]

In a thrilling climax England won 3-2 in the final match.

'The ups and downs of cricket form one of the charms of the game' wrote Tom Horan in the *Australasian* when Australian spirits were high at the end of the first day of the fifth Test in Melbourne following an unbroken partnership of 140 by Darling and Syd Gregory which had taken the score to 4-282. With Darling on 72 and Gregory 70 each man must have been eyeing a century but both left for the addition of just four runs. Darling was first to depart at 284, caught brilliantly by Ford in the slips off Peel, and Gregory caught behind off Richardson. Darling batted 115 minutes for his 74 which included nine fours. John Darling had arrived from Adelaide and

---

13 *Referee* 6 February 1895, p. 8.

Australian team which levelled the series after winning the fourth Test in Sydney in February 1895. Back row: C Bannerman (umpire), FA Iredale, H Moses, W Bruce J Jackson (scorer), CE McLeod. Seated: AH Jarvis, J Darling, G Giffen (captain), AE Trott, GHS Trott. Front row: H Graham, CTB Turner, SE Gregory. Melbourne Cricket Club Collection

said he would give his son a gold watch and chain if he reached three figures but relented and made the award for him topping the run scorers.[14]

Australia's 414 led England's 385 narrowly on the first innings and posted a competitive second innings of total of 267 in which every player except Albert Trott reached double-figures, but the highest scores came from Giffen with 51 and Darling 50. Darling entered for his second innings at 4-149 on the fourth afternoon and he was the backbone of the lower order as he was at the wickets while 99 runs were added, a performance which drew rich praise from a hometown critic in the Adelaide *Observer*.

> Joe Darling carried off the individual batting honours of the match on the Australian side. What a meteoric rise to eminence his has been. Two years ago he was managing a farm in the country playing cricket rarely against the greenest of bucolics. Now he is in the topmost branches of the tree of Australian batsmen, with not three finer batsmen in the colonies. George Giffen and Harry Trott by virtue of their greater experience are still his peers, but give me Darling in preference

---

14 *Australasian* 9 March 1895, p. 18.

to either Iredale or Gregory for he combines defensive and hitting powers in a more remarkable degree than either of them.[15]

A fourth innings target of 297 was sizeable and especially on a crumbling wicket. In addition they began batting on the evening of the fourth day when Brockwell departed with just five runs on the board although the total was 1-28 at stumps. A fifth day crowd of 14,000 pushed the total attendance passed into six figures for the first time and the excitement was intense. Much depended on Stoddart's performance on the final morning as he had been batting consistently throughout the tour.

Punctually he and Albert Ward, the not out batsmen, came out to face the bowling of McKibbin and Harry Trott. A pin might have been heard drop as Stoddart took guard and had a final look around the field before receiving the first ball. How's that? Up went the finger and out he went lbw at 2-28. Up went the hats from crowd, yells of delight came from home supporters as an Australian victory now seemed a formality but they had overlooked the qualities of sturdy little Yorkshireman Johnny Brown who was next in. He went to the wicket with a smile on his face and there was a rapid turnaround as he thrashed the attack to raise his half-century in 28 minutes (the fastest in all Test history) and his hundred in 95 minutes. Brown smote Giffen, Harry Trott, Albert Trott and Tom McKibbin as though they were mere village bowlers in a display Darling might have borne in mind for his own heroics four years later. Brown and Ward's third wicket stand of 210 in 145 minutes put the issue beyond doubt as England cruised to a six wicket win.[16]

Andrew Stoddart

Johnny Brown whose dashing century to win the Ashes Joe would emulate four years later.

There were astonishing individual performances on both sides during the series. For the winners the star performer was fast bowler Richardson with four 5 wicket hauls and 32 wickets at 26.53 and he was well supported by Peel and Briggs with the ball. Opening batsman Albert Ward was the leading run scorer with 419 runs at 41.90 but others weighed in heavily at important times: captain Stoddart with 173 in Melbourne, MacLaren (after a poor series) with a century in the first innings of the last game in Sydney, and Johnny Brown with his superlative 140 in the second innings of the same match. For the losers Giffen was in the most wonderful all-round form of his career with 475 runs at 52.77 and 32 wickets at 24.12 while others to shine were Albert Trott on his debut in Adelaide where he scored 110 runs without losing his wicket and took second innings figures of 8 for 43;

---

15 *Observer* 9 March 1895, p. 22.
16 Webster, *First-Class Cricket, p. 206; Referee* 25 July 1923, p. 16.

Gregory, of course, for his double-hundred in the first game; Iredale for a second innings century in the third match; and Harry Graham for his century in the fourth match in Melbourne. Erratic selection policies cost Australia dear and especially when Charlie Turner, who had captured 18 wickets at 19.38 and together with Giffen bowled Australia to victory in the fourth Test, was omitted for the final game.

For the rest of the summer Darling made steady contributions for South Australia and finished the season with the creditable figures of 709 runs at an average of 39.38.[17] In club cricket he finished with 190 runs in four completed innings at an average of 47.50 and was a member of North Adelaide's premiership team.

George Giffen's superb all-round efforts ended up in a losing cause.

1895-96

An English tour by a ninth Australian team would concentrate Darling's mind during the 1895-96 domestic summer but the South Australians had two disappointing Sheffield Shield losses on their home ground and Darling's first-class form was only moderate with innings of 6, 50, 7 and 33. Fortunately selectors Giffen, Tom Garrett and William Bruce put these figures aside when the Australian side was picked on 28 January at Garrett's Strathfield home after a day in which Darling and Clem Hill scored heavily in Sydney.[18]

Clem Hill at 18 became the youngest player to record a double-century in Australia.

Losing both opening batsmen for ducks on the first morning, Darling joined Giffen and immediately went on the attack, taking three boundaries from one over by Charlie Turner, before losing his partner. When joined by Hill, Darling maintained his urgency while his partner played with ease leading up to lunch although both batsmen collared the bowling in the afternoon. The pair added 169 runs in 130 minutes for the fourth wicket and though Hill went on to gain the richer plaudits for becoming the youngest player at 18 years and 348 days to reach a double-century in Australia in carry his bat for 206, Darling's initiative had wrested control of the attack away from New South Wales before departing for 121 in 169 minutes with two fives and 15 fours. As the *Referee* reported 'his driving was very powerful and his cutting could not have been excelled, the ball travelling like a shot from the bat'.[19]

---

17 Webster, *First-Class Cricket*, p. 188.
18 Webster, *First-Class Cricket*, pp. 210, 213; *Referee* 29 January 1896, p. 8.
19 *Referee* 4 March 1896, p. 8.

Darling's overall first-class form was sound with 321 runs at 36.33 and his statistics were remarkably similar in club matches. After opening with an attractive 41 in the first round for his new club Adelaide, he totalled 216 runs at 36.00. Darling rarely bowled and in 202 first-class matches he would take just a solitary wicket. However, on 1 February for Adelaide the sturdy batsman came out of his shell as a fast bowler against Port Adelaide by securing 4 wickets for 53, before batting vigorously for 40 not out in a fresh game against Norwood on the same day, making his runs at a run a minute.[20] On the following Saturday he converted that beginning into a score of 120.[21]

Darling was ready, but because he prided himself on his play in adverse conditions, he would now and before all his English tours, arrange for Adelaide Oval curator Charlie Checkett to prepare difficult wickets for him in the nets, and practise against good quality bowlers.[22]

Charlie Checkett

---

20 *Town and Country Journal* 15 February 1896, p. 40; *Observer* 8 February 1896, p. 20.
21 *Observer* 15 February 1896, p. 19.
22 Darling, *Test Tussles*, p. 4.

Cover of 1896 Australian tour brochure published in London.

FIRST ENGLISH TOUR 1896

Australian Cricket Team 1896

Confidence was not necessarily high when Harry Trott's team departed for England. The absence of his brother Albert was a grave omission by selectors William Bruce, George Giffen and Tom Garrett while that of Charles Turner, who had been a devastating performer on three previous tours, also weakened the side.[1] The team which left Adelaide's Outer Harbour aboard the ss *Cuzco* on 14 March consisted of Trott's fellow Victorians Hugh Trumble, Harry Graham and Alf Johns; Syd Gregory, Frank Iredale, Harry Donnan, Jim Kelly and Tom McKibbin of New South Wales; Tasmanian Charles Eady; and the four South Australians Giffen, Ernie Jones, Joe Darling and Clem Hill who were last to board; plus manager Harry Musgrove.

For the first time the Australian party stopped at Colombo long enough to play a one day

---

1 Bernard Whimpress, *On Our Selection: An alternative history of Australian cricket*, Bernard Whimpress, Adelaide, 2011, pp. 44-50, 228.

game against Ceylon and arrived in England in the third week of April.[2] It is sometimes difficult to ascertain the flavour of such tours, but Hill remembered that pith helmets were supplied to team members for the Colombo match and Graham providing much merriment by using his to catch the ball in the outfield. While this action delighted spectators it disgusted the owner as the ball passed through the hat and fell to the ground.[3]

In a leisurely age the team took time settling into their accommodation in London and spent a fortnight in practice before the traditional opening match against Lord Sheffield's Eleven at Sheffield Park on 11 May. The weather was perfect and as the gates were thrown open to the public, a crowd of nearly 25,000 passed through them including the Prince of Wales in the first carriage. Darling was quickly into form, top scoring in the Australians first innings with 67 as well as getting the opportunity to appreciate the talents of WG Grace and KS Ranjitsinhji who took the brunt of Jones' fierce attack on a fiery wicket in the first innings, as well as Stanley Jackson who made 95 not out in the second innings of a drawn contest. It was also the game over which there has been dispute concerning the famous incident of Jones bowling the ball through Grace's beard and then offering the apology, 'Sorry, Doc. She slipped.' A number of accounts have placed this in the mid-summer match against the Gentleman of England at Lord's but it is much more likely that it was this late-spring occasion. In any event, for Darling the atmosphere and setting at Sheffield Park must have been an exhilarating introduction to the English game.

SS Cuzco on which the 1896 Australian team travelled to England. SLSA B 11793

Darling raised his first century on English soil in the fourth match ten days later against Eleven of the South at Eastbourne when he and Giffen posted identical scores of 115 but the game was drawn. Darling opened the innings with Donnan but his partner left before a run was scored so that he was then joined by Giffen. The younger man was vigorous from the start while Giffen exercised caution although by lunch the total stood at 112 of which Darling had scored 64. Resuming after the break a brilliant exposition of batting was given by both South Australians. Darling's hitting was powerful although Giffen with beautiful all-round strokes began to overhaul him. Darling reached his century but then fell to the part-time fast medium-pace of Jack Mason when the score had reached 213. He hit 16 fours, but luck went his way as he gave three chances during his innings.[4]

---

2 Peter Wynne-Thomas, *The Complete History of Cricket Tours at Home and Abroad*, Hamlyn, London, 1989, p. 227.
3 Bernard Whimpress (ed.), *Clem Hill's Reminiscences: The 'Unwritten History' of his Test Career 1896-1912*, Association of Cricket Statisticians and Historians, Cardiff, 2007, p. 19.
4 *Observer* 30 May 1896, p. 21.

He continued in the runs with another half-century in the following innings win over Yorkshire at Sheffield. Until the second week of June the Australians were in brilliant form with seven wins and two draws from nine games, but a severe reversal came on the first morning of their first appearance at Lord's against the Marylebone Cricket Club when Leicestershire medium-pace off-spinner Dick Pougher with 5 for 0 and Middlesex medium-pacer JT (Jack) Hearne with 4 for 4 ran through the side on a sticky wicket for 18 including six ducks. Darling's consolation was to finish with 0 not out in the first innings and the top score of 76 in the second when Hearne captured 9 for 73 to finish with outstanding match figures.[5]

Joe Darling

The summit of every cricketer's ambition is to play in a Test match at Lord's and this now came for Darling in the thirteenth match of the tour beginning on 22 June. Unfortunately the visiting team made another dismal beginning at cricket's headquarters before a crowd that grew to 30,000 by being dismissed for 53 on the first morning. With Donnan run out for 1, Giffen caught behind from the first ball he received from George Lohmann for a duck, and Trott bowled by Tom Richardson without troubling the scorers, it was a dire start. When Darling was joined by Gregory the hopes of the Australians briefly revived but when the Surrey express found a weak spot in Gregory's defence and he retired for 14 it brought a second tumble of wickets: Graham clean bowled by Richardson's succeeding delivery, and Hill and Trumble both playing on against Lohmann and Richardson. Darling scored consistently from every ball that offered the slightest chance until he too fell victim to Richardson for 22, the highest contribution to the innings but as Giffen commented, 'nothing can be said in extenuation' of such a 'miserable batting failure'. The ball which dismissed Darling was a magnificent one and just took the bails. Perhaps he deserved an ounce of luck. After England's 292 gave them a lead of 239 the Australians again opened poorly with Darling falling to Richardson in the first over and Eady following soon after. However, grand centuries by Trott and Gregory at least posted a strong total of 347 and gave the home side 109 to chase for victory, a task they might have found beyond them if not for faulty fielding on the final morning.[6]

The tourists won their next six matches, three by an innings, and Darling became the first

---

5 Cricinfo season archive 1896.
6 *Observer 27 June 1896*, p. 20; George Giffen, *With Bat and Ball*, Ward Lock, London, 1898, p. 142.

Australian player to reach 1000 first-class runs. The milestone came in the nineteenth match (against Leicestershire) and he beat Gregory to the target by half an hour.[7] It also came in the course of reaching 194, his highest first-class score to that time, while Gregory made 102 in the team total of 584, and Giffen captured match figures of 14 wickets for 119 on the way to a win by an innings and 317 runs. On his first visit to England, Darling was proving as reliable a batsman on all wickets as the team possessed.

Given their good form it was pleasing that they won the second Test at Manchester's Old Trafford ground in mid-July although it was a near-run thing and might have repeated the result from Darling's first match at Sydney in 1894. The Australians opened with 412 and two of the batsman from the former match again scored heavily, Iredale with 108 and Giffen 80. When England started their innings Harry Trott was praised for his inventive captaincy although there are varying reports on how he came to share the attack with Ernie Jones.[8]

According to Darling, in an article titled 'How Trott beat Dr Grace' he noticed that WG Grace was becoming slow in his footwork and did not play Trott's slow leg breaks well, and that Stoddart, who opened the innings with him had shown a similar weakness in Australia in 1894-95. Trott generally opened the bowling with Jones one end, and either Giffen or Trumble at the other but Darling's suggestion was that Trott go on himself in order to dismiss these great batsmen before they got set. The advice was accepted, Trott had both Grace and Stoddart stumped off his own bowling by Kelly in his first two overs, and this had a lot to do with the result of the game. Darling gives the example of Trott's good captaincy and his willingness to take advice from other members of the team. Darling added that the newspapers and *Wisden* made favourable comments on Trott's great generalship, but his version of the event was corroborated in a separate article by Hugh Trumble headed 'Joe Darling's Stroke of Genius' which appeared in *Life* magazine of 1 January 1921.[9]

Memories, of course, are unreliable and a variation comes from Clem Hill writing of the Manchester game in his reminscences in the Adelaide *News* in 1933 under the heading 'Clever tactics by Harry Trott':

> Just to show clever he was, examine the tactics in the first innings of the Englishmen. Ernie Jones opened the attack at one end, and Trott put himself on at the other. It was most unusual for his type — a slow leg break bowler — to go on with a new ball. Nobody passed a remark, but we all chuckled to ourselves. His head was deeper than ours. Grace was stumped by Kelly off him for two and Stoddart went in the same way when he had 15 against his name. Then without the faintest suggestion of a smile on his face, he threw the ball to Trumble, and quietly remarked, 'I felt certain I could wheedle those two out; now, you have a go.' He went back to his usual position at point, in which place he was one of the greatest fieldsmen.[10]

---

7 *Evening Journal* 15 July 1896, p. 2.
8 Cricinfo season archive 1896.
9 Darling, *Test Tussles*, pp. 41-2.
10 Hill, *Reminscences*, p. 23.

As it turned out England was dismissed for 231 in its first innings, the follow-on was automatic and Prince Ranjitsinhji's 154 not out on debut in the second innings was as fine a display as many people had seen, his leg side play in particular being a revelation. Batting last, the task confronting the Australians was 125. That they lost seven wickets in reaching that mark showed that it was accompanied by difficulty, particularly from Richardson who took six of the wickets in reaching the century and had thus claimed 24 victims in two matches. Fortunately the steady heads of Trumble and Kelly saw Australia home.[11]

Harry Trott

With the series tied, Trott's team had everything to play for in the final Test at The Oval in early August but sadly that game which has been described as 'a wretched match played in the mud' was a farce with England defeating Australia on a pitch that for the most part was sticky and the bowlers in control. However, there also appears to have been skulduggery involved during the match.

The game was due to begin on the Monday, but as it rained practically all the preceding day the promise of the match starting on time was doubtful. Trott duly lost the toss to Grace and from then it rained until mid-afternoon. There should not have been any play on the first day, but as there was a large crowd clamouring for action, the umpires were influenced to begin at 4.30 even though the bowlers could hardly stand on the wet ground and the ball was greasy. In conditions which heavily favoured the batsmen, England lost 1-66 when Grace was caught off Giffen, and these runs cost the Australians the match which otherwise would have been played on equal terms. England scored 145 but after a strong start by Darling and Iredale, in which 78 runs were added for the first wicket, Australia collapsed to be all out for 119. At the end of the day, England had lost five wickets and led by around 80 runs, so that after a fine night the tourists were confident of gaining a win the next day. Imagine then their dismay when they discovered a damp centre pitch area which was especially mysterious when the lower practice wickets on the edge of the ground were remarkably dry. In their second innings England was dismissed for 84 meaning that 111 runs were needed to win, but the Australians made just 44.

KS Ranjitsinhji, a brilliant debut for England at Old Trafford.

---

11 *Observer*, 25 July 1896, p. 12.

Without doubt the wicket was at its absolute worst during the fourth innings and Bobby Peel captured 6 for 23 in his last Test for England and JT Hearne 4 for 19.[12]

While Australia lost the series 1-2, Trott's team won 20 of its 34 matches with six draws and eight losses by the time the final game was completed at Hastings in September. Seven Australian batsmen in Darling, Gregory, Iredale, Trott, Giffen, Hill and Donnan topped 1000 runs and a quartet of bowlers in Trumble, Jones, Giffen and McKibbin passed 100 wickets. Darling had played in 32 matches, finished at the head of the aggregates and second in the averages with 1555 runs at 29.90 with three centuries and 11 half-centuries.[13] In the Tests, Darling's innings of 22, 0, 27, 16, 47 and 0 might appear negligible with an aggregate of 112 runs at 18.66 but he got starts four out of six times and top scored twice, his first innings in the last game being a brilliant display of 50 minutes batting.

The team was one of the happiest Australian parties and one of the few downsides related to an ugly rumour which tarnished Darling's name. The rumour was that when the team was originally selected he had voted against the inclusion of his South Australian team-mate Clem Hill. It was vehemently denied by Darling and scotched by George Giffen who as one of the selectors stated that such an accusation was nonsensical because Darling (as a junior member of the side) had no say in the selection of the team.[14]

Trott's team (like the 1893 side which preceded it) came home via America where it played three matches against the Philadelphians who won two, the first at Manheim by 123 runs and the second at Elmwood by an innings, before losing the third at Haverford also by an innings where the Australians were outswung. The American trio of bowlers, Barton King with in-swing and Percy and EW Clark were able to make the ball swing from the leg to the off-side. The pitch was soft and the Australians were dismissed for 121 and 101 while the Philadelphians made 282. The Australians then travelled to the west coast by rail as George Giffen recorded in *Bat and Ball*:

> The journey across America was very enjoyable. There were a number of magnificent sights, and the railway companies spared no trouble to ensure our comfort. Despite the comfort and the sights, however, the long train journeys sometimes became a little monotonous, so we decided to relieve the tedium by improvising a prize-fight at one of the wayside stations. Here Hugh Trumble and little 'Tich' Gregory were matched, with Erny [sic] Jones and Johns holding the sponges. They had a desperate 'mill' and several of the team brought their kodaks to bear upon the group. The authorities did not seem to mind one bit that such a struggle was going on in the main street. Several rounds were contested, and the townspeople who gathered thought it a great shame that we should have stood quietly by and allowed our Giant to hammer the Midget. Syd, however, was not so concerned, and with his usual dexterity emerged from the contest without a scratch.[15]

---

12 Darling, *Test Tussles*, pp. 30-31; Hill, *Reminiscences*, p. 26.
13 Wynne-Thomas, *Cricket Tours at Home and Abroad*, p. 227.
14 *Evening Journal* 9 August 1896, p. 7.
15 Giffen, *Bat and Ball*, pp. 97-8.

Australian team pictured on the steps of the Germantown Cricket Club, Philadelphia. The 1896 party like that of 1893 came home via America and on each occasion lost a match in Philadelphia. CC Morris Library

Their arrival in San Francisco, however, produced one qualm as Frank Iredale revealed:

> This city rather pleased us, for it appeared more restful than New York or Chicago. The people were more contented and less inclined to rush. The lawlessness however was rampant, and several people were shot during the time we were there. This indiscriminate shooting in the cities in America amazed us, but what amazed us more was the indifference of the people to the fact![16]

The final leg across the Pacific Ocean on the *Mariposa* from San Francisco to Auckland was a rough trip, however they stopped over to play five second-class games in New Zealand. The team had been due

Famous South Australian cricket quartet at same venue as above. From left: Joe Darling, George Giffen and Ernie Jones. It seems likely that the photographer took separate shots of New South Wales, Victorian and South Australian representatives after the team picture.

---

16 Iredale, *33 Years in Cricket*, p. 144.

home on 30 November but made another detour to Tasmania before arriving in Melbourne from Launceston on the *Pateena* on 15 December.

Darling had an enviable experience on his first trip around the world, gaining renown for his big hitting on classic English grounds. He crossed the Indian, Atlantic and Pacific oceans and with rich batting honours and several hundred pounds in his pockets, was a popular figure on his homecoming. The days spent mostly in the sun left him in good health although continuous cricket could be hard work. In speaking to the newspapers, Darling considered that the team was well managed and the players got on well together, but were disappointed to lose the last Test after having the worst of the wicket. On the performances of his South Australian team-mates he considered that George Giffen was in splendid form throughout the tour and his innings of 80 at Old Trafford was the best he had seen him play. He regarded Clem Hill as a wonder, although he fell now and then to balls which kept low. On Ernie Jones he thought the fast bowler kept a splendid length and that the suspicion of throwing was nonsense written by the English press.[17] He cut his long tour short by returning to Adelaide instead of playing the Tasmanian games in December because of the need to look after his sports store and before embarking on a three week intercolonial cricket tour to play Sheffield Shield matches.[18]

SS Mariposa which conveyed the Australians across the Pacific Ocean on their homeward trip in 1896.

---

17 *Evening Journal* 8 December 1896, p. 2
18 *Evening News* 16 December 1896, p. 2.

ASCENDING THE PEAK 1896-99

Adelaide Cricket Club 1896-97 in the final year before the establishment of the electorate cricket system. Back row: DF Hay, RG Neill, JN Hines, CH Winnall. Seated: AVH Rosman, RG Bowen, J Darling, BV Scrymgour, RJ Hill, WJ Gunn, A McKechnie, AW Pettit (secretary). Front: P O'Donoghue (scorer), H Hay, Frank Darling.

The 1896-97 first-class season began late on 19 December to accommodate the return of the Australian players and the first game was South Australia's home Sheffield Shield match against New South Wales who boasted eight Australian representatives plus Bill Howell and Monty Noble who would make their Test debuts the following summer. Given the class of their opponents, SA was competitive in losing by 51 runs but Darling had a poor match, succumbing in each innings to the prodigious off-breaks of Tom McKibbin for 19 and 0 as the bowler gathered a match haul of 15 wickets for 125 runs.[1]

Darling was in better touch against Victoria in the match starting at the MCG on New Year's Day with scores of 25 and 65. Despite the heroic fast bowling stamina exhibited by Ernie Jones in delivering 85 overs for 12 wickets for 206, the South Australians fell 49 runs short chasing 345

---

1   Webster, *First-Class Cricket*, pp. 219-20.

Joe Darling's Sports Depot had its second location on the Gawler Place (right hand side) of the YMCA Building which stood on the corner of Grenfell Street and Gawler Place until the 1970s. SLSA B 43309

in their fourth innings. In a limited season, Darling had to make do with 24 and 4 in an innings loss against NSW in Sydney, but found better touch on the Adelaide Oval against Victoria with 75 in a slashing opening 184 run partnership with veteran Jack Lyons which was posted in just two hours. Unfortunately for Darling he was caught on the bicycle track which surrounded the ground. Local rules deemed a ball in the air as live whereas a boundary was registered when a ball struck along the ground reached the track. In the event the home side gained a lead of 148 runs and when rain freshened the wicket brought a victory by an innings and 70 runs. [2] In four matches he finished with 212 runs at 30.29.

The highlight of Darling's summer undoubtedly came on 20 March when in a club game for Adelaide he treated the Port-Australs to leather hunting like they had never experienced before. When play resumed, Adelaide was 6-129 and Darling 75, but for the rest of the afternoon only two more wickets fell while adding 223 runs of which the great left-hander made the enormous proportion of 160 to reach 235 not out at stumps. Realising that the position was desperate he

---

2 Chris Harte, *The History of the Sheffield Shield*, Allen and Unwin, Sydney, 1987, pp. 44-5; Webster, *First-Class Cricket*, pp. 220, 222-3, 226.

adopted bold tactics from the outset and made some magnificent hits. One struck the top of the fence which surrounds the Oval, three sailed over the scoreboard on the north mound which preceded that erected in 1911, while several other strokes landed over the boundary chains. In addition, he executed cuts and drives in his best style along the ground. His batting was a treat to watch as he recorded 42 boundary hits in his biggest innings since his 252 in the intercollegiate match of 1885.[3]

At the end of the season Darling did not stop, and the autumn of 1897 was a novel experience for the cricketers of George Giffen's Eleven which toured Western Australia during April and May and returned to Adelaide aboard the steamer *Orient* on 11 May as team manager Mostyn Evan explained in an interview. The party, organised and captained by Giffen had left Adelaide on the RMS *Parramatta* on 7 April, arrived in Albany at midnight on 12 April where they were supposedly quartered in hotels, but half the team found themselves sleeping on wooden benches in an iron shed. It consisted of nine members of the 1896 side which toured England — Harry Trott, Harry Graham, Syd Gregory, Jim Kelly, Tom McKibbin, Clem Hill, Darling, Ernie Jones plus former Test player Jack Lyons, and South Australian cricketer and footballer Alby Green who the following year would be the inaugural winner of the Magarey Medal for best and fairest player in the winter sport.

Evan stated that the trip had been exceedingly pleasant and the players had seen everything there was to be seen in Fremantle, Perth and the goldfields. From a cricket point of view it was a great success. Although the team lost the first match against a Fremantle Eighteen by 19 runs, they defeated a Western Australian Eighteen by ten wickets and a Coolgardie Eighteen by 125 runs. Draws then followed against a Kalgoorlie and District Eighteen and a Western Australian Twenty Two before a final victory in a one day game against an Eastern Districts Twenty-Two at Northam. In the final match on the Jubilee Recreation Reserve, the Eastern Districts team was dismissed for 123 to which the eleven responded with 6-304 and Clem Hill made the only century (122 not out).

Among Giffen's team's experiences was the wicket in the first match at Fremantle which consisted of asphalt over which a blanket was laid before coconut matting was stretched on top. The presence of the blanket gave the wicket an irregular pace and the batsmen were completely puzzled. For the turf wicket in Perth, the soil was obtained from the Merri Creek in Melbourne and although it had been down for a few months it played splendidly and Darling reckoned there was not an easier place on which to bat. At other places, matting was stretched over asphalt and on large grounds batsmen attempting to hit the ball over the eighteens and twenty-twos found it difficult to score. The Western Australians were certainly keen to develop their cricket and at Kalgoorlie the ground had been a waste of scrub only three months before being cleared, fenced and a grandstand erected. The drawback, however, was the shocking amount of dust owing to the lack of water. At times, players had to stop play and turn their backs to the dust and wait until the atmosphere had cleared. The ground at Perth was well situated with the Swan River

---

3   *Observer* 27 March 1897, p. 19.

flowing by and a range of hills in the background. While Hill topped the batting averages with 248 runs at 35.42, Darling was the most consistent batsman, only twice failing to reach double figures, and finishing with 270 runs at 34.87. McKibbin and Jones did the bulk of the bowling with McKibbin taking 73 wickets at 5.77 and Jones 54 at 4.38. However Jones was not able to bowl at top pace because it would have been dangerous for the inexperienced batsmen.[4]

Dominant batsman 1897-98

A clue to the operation of Joe Darling's Cricket and Sports Depot, operating at Gawler Place, was offered in an advertorial piece which appeared in the Adelaide *Observer* on 3 April. After his English tour, Darling had acquired a number of significant items which were sent out to him. Among these were Wisden Crawford Exceller bats from leading English players Bobby Abel, William Brockwell, and Tom Hayward of Surrey who had all provided endorsements. Abel had written, 'I made in three successive matches: 138 v Warwickshire, 152 v Leicestershire, 131 v Essex, and nearly all my runs in 1890 with this bat.' Brockwell wrote: 'During 1896 I made nearly 1500 runs with this bat, and it could have made as many more.' And Hayward remarked: 'A magnificent bat. I made in all my matches nearly 2000 runs With it.' Darling also obtained Wisden's Special Crown cricket balls which were used in the Lord's and Old Trafford Tests as well as tour games against Kent, the South of England, the MCC and the Oxford v Cambridge intervarsity match at Lord's. These objects, which were used in feature displays, assisted Darling in selling sporting materials which also included shipments of footballs, cricket, lacrosse, golf and tennis ware.[5]

Now as the new cricket season approached in August came an emphasis on the fine selection of bats Darling could offer players. When in England he, with the player/umpire Jim Phillips, selected 1400 Wisden bats with the Crawford patent handle mostly used by the leading English players Grace, Stoddart, Jackson, Ranjitsinhji, and Hayward as well as Giffen and Hill among the Australians. The store had a splendid and well-ventilated cellar in which all the bats intended for the coming and the following season were stacked and each was regularly inspected and oiled and when thoroughly seasoned were placed in the shop for sale. Four hundred were in the rack, and each one had been nine months in stock. In addition were the several curiosities in the shape of the bats which had been presented to him plus his own from the English tour. The repairing department was another feature of the establishment. New blades were fitted to old handles; and the former came from both England and Lobethal where they were made from colonial willow. He had also secured a machine in England for sewing balls that had succumbed to wear and tear. These could be resewn and made practically as good as new which was a considerable saving to clubs as they proved a heavy item of expenditure.[6]

---

4   *Observer* 15 May 1897, p. 20; Alf James, 'Giffen's mission to the 'Golden West' in 1897', *Between Wickets*, 7, Summer 2016/Winter 2017, pp. 92-101.

5   *Observer* 3 April 1897, p. 22.

6   *Express & Telegraph* 28 August 1897, p. 7.

Cricket, of course, was not the only summer sport and lawn tennis was very much an important part of Darling's trade. His English tour also provided the opportunity for him to learn the importance of repairing and stringing racquets, visiting leading factories in order to obtain racquets and nets made by companies such as Slazenger, Ayres, Moore, Tate and Wisden, and to arrange a monthly shipment of tennis balls. Sporting apparel, gloves, clubs and gymnastic equipment were among other items in stock.[7]

The Melbourne Cricket Club and Sydney Cricket Ground trustees combined to invite Andrew Stoddart to bring a second side to Australia and he chose just 13 men, insufficient for an arduous tour of 22 matches, and with insufficient bowling strength. The Englishmen were aiming for their fourth consecutive series win, but a restricted four day opening game against South Australia beginning on 28 October proved inconclusive as the tourists were more intent in reaching Victoria in time for the running of the Melbourne Cup. Brilliant batting by Clem Hill (200) and Ranjitsinhji (189) were pointers to the Tests ahead as were the seven wicket hauls by Tom Richardson and Ernie Jones. On the other hand Archie MacLaren's duck and Joe Darling's two innings of 0 and 1 simply underlined what a strange thing cricket form can be.

Darling had played only one innings for his new club East Torrens before that tour game when he opened the batting with Jack Lyons in their first appearance in the newly organised electorate cricket competition. On that occasion he made 68 but his only other knocks before the first Test match in Sydney six weeks later were 11 runs against North Adelaide, and 33 against Victoria, in early November. Stepping into the Test arena he was underdone but might have been buoyed by a poem titled 'What Ho, Joe?' which appeared in the satirical Adelaide magazine *Quiz and Lantern* on 4 November beneath a heading 'Short Stories'. Written by a correspondent 'Mosquito' it would definitely prove prescient:

What have you done to your hands, Joe Darling?
You caused us dismay in the Stands, Joe Darling.
You regarded the ball as a brick,
And dropped it too mightily quick,
We'll give you some birdlime to stick, Joe Darling.

What have you done to your bat, Joe Darling?
Is it square, is it round, is it flat, Joe Darling?
With Giffen laid up 'mid the wrecks,
We watched you, all craning our necks,
And you just missed a couple of "specs", Joe Darling.

---

7   *South Australian Register* 7 September 1897, p. 6; 2 December, p. 6.

When do you mean to retrieve, Joe Darling?
Have you got something stowed in your sleeve, Joe Darling?
We know you were not at your best,
But we trust you far more than the rest,
And we're sure you will shine in the test, Joe Darling.

Darling's position and standing in the Australian game was also secured by George Giffen's decision to stand aside from the series over a money dispute with the tour organisers. So Darling took his place as South Australia's representative on the selection panel along with Victorian Harry Trott and New South Welshman Frank Iredale.

The first Test match was due to begin on Friday 10 December, but was put back until the Monday because of poor weather and English captain Stoddart withdrew because he was grieving over the death of his mother. The tourists were led by MacLaren who began with a brilliant century (109) opening the batting, and supported by a scintillating 175 from Ranjitsinhji, saw their side to 551 in seven and a quarter hours at the crease to set up a nine wicket victory. Opening the innings with his club and state team-mate Lyons just before 4 o'clock on the second day before a crowd of 19,000 was a daunting task and Richardson made a quick double break, removing Darling for 7 and Lyons for 3 as five wickets tumbled for 86 at stumps. On the third day only a 90 run eighth wicket partnership between Hugh Trumble and Charlie McLeod enabled Australia to reach 237 but they still faced a deficit of 314 when following on. Trott juggled the batting order and sent Iredale in with Darling to open the second innings.

Sydney Cricket Ground — Ladies' and Members' Pavilions

Archie MacLaren made a brilliant century to start the 1897–98 Ashes series.

It could be said the last session of the third day belonged to Darling as he reached 80 out of 1-126. Hardly a soul stirred to leave the ground in the last hour as they were enthralled by Darling's play. MacLaren had been stylish and Ranji masterly but Darling hit clean and hard, scarcely raising the ball from the turf, and when he did loft the ball did so safely. After Iredale's dismissal in the 64 minutes he batted with McLeod he scored 63 runs and his hits were 1,4,4,1,4,4,1,1.4.4 4,4,4,1,4,4,4,1,1,4,4. But what added to the quality of his display was that if he had failed there would have been calls for him to be dropped from the team.

What a difference a night would make. The Australians might have indulged in dreams of compiling 500 runs, but with Richardson bowling with a strong northerly wind behind him, the Englishmen were intent on maintaining pressure and the fast man at one point sent down five consecutive maiden overs while only eight runs were registered in the first half hour. Although Hill got quickly into stride after McLeod's run out, Darling was unrecognisable from the previous day as he posted just eight runs in the first hour, and batted for his hundred as well as his desire to take a firm root. Finally, however, he drove successive balls from Johnny Briggs to the fence, and struck a third boundary from Hearne to the square leg boundary to raise not only his first century in Test cricket in three and a quarter hours with 19 fours, but also the first by a left-hand batsman after 53 matches, before holing out for 101. In the end Hill made 96, the first of five scores between that and a hundred in home Tests, Australia's 408 was a creditable total, but England had no trouble reaching their victory target.[8]

Melbourne would begin a reversal of fortunes in the second Test which began on New Year's Day. Darling began with a rapid 36 out of 43 runs and all the top-line Australian batsmen scored well to pile up 520 runs in their only innings. England had to struggle on a cracking third day wicket for 315 and even harder on the fourth day when the crumbling surface helped Monty Noble to mark his Test debut with 6 for 49 out of a total of 150. Ernie Jones also made a mark in a different way by becoming the first Test bowler to be called for throwing. Umpire Jim Phillips made the call and while Jones did not bowl in the second innings it did not interrupt his career as he obtained 11 wickets for 125 runs in the Sheffield Shield game against New South Wales at Adelaide Oval in the week before the third Test.

Darling had warmed up for the match with scores of 8 and 74 against NSW and the English team arrived in Adelaide by train from Victoria two days before play began on Friday. Opening in cool weather, more like autumn than summer, McLeod made a delicate late cut for three runs from Richardson's first ball and the fast bowler's length was erratic in his first spell as 25 runs came from his first five overs, mainly on account of some fine cutting by Darling.

---

8   *Observer* 18 December 1897, p. 20.

Cartoon from Quiz and Lantern *in 1898 following Joe Darling's assault on England left-arm spinner Johnny Briggs and suggesting an imaginary conversation between Briggs and captain Andrew Stoddart.*

By contrast, left-arm orthodox spinner Briggs bowled well-controlled off theory from the other end and his first six overs yielded only a single run before Darling lofted him into the crowd for five.

Darling was a remarkable batsman with the knack of playing two types of game. If his side was in difficulties he could stonewall for hours, but when the wicket was good he could hit out brilliantly. This Test afforded him the opportunity to attack and he brought up his half-century with the total at 64, and by lunch when the total was 70 he had made 54. During the afternoon he played one of the great innings of Test cricket. At 97 he lost McLeod but was then joined by Hill and the two South Australian left-handers flayed the English attack by adding 148 runs in 98 minutes. Darling gave two difficult chances at 86 and 98, but celebrated his second escape by swinging Briggs over square leg and out of the ground for six. In the hour before tea, 98 runs were added to take the score up to 1-195 with Darling 117 and Hill 45. After the interval, Hill leapt into action, adding 36 in even time before tipping Richardson into the keeper's hands after which Syd Gregory sedately established himself at the crease. For a time the pace slackened, but after Darling passed 150, a late flurry of strokes took the Australian total to 2-309 at stumps with Darling 178 and Gregory 16.

Darling's undefeated 178, including 26 fours, two fives and one six, earned him a tremendous ovation from the crowd of 10,000 as he returned to the pavilion. His strokes had been crisp and splendidly timed, and only Bill Murdoch's 211 at The Oval in 1884, and Syd Gregory's 201 at Sydney in 1894, stood above him as records to be surpassed. Loyal fans believed he would smash those records and many people also believed that Australia's 586 at Sydney in 1894 would also be surpassed. Some optimists' hopes were as high as 800.

Most hopes dissolved when England wicket-keeper William Storer caught Darling from Richardson's fifth ball of the morning and performed a war dance for the benefit of the spectators. Although Gregory and Iredale then gathered half-centuries, and there were useful contributions from Noble and Hugh Trumble, the innings of 573 spread over nine hours and 20 minutes eventually petered out on the third morning. Even so it was sufficient to establish an innings win as England fell for 278 and 282 as only Tom Hayward (70) and George Hirst (85) offered major resistance in the first innings, and MacLaren (124) and Ranji (77) were able to do so in the second.[9]

When Australia's score stood at 6-58 on the first day of the return Melbourne Test, the English

---

9 Bernard Whimpress and Nigel Hart, *Adelaide Oval Test Cricket 1884-1984*, Wakefield Press, Adelaide, 1984, pp. 20-2.

Clem Hill

team must have fancied their chances of squaring the series only for a 165 run seventh wicket partnership between Hill and Trumble to restore the position as part of an eventual total of 323. Not only was this figure competitive, but the 20-year-old Hill's superb innings of 188 altered the series as England replied with 174 and 263 to lose by eight wickets. Darling had a quiet match in returning scores of 12 and 29 although his second innings was part of an opening partnership of 50 with McLeod which ensured an easy path on the final day. In the month between the fourth and fifth Tests, South Australia undertook its tour of the eastern colonies, losing narrowly to Victoria and then trouncing New South Wales. While Hill reached centuries in both matches Darling contributed solid scores of 34, 16, 75 and 16.[10]

With nothing to inspire them in the final Test except honour, MacLaren and Edward Wainright put on 111 runs for the first wicket. After even contributions from the middle order, and inspired by typically lion-hearted fast bowling by Richardson with career-best figures of 8 for 94, they had a 96 run lead when the first innings of each side was completed. The loss of MacLaren caught Darling off Jones to the first ball of the second innings, however, signalled a collapse for 178 although a victory target of 275 on a fourth day wicket still loomed as a significant challenge.

Following the relatively quiet cricket of the first three days, now came a finish to be remembered. When the Australians started their task on the Wednesday before a crowd of 13,000 there were threats of rain, but they never got beyond that as the home side got off to a poor start with McLeod playing across a straight ball from Hearne, and Hill attempting to turn Richardson off the middle stump and touching it lightly on to his leg stump. Although these two had made only six runs between them, Darling hit so hard that the total had reached 40 when Hill departed. The Englishmen were delighted at obtaining these wickets and may have fancied they had the game in their grasp. Instead, they spent a long time waiting for their next wicket as Darling and Jack Worrall added 193 runs for the third wicket and the game was practically won when they were parted. Darling's fierce striking roused the spectators to the highest pitch of enthusiasm.

Before the match began, Darling had said, 'I'll fancy I'll have a go at Tom Richardson. I feel sure I can hit him.' For most batsmen such a remark would have been mocked as a shallow and amusing boast, but Darling did hit him as he had never been hit before. He had luck to begin with for at 17 he drove hard to the off which Briggs stopped as it was going over his head and had not the

---

10 Webster, *First-Class Cricket*, pp. 240-3.

Joe Darling

force staggered him he would have caught it at the second attempt. A second chance came at 58 from a low hard off drive which was swerving as Hayward came in from near the fence and lost control to his right and he survived an lbw appeal from Richardson which the Englishmen felt was out. Having survived these perils, Darling made his last hundred runs with cricket that would live in the memory of all who saw it. In one over he hit four successive boundaries from Richardson and the fast bowler, determined that he should not have a fifth, bounced him and he had to duck to save his head.

To return to the partnership between Darling and Worrall, however, the Australian 100 was raised in 66 minutes and Darling reached his century in an hour and a half, the fastest in Test cricket, of which 80 had come in boundaries. His rate of scoring can be better gauged by the fact that he had 103 when the total was 130. Richardson persevered until 84 runs were hit off him, Darling being consistently more severe than any other bowler. Briggs' plan was to toss the ball up and posted three men on the fence for on side drives, but Darling drove him three times beautifully along the ground to the off side fence, his cover hitting and driving over and on either side of the wicket being a feature of his innings. He scored off his own bat at almost the rate of a run a minute as his 160 came in 171 minutes with 30 fours, an even more remarkable performance than his 178 in the Adelaide game.

Giving another perspective on the innings, an article for *The Cricketer* magazine in 1921, Archie MacLaren, who captained England in place of Andrew Stoddart, observed:

> … Darling commenced one of his furious onslaughts, the left-hander letting drive at everything Richardson sent along, his most telling stroke being in the direction of the covers, and once little Johnny Briggs jumped his full height to knock a terrific punch up over his head, only to fall as he came down—enough to prevent his reaching the catch at the second attempt.
>
> After this happened I brought up a second cover point, right on the boundary line, as Darling gave me the impression he would ignore placing of fieldsmen and trust on his arm. Sure enough, he hit one straight down the line to the deep cover immediately afterwards, only to see the ball put on the carpet, which sent up a wild scream from those excellent judges of the game who occupied the ladies' pavilion.
>
> Then Tom [Richardson] and the wicket-keeper, Storer, roared 'How's that?' when Joe missed his drive, but the decision was in the negative.
>
> Although Worrall made some fine hits they were put in the shade by Darling's maximum batting. He hit like a horse kicking and it was only after he had put up 160 and the game was practically won that Tom eventually got him caught by Ted Wainright … Darling never hit harder than on this occasion, and I spotted my bat in his hands, which was given by me to Jim Kelly, and I well remember wondering if the gift of that bat had lost us the fifth Test match and

I had to wonder as Joe Darling told me he had never used a better. A driving bat to a good player in form enables him to know how far he can hit the ball and consistently avoid certain fieldsmen.[11]

For his part Worrall played an unselfish innings and only lost his self-restraint in one over from Briggs when he hit three boundaries in succession. At that stage, however, the score was past 200 and he admitted remarking, 'I couldn't help it, Joe', by way of apology to his partner. Later he added, 'When Joe was cracking them all over the field my blood was just tingling to have a go as well' but instead he played the game for his side. Though his scoring rate might only be half that of Darling, Worrall's 62 came in two hours with 9 fours and was praised for the triumph of discipline over impulse. In the end both men fell just before the target was attained and there was felt to be some justice that Richardson should have gained Darling's wicket as he paid heavily for it.[12]

Tom Richardson

Darling's brilliant season was a puzzle to many including the astute *South Australian Register* journalist Clarence Moody who observed the final Test and watched him thump Richardson as though his deliveries were 'the simplest garden stuff' instead of a man who the day before had taken figures of 8 for 94. To recapitulate, he set several astonishing records: he became the first left-hand batsman to record a Test century; he was the first Test batsman to make two centuries in a series; he hit the first six in Test cricket; he hit the fastest Test century; he was the first player to make 500 runs in a Test series; and he was the first player to record three centuries in a Test series.

Moody offered that when Darling went in 'you can never tell whether he is going to bang or play the barn door game. Similar circumstances affect his play variously. Basing my judgment on his batting in previous matches this season, I thought that at Sydney he would have played keeps on Wednesday in the face of the serious situation. But he lashed out and played the most brilliant innings of the season'. Quoting George Giffen to the effect that Joe was 'meant to be a forcing batsman', Moody concluded he would be more successful if he pursued that path and never tried to stonewall. However, his feat of scoring 537 runs in eight innings against the English bowlers including three centuries revived the argument of whether he or the younger Clem Hill (who had made 452 runs in the Tests) was the better batsman. Over the 1897-98 first-class season, Hill topped the aggregates and averages with 1196 runs at 66.44 ahead of English Test men MacLaren and Ranjitsinhji who also topped four figures. Darling finished in fourth place with 978 runs at 51.47. He ended up playing just two innings for his club, an early instance of a great player being divorced from his roots.

---

11 *Register 26 November 1921*, p. 9.
12 *Australasian 5 March 1898*, p. 21.

No matter how people differed regarding the respective merits of the two left-handers, it certainly left South Australians rejoicing that with Giffen's career winding down and Jack Lyons best days having passed, the likelihood of the two young players rendering splendid service in the future was an exciting prospect. Certainly, most cricket followers approved the presentation to Hill with a testimonial on his twenty-first birthday, although a significant number of supporters also felt the South Australian Cricket Association should offer financial support to players in return for past services rendered. Leading players received compensation for loss of time involved in taking part in intercolonial matches but players such as Lyons and Affie Jarvis were insufficiently rewarded.[13]

It is assumed that Darling's sports goods business made increased profits because of his international fame. Yet, he was almost certainly the victim of captive marketing as it is doubtful that he profited from the shrewd advertisement headed JOE DARLING and which followed with 'The cricketer is very popular among sportsmen but "Darling" brand of cigars are popular amongst all smokers. Obtainable at F Bennett's wholesale and retail tobacconist, Bundaberg.' The advertisement ran twice weekly for two months in the *Bundaberg Mail and Burnett Advertiser* from March to May 1898. Advertisers were ever looking for the main chance and the incident brought to mind another connected with Clem Hill around the same time. On that occasion a tobacco firm wrote to him asking for permission to advertise on some scoring sheets that he smoked a certain brand of cigarettes. Hill denied this but it did not prevent 500 cigarettes being delivered to him and the advertisement duly appearing.[14]

One additional source of personal income related to Darling's cricket, however, did come from his father, John, who never knew how to play and at one time had contempt for the game. Now, however, he began by giving his son £1 for every he run he made in big matches. Whether the extrinsic reward played any part in Joe developing the facility for making centuries is not known but it is noteworthy that as a born Scotsman, John, revised his method to giving the £1 for every run over 100. When Joe made his two big centuries it was felt that John might raise the bar to 150, then to 200, and so on. A nice way to teach a son about economics as well as the niceties of cricket.[15]

A final point should be made here about economics. The three stars of the 1897-98 series were South Australians Darling, Hill and Ernie Jones who took 22 wickets at 25.14. Before the matches began, the SA players were described in some quarters as 'difficult' in discussion with the promoters over match payments and George Giffen withdrew his services altogether. Various accusations were levelled at the group which were not finally made clear until the following signed letter appeared in the *South Australian Register* sixteen months later.[16]

---

13 *Evening Journal* 5 March 1898, p. 4.
14 *Observer* 20 January 1900 p. 19.
15 Western Australian *Sunday Times* 15 May 1898, p. 6.
16 *South Australian Register* 23 March 1899, p. 6.

GIFFEN AND INTERNATIONAL CRICKET.

To the Editor.

Sir— As occasion has previously been taken during our absence from the colony to publish a garbled statement as to the facts which led up to Mr. Giffen not taking part in the test matches against Mr. Stoddart's team in 1897-8, and as the same thing may be done again, we wish to give a plain statement without comment of the true facts of the case.

Shortly stated they are us follows:— When the time for arranging terms with players for test matches was approaching a meeting of South Australian players, consisting of Mr. Giffen, Mr. Lyons, and the undersigned, was held, and it was then decided that we should act in concert. We also decided what terms we would ask from the promoters of the team for playing in the test matches. This we did. and our terms were at first refused, and during correspondence between our Association and the promoters of the English team the former were threatened that unless terms with the South Australian players were promptly arranged no test match would be played in Adelaide.

The Committee of the Association thereupon, without consulting us, came to the decision that if we left the matter of terms in their hands they would guarantee to us that we should get the terms which we asked, and Messrs. Evan and Creswell interviewed us and urged us to agree to this as it was the wish of our Association, at the same time informing us that they were satisfied that if the matter was left to them they would obtain without difficulty from the Melbourne Cricket Club and Sydney Trustees the terms we asked. Entirely with a view of assisting and trusting it to our Association (as we had no doubt of the strength of our position) we at length consented to this course, and it was arranged that the Association should send Mr. Creswell to Melbourne to fix matters up. The Association, although guaranteeing us all we asked, assured us that they were satisfied they would not have to pav anything in the long run; this proved to be so, as the Association was not called upon to pay anything on our account.

We, the undersigned, and Mr. Lyons, all gave Mr. Creswell authority to act for us, but Mr. Giffen declined to do so. Mr. Creswell went to Melbourne and arranged for us the terms we asked in every particular, but as Mr. Giffen had distinctly declined to give him any authority to act for him nothing could be done in his case. We hold that it was our duty to be loyal to our Association, and it was only at their earnest request that we allowed them to take the matter in hand for us, and we also hold that as there were five of us interested in the matter, and as four had very strong opinions one way and one held an equally strong opinion the other way, it was expecting too much that the four should defer to the one.

The above statement has been shown to Messrs. Creswell and Evan, who vouch for its entire correctness so far as it relates to negotiations between the Melbourne Cricket Club and Sydney Trustees and the Association, and our players and the Association.

JOE DARLING.
ERNEST JONES.
CLEM HILL.
Adelaide, March 20.

East Torrens CC premiership team 1897-98. Back row: AJ Bleechmore (treasurer), F Colliver, R Evans, EA Peters, R Homburg, WO Whitridge (secretary). Seated: WJ Gunn, JJ Lyons, Sir ET Smith (president), J Darling, AEH Evans. Front: PM Newland, PW Stuart. SLSA B23092

With a heavy first-class season, Darling's club appearances for East Torrens amounted to just two matches and two innings for 79 runs but as the club took out the premiership it was sufficient for him to take his place in the team photograph.

1898-99

Darling would have delighted in a fuller Test match program when at the peak of his powers. Before the 1898-99 season got underway, however, there was considerable discussion about the role of the Australasian Cricket Council (ACC) and its control over the Australian Elevens of the future. Some disquiet had been expressed by prominent cricketers with the work of the council which they regarded as practically useless. At issue was the fact that the players had banded together with the object of forming a team to tour England in 1899 and wanted to rid themselves of any control by the council. Referring to overseas tours, a manager appointed by the council should be its servant although still a partner with the cricketers and therefore accountable to his employers. The council contended that if a team of players leaves Australia and appears in England as a representative Australian Eleven it should not depart from home without the hallmark of authority. The council was extending its powers and was beginning to occupy the position of the governing body of Australian cricket. In the words of South Australian cricket administrator

Mostyn Evan, who had worked hard to set the council in its proper place, it was not about to exercise its extended powers in an 'arbitrary manner' nor to run counter to the wishes of the players. From its point of view, it simply seemed reasonable that the governing body of any sport, in any country, should direct the operations of a representative team.[17]

In the event reasonableness did not win. As a result of the appointment of a subcommittee, the council met representatives of the Melbourne Cricket Club regarding the forthcoming tour of the Australian Eleven to England. A telegram was then sent from the council to the club notifying that players should be elected on the council. Players selected from the last Australian Eleven should also choose the next team to England; and the team when completed should select its own manager. These were actions the club heartily approved. In effect, the status quo was maintained and the next team would go to England under the auspices of the Melbourne Cricket Club.[110]

Mostyn Evan

When club cricket began, Darling's early form for East Torrens was poor, scoring just 6 and 4 in the first match against West Torrens, and missing the first week of a low scoring match against Port Adelaide due to illness. After Port was dismissed for 57 and East Torrens for 76 the harbour team's 94 in its second innings left an easy target of 75. It might have been expected that Lyons and Darling would take the time for easy batting practice but Lyons burst out of the blocks with such explosive energy that he belted 14 fours in reaching 64 in half an hour and left his partner the opportunity to gather a mere 11 runs in a ten wicket win.[18] Darling was due to make his first appearance for South Australia in the Sheffield Shield match against Victoria on 12 November but withdrew the day before following the death of his youngest daugher that morning.[19]

While he missed the game, Darling's increased standing in the game is evident by his attendance at an informal meeting of the Victorian and South Australian members of the ACC held in Adelaide during the visit by the cricketers. Among the others present were JT Lipscombe, Jack Worrall and Hugh Trumble representing Victoria and William Whitridge, Mostyn Evan and Bernard Scrymgour for South Australia, and one of the key issues discussed was the representation of players on the council.[20]

Darling was back in batting form at the end of November. After heavy rain had fallen on the Friday and Saturday no one who went to Adelaide Oval on Saturday expected to see one team occupy the wickets for any length of time on either the divided main ground or the Neutral Ground behind the western grandstands. Sturt and West Torrens were engaged at the northern end of the main ground and scientific batting was out of the question as West Torrens were skittled in quick time for 55. While this was occurring, however, Darling showed how to play

---

17 *Observer* 30 July 1898, p. 20.
18 *Observer* 12 November 1898, p. 19.
19 Melbourne *Age* 12 November 1898, p. 11.
20 *Observer* 26 November 1898, p. 18.

high-class cricket in adverse conditions in the match against East Adelaide. When the ball was not bouncing off his body or gliding off his legs it was travelling through the air at a rate of knots from his bat which was wielded with power and skill. The batsman recognised there was little use pottering about with defensive cricket to make half a dozen runs in half an hour and playing the ball along the ground would only bring singles on the wet turf. Instead, he threw caution to the winds and in an hour and a half compiled 76 runs by magnificent hitting, including 15 strokes which reached the boundary. Not only did his innings allow East Torrens to establish a strong score of 205 it transformed his own season.[21]

In the peculiar way in which club matches were sometimes organised, East Adelaide replied in fine conditions with 160 and East Torrens scored 5-203 with Darling making another powerful 94 not out a fortnight later on 10 December but the match would not conclude until 21 January. In between New South Wales would play a Sheffield Shield match at the Oval and South Australia would visit the eastern colonies.[22]

The second of the season's intercolonial contests saw Darling captain South Australia for the first time, replacing Jack Lyons. This was a forbidding task, even on home soil, as in the first match they had met with a severe reverse at the hands of Victoria, and NSW had just trounced the Tasmanians by an innings and 487 runs. Darling and Noble began the batting against Monty Noble operating from the Cathedral end and no doubt many observers would have discussed Noble's recent decision to resign his position in the English and Scottish bank rather than prejudice his chance of a trip to England. The public demand for high standards and the pressure of business versus the call of play meant that one would inevitably give way, but even so it seems incredible that at the time some journalistic opinion was proffering that professionalism was inevitable. The one sensible argument was that when it eventually came to Australia it should have none of the snobbishness associated with the amateur–professional divide in England, and particularly not with gentlemen styled 'Mr' entering from one gate and working cricketers from another. As it turned out in the first innings, Noble did the working man's load in taking 6 for 129 out of 334 with Jones (as a batsman) making a mess of everyone's figures with a career-best innings of 82 scored in 65 minutes as he blasted the ball in all directions. Harry Donnan carried his bat through the innings for 160 not out to give NSW a 40 run lead but Darling (70) and Hill (109) made a crucial second-innings partnership of 150 which enabled them to set a fourth innings target of 230 and gather a win by 57 runs after a vintage bowling display by Giffen.

Darling's captaincy thus began in brilliant fashion and he was described in the first innings as handling 'his team of bowlers capitally' although in the second innings he relied almost totally on Giffen and Jones. In the after the match celebrations for players and friends, South Australian Cricket Association chairman William Whitridge was perhaps being generous in attributing SA's win to Darling winning the toss. However, NSW captain Syd Gregory thought it was the

---

21 *Observer* 3 December 1898, p. 19.
22 *Observer* 17 December 1898, p. 18.

local team's play and manager JC Wilson considered it was Giffen's return to form in gathering 10 wickets for 194 runs that won the game.²³

South Australia's tour of the eastern colonies began on New Year's Eve and after experiencing a crushing innings defeat in Melbourne, the side lost narrowly to New South Wales, before meting out harsh punishment to Queensland in their first-ever meeting with the northern team. Darling continued to work Jones and Giffen hard and the bowlers returned the dividends although the intense heat of the first day at the Melbourne Cricket Ground took its toll on the fast man who had to be assisted from the field at the end of play suffering from heat stroke. The MCG wicket played well on the second day, but rain through the night created such strife that 17 SA wickets tumbled on the final day. Darling's scores were 62 and 1 in Melbourne, and 10 and 34 in Sydney, before making the highest innings of his first-class career in Brisbane.²⁴

George Giffen's vintage bowling display underlined claims for selection on the 1899 English tour.

The South Australians arrived on the Thursday night and were accorded a hearty welcome by around 600 people who assembled at the Central Station. The platform was crowded and as the train steamed in there were loud cheers for Clem Hill and George Giffen in particular. The team was then welcomed again by the Mayor of Brisbane at the Town Hall for lunch on Friday when a large gathering of all branches of sport attended. Loud calls were made for Giffen to say a few words and he spoke of the great ability of Darling, Hill and Jones and predicted that their performances on the cricket field would outshine those of himself and the older brigade.²⁵

The inaugural contest between South Australia and Queensland cricketers at the Woollongabba ground was welcomed in quaint terms as the 'joining of hands' between the Bananalanders and Wheatfielders, and was justified by the splendid attendance of nearly 10,000 on the first day who welcomed as heroes Giffen, Hill, Darling, Lyons and 'Jonah' Jones — players whose deeds they had only heard about from afar. Although bowled out for 100 in just

Joe Darling recorded the highest score of his career against Queensland.

---

23 *Observer* 24 December 1898, p. 18.
24 Webster, *First-Class Cricket*, pp. 253-55.
25 *Queensland Times* 14 January 1899, p. 4.

over two hours, they were sanguine about that total, comparing it to SA's recent 164 against New South Wales and the Tasmanians 130 against NSW's 839.[26]

Perhaps more ominous for the purpose at the time was the South Australians reaching 582 in seven and a quarter hours batting over three days with Darling providing a perfect treat with strokes all round the wicket in making 210 in 265 minutes, Hill smashing 78 in just over an hour before being run out, and Giffen playing a more sedate but chanceless innings of 115 in three hours. Darling had reached his century just before the close on the first day and on resumption he and Giffen gave a fine exposition of batting in adding 202 runs for the third wicket. At one point the two batsmen progressed so smoothly that it appeared doubtful if a separation would ever be effected, but eventually Darling was disposed of although not before crashing 36 boundaries in the sole double-century of his first-class career. As the *Brisbane Courier* recorded:

> The retiring batsman on returning to the dressing-room was accorded an ovation. And he deserved it, for a more brilliant innings has never been seen in Brisbane. He was at the wickets for exactly four hours and during his long innings gave only one chance, a rather easy one to Carew when his score stood at 35. After that there was not a fault in his batting. His driving was a treat to witness, the ball flying off the bat at a terrific rate. His glancing and late-cutting were also of the highest possible order.[27]

As for the team, the South Australian players duly found themselves commemorated in limerick verses,[28]

> Clem Hill is an Adelaide kid.
> In a bushel his talent's not hid.
> When the field missed him twice,
> He muttered 'How nice!
> But I want to get out" — and he did.

> The pick of the Adelaide men
> Was Darling, undoubted, but then
> He gave one great chance
> Which did not enhance
> His score of two hundred and ten.

---

26 *Queensland Times* 17 January 1899, p. 6.
27 *Brisbane Courier* 17 January 1899, p. 5.
28 *Observer* 4 March 1899, p. 19.

The notable warrior, Giffen,
Whom Queensland was anxious to stiffen,
Left his ground rather madly,
And was stumped by Bill Bradley,
Which occurred after luncheon (or tiffin).

An Adelaide cricketer, Hack,
Smote the ball an astonishing whack,
Then he shouted, 'Oh, heavens!
I am caught out by Evans,'
And the dressing room saw him come back.

Darling did not add to his score of 94 not out when the electorate match between East Torrens and East Adelaide resumed on 21 January after a six week break and he finished his club season with a score of 158 against Sturt on 4 February to give him 349 runs at 69.80 in that form of the game.[29] His dramatic rise to the Australian Eleven captaincy came when he was unanimously elected to lead the team on its 1899 tour of England. That he should have had just four first-class matches in a leadership role was obviously viewed as no impediment, but succeeding Harry Trott would no easy task as Trott always seemed to make the right bowling change at the right moment and dispose his field with fine judgment to counteract the strokes peculiar to each batsman. In the opinion of many English cricket followers, Trott's captaincy of the 1896 team was so good that they placed him highly as a tactician. As Trott's successor, Darling had several things in his favour: youth — he was aged 28, an iron will, keen judgment, and spirited courage.[30]

Farewell dinner menu, 1899.

Before leaving Australia however, Darling almost doubled his first-class matches as captain by leading the Australian Eleven in three games in Sydney, Melbourne and Adelaide against a team styled as The Rest captained by George Giffen. At the time the first match began on 3 March, the Australian party had not been finalised. Nine players were chosen by the selectors: Darling, Hugh Trumble and Syd Gregory on 4 January, joined by Iredale and Bill Howell who were selected along with Frank Laver and Alf Johns after the second match on 13 March. Fortunately, the Australian team won all three matches by seven, nine and four wickets to avoid embarrassment, although

---

29 *Observer* 28 January 1899, p. 19; 11 February 1899, p. 19.
30 Bathurst *National Advocate* 9 March 1899, p. 2.

Victor Trumper only won the last tour place as a result of his polished innings of 75 in the first innings of the third game. Darling's own scores in these matches were 36, 104, 49, 69 and 3 which placed him fourth in the first-class aggregates and fifth in the averages with 675 runs at 56.25.

For England, 'OME, and BOOTY.

THE BOY (to Captain Joe Darling): "Ta-ta, Joe—wish you well, though "13" IS an unlucky number."

SECOND ENGLISH TOUR 1899

Australian Cricket Team 1899. Melbourne Cricket Club Collection.

The tenth Australian side, under the management of Melbourne Cricket Club secretary Major Ben Wardill, departed Largs Bay on the steamer *Ormuz* on 30 March. As on the previous tour, there was a party of South Australian cricket officials to see them off. In addition, was the sizeable Hill clan, his father John and five of his brothers. A dense crowd gathered at Adelaide Railway Station and it was with difficulty that the cricketers made their way to the train which was to convey them to their ship. There was a hearty cheer for Giffen when he stepped into a carriage, and the train left amid mixed cheering and hooting. George's supporters were doing the

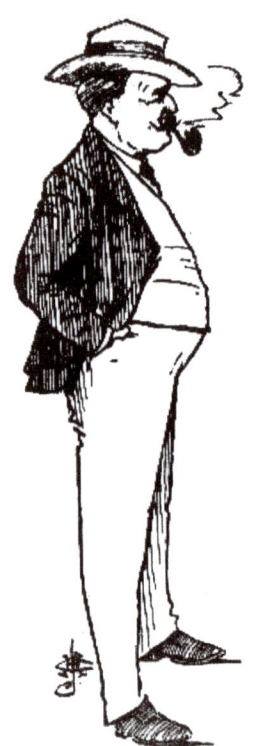

Caricature of Major Ben Wardill, manager of the 1899 Australian team.

hooting as there was strong feeling that the old warrior should have been part of the tour party and not merely a member of the farewelling brigade.[1]

Giffen's form in the 1898-99 first-class season was sound. In five matches during the main part of the season against the other colonies he scored 229 runs at 25.44 and took 28 wickets at 29.61 before captaining The Rest against the Australian Eleven in three matches during March when final selections for the touring party were made. Rumours that there was prejudice against him going back to the previous summer, and that Wardill would not manage the team if he was selected, were dismissed by selector Joe Darling in early February. In the end, however, Giffen's three successive half-centuries in Sydney and Melbourne, and seven wickets in Adelaide proved insufficient to gain him a berth.[2]

Darling and Hill each provided reminiscences of this voyage, and on the second night the ship ran into terrific seas in the Great Australian Bight, several passengers were injured and damage was caused to the upper deck. After three or four days, the sea calmed down, but some players did not travel as well as others, so that when Hill, Howell and Iredale made their first appearance on deck it was the signal for a popular demonstration.[3]

A story told about Darling was that he was fond of a cream pair of trousers. He had them on his first tour of England in 1896, but when as captain on this tour, fellow team members saw the same pair, they conspired to get rid of them and held a meeting to draw lots as to who should steal and throw them overboard. Darling was furious when he discovered his loss, but not for many years did he discover their fate. Because he had a reputation for direct action, the players felt that the culprit, if identified, would find himself despatched overboard.

SS Ormuz which transported the 1899 Australian team to England

Unlike the previous tour, no match was played at Colombo on the way over. The players elected to see some of the sights of Ceylon rather than suffer heat exhaustion under a scorching sun and in energy-sapping humidity. Once the *Ormuz* anchored on 5 April, the cricketers spent a brief time at the magnificent Grand Oriental and Bristol hotels

---

1. Bernard Whimpress, *Ernie Jones: Australia's First Fast Bowler*, Association of Cricket Statisticians and Historians, Cardiff, 2007, p. 42.
2. *Advertiser*, 3 February 1899, p. 4; Webster, *First-Class Cricket*, pp. 260-2.
3. Darling, *Test Tussles*, p. 50.

Clem Hill and fellow passenger astride a beam and playing a shipboard game.
Frank Laver photo, National Sports Museum.

Victor Trumper awaits participation in a skipping game.
Frank Laver photo, National Sports Museum.

before engaging rickshaws to drive to Mount Lavinia and a relaxing time at another superb hotel with spectacular views.

A number of English army officers and their wives, who were returning home after a tour of duty in India, joined the ship and a happy atmosphere altered as they did not think the colonial cricketers were of their class and arranged a concert snubbing the players. To get their own back, the cricketers then organised a fancy dress ball to which all passengers were invited. This proved such a success, that an entertainment committee was established with Frank Laver as secretary, and everyone became friendly for the rest of the voyage. Every day some sort of entertainment occupied attention, sports, games and competitions. Practically all the prizes were won by the cricketers with Ernie Jones scooping the pool.

The ship arrived at Naples on 21 April where Noble, Iredale and Laver disembarked, although it is most likely that all visited the nearby ruins at Pompeii. Darling then left the ship at Marseilles with Johns, Kelly, Gregory, Hill and Jones which meant they probably viewed Paris from the top of the Eiffel Tower and visited the Can-Can as well. The remaining five members of the team — Worrall, McLeod, Howell, Trumble and Trumper — continued by sea to England.[4]

Darling's first Australian team was similar to the side which had won the 1897-98 series, so in spite of what was viewed as the absence of a star batsman and bowler, and a hitter like Hugh Massie, George Bonnor or Jack Lyons, their general all-round ability gave them great expectations of success. Hill was notably regarded as the boy wonder of Australian cricket in a pre-tour judgment of the players by English observer WJ Ford, but Darling was considered only little inferior because of his resourcefulness and severe attacks on fast bowling. Because for the first time five Test matches were scheduled, it meant that the first Test would be played three weeks earlier than the previous tour and thus consist of just seven lead-up matches instead of 13.

Bill Howell made a sensational debut in English cricket.

Proceedings which opened with a drawn game against South of England organised by WG Grace at Crystal Palace, and apart from a shock 126 run loss to Essex in the second match at Lleyton where left-arm medium-pacer HI 'Sailor' Young captured match figures of 11 wickets for 74 runs on a tricky wicket, proceeded smoothly enough. Medium-pacer Bill Howell's astonishing 10 wickets for 28 runs in the first innings of his match on English soil produced an innings win over Surrey as he also gathered 5 for 29 second time around. This was followed by a win over an England Eleven at Eastbourne, a rain-ruined draw against Yorkshire, an innings win over Lancashire, and a draw against Oxford University. As fast bowler Jones was the spearhead of the attack, Darling let him loose in the first match where he took 9 for 156, but then wisely limited him to three appearances in which he delivered just 100 overs for 14 wickets at 19.28 before the main games. Darling's own batting form was poor with scores of 24, 5, 15, 10, 22,

---

4   Wynne-Thomas, *Cricket Tours at Home and Abroad*, p. 229.

15 and 16 revealing that he had been getting starts, but not converting them to substantial scores while opening the innings. Dropping himself to number six in the batting order, he then tuned up for the series with 35 and 106 not out in the Oxford match at The Parks where Noble also completed an undefeated 100.[5]

What was most admirable about Darling's captaincy was his love of fair play, an example of which was expressed in the Surrey match mentioned above. After Howell's first innings mayhem, Tom Richardson was bowling when he cut a deep hole in the soft turf with his left foot in the act of delivery. After a shower drove the players from the field, one of the umpires held an umbrella over Richardson's head while the fast bowler gathered handfuls of sawdust to put in his foothold and the umpire assisted by carrying and pressing the mixture down to make it secure. Although the Australians had never seen this done before, Darling made a mental note for future use, which came at the end of the tour in a match against CI Thornton's Eleven at Scarborough.

Australia won the Test series 1-0 with four matches drawn, but felt they were deprived of victory in the first game due to faulty umpiring. Nottingham was hosting its first match, and the Trent Bridge ground was an historic site. Approaching it from the city, a noticeable building was the small inn close to the entrance gate built by the celebrated professional bowler and cricket entrepreneur William Clarke, and the one tree inside the arena was known as George Parr's tree because of the number of times he struck leg side hits into it. When he died, a branch of the tree was said to have been placed on his grave.

The weather was glorious on the opening day and the Australians batted grittily on a hard and true wicket to make 252. After Iredale's early exit, Darling and Noble, the batting heroes of the second innings at Oxford, established themselves although each were appealed against for lbw by Grace before taking the total to 82 when Darling was bowled by Hearne for 47 in a sound and defensive innings which occupied two and three quarter hours. England trailed by 59 on the first innings, so when Darling declared at 8-230 on the last day, the home side was left to make 290 in under four hours.

Howell started the ball rolling for Australia by dismissing Grace and Stanley Jackson with beautiful off-cutters, so when Charles Fry was caught off Trumble, and William Gunn was bowled by Jones, the score was 4-19 and the Englishmen looked well beaten. In Hill's recollection of the match, this became even more likely when the Australians thought they had Ranjitsinhji run out for 30 and he had begun to jog to the pavilion. To the surprise of the team, umpire Barlow then called 'You're not out' and, on his return, the Indian batsman made 93 not out of a total of 7-155, which together with the two sharp chances dropped by Darling at short leg allowed England to escape with a draw.

Darling also recalled the incident, but had Ranji on 48 when was 'run out by fully three yards'. He does not mention dropping any catches, but refers to Hill's first innings run out dismissal: 'The wicket was hit in the throw in and Barlow, before anyone had time to appeal, jumped up in

---

5   Wynne-Thomas, *Cricket Tours at Home and Abroad*, p. 230.

the air just as an excited player does in a close match with his arms stretched out and yelled for all he was worth, 'OUT!'[6]

The Ranji run out incident had an aftermath with Laver, who had been been fielding close to the wicket and returned the ball to keeper Kelly to effect the dismissal, accusing the official of cheating. The Australians then expressed their dissatisfaction to the Marylebone Cricket Club (MCC) after which a special meeting involving Lords Harris and Hawke promised Darling that Barlow would not be appointed to any more of the team's matches. That was his first and only Test match in such a capacity.

As an aside it should be mentioned that Dick Barlow was the former Lancashire opening batsman and left-arm slow medium bowler who had played 17 Test matches for England in the early 1880s and was twice celebrated in famous cricket literature, first in the poem pasted on the side of the Ashes urn.

> When Ivo goes back with the urn, the urn;
> Studds, Steel, Read and Tylecote return, return;
> The welkin will ring loud,
> The great crowd will feel proud,
> Seeing Barlow and Bates with the urn, the urn;
> And the rest coming home with the urn.

and later in Francis Thompson's much superior 'At Lord's' which ends.

> As the run-stealers flicker to and fro,
> To and fro:—
> O my Hornby and my Barlow long ago!

Joe Darling on his first mission as Australian captain in 1899

Darling had a good batting double of 71 and 53 in an eight wicket win over the MCC at Lord's and followed with an undefeated 60 in the second innings of a ten wicket win against Cambridge University. However, single figure scores in each innings in a second game against Yorkshire at Bradford were disappointing.[7]

At this point, however, it is important to distinguish between individual and team momentum, as the Bradford match proved more exciting and a bigger occasion than many Test matches. It was a remarkable game in many ways. In the first place play ceased an hour earlier on the final day to allow the Australians to go straight to their train for London which they reached at 1 o'clock in the morning on the day of play. A second notable

---

6   Darling, *Test Tussles*, p. 48.

7   Cricinfo season archive 1899

incident was that on the previous English tour of Australia, Hirst had taken only two wickets for more than 300 runs in four Tests but now he made the ball fly, taking 8 for 48 in the first innings and 5 for 101 in the second, clean bowling Clem Hill in each innings. 'My word, George', said Clem, 'I will get even with you before the tour is ended.' 'Don't worry about that, Clem', came the reply, 'For I have a long way to go before I catch up with what you did to me in Australia.' The third incident was that Johnny Brown played the best hand against the Australians on the tour following a first innings of 84 with 167 in three and a half hours in the second. As he banged the ball against the fence it was returned like lightning as Yorkshire were forcing the game for a win. There were 22,000 spectators present and so great was the crush that in parts of the field they were seven or eight deep. 'Hit 'em hard, Johnny' came the cry with one voice but when he departed and all hopes of a win had gone they played for all they were worth for a draw and achieved that objective. Fours were few and far between after Brown left but every time the ball reached the boundary the crowd yelled out, 'Coom and get it thyself, lad' and would not throw it in. At the time it annoyed the Australians but afterwards they saw the joke and appreciated it.[8]

The Test match at cricket headquarters brought Australia the win it deserved in the most emphatic fashion. Jones was irresistible in the first session of play with four of the six wickets which fell for 66 and he cleaned up the tail to finish with his best Test performance of 7 for 88 as England were shot out for 206 on the first day. At 3-59 Australia might have slipped to a similar score but for the resilience and then brilliance of youngsters Hill and Trumper who each scored 135 runs, with Trumper remaining undefeated in a tally of 421 and a lead of 215. When England could only manage 240 in its second visit to the crease victory was accomplished by ten wickets. While England's performance represented a tale of woe, the newspapers made special reference to Trumper's masterly stylish batting which amply justified the selectors asking him at the last moment to join the team, and the absence in the home team of a high-class fast bowler to match Jones whose second innings figures of 3 for 76 giving him match figures of 10 for 164. Critics freely admitted that Australia's bowling and fielding was high-class and far superior to their opponents. As a batsman, Darling played only a minor role with innings of 9 and 17 not out in a quick run chase at the end.

Ernie Jones captured 10 wickets for 164 in the first Test match.

Darling had opened the batting throughout the tour, but his authoritative home form of the last couple of seasons was missing. When he followed the match with innings of 12 against Oxford Past and Present and two single figure scores against Leicestershire, he dropped himself to number six at Derby where he scored 134 not out in an innings win. With only a couple of exceptions, he remained in the middle order for the rest of the summer.

The last three Tests were all drawn and in the first of these, the first-ever Test match at the

---

8 *Australasian* 16 June 1928, p. 7.

Headingley ground in Leeds, Australia had both bad and good luck. Bad luck to bat first on a slow treacherous wicket and be dismissed for 172 by 'Sailor' Young, who had wreaked havoc at Lleyton early in the tour, and experienced spinner Johnny Briggs. England replied with 220 and Darling, having made only 9 at number six in the first innings, promoted himself to open in the second. As he and Worrall pushed the total to 34, confidence built, then four wickets fell without addition to the score. Worrall's departure, caught at long-off from Young, was immediately followed by Hearne taking one of cricket's great hat-tricks, his wickets being Hill, Gregory and Noble for ducks. When Darling followed for 17 as Young's second victim at 5-39, Australia still trailed by nine runs and a home win seemed a formality.

Good luck to Australia came in two forms. First, Briggs suffered an epileptic seizure in the Empire Theatre on the first night of the match and took no further part in the game, or Test cricket in the future and as a result. The Australian lower order was able to summon enough resolution to recover to 224 and a lead of 177, a target reduced to 158 at the end of play. Second, rain washed out play entirely on the final day.[9]

England totally dominated the first half of the fourth Test at Old Trafford. They scored 372 and had Australia 7-57 in the first innings with Darling (batting as low as number eight) before Noble's obduracy saved them twice, with an undefeated 60 out of 196 and 89 following on in a score of 7-346 declared. In all, Noble's 149 runs occupied eight and half hours and Darling's 39 at number six in the second innings was an important contribution to his team's safety. With a lead of 150 runs and around two hours to play, Ray Robinson tells a story of Lancashire secretary 'Monkey' Hornby offering £250 if they would declare to provide an exciting finish and of Darling replying, 'Make it £500 and we'll consider it.'[10] In the event when his declaration came it was a futile gesture as England was left with 171 runs to chase and little over an hour to bat.

Seven first-class games were contested before the rubber would be decided in the fifth Test at The Oval, and most players would have preferred to miss the next match against WG Grace's Eleven at Crystal Palace. An hour after the Manchester Test ended the players were transported to London on the Great Central Railway. Dining on board they reached their Inns of Court Hotel at 2 a.m.

This hotel in Holborn provided delightfully comfortable quarters for the team while based in London over five

Inns of Court Hotel

---

9 Cricinfo season archive 1899

10 Ray Robinson and Gideon Haigh, *On Top Down Under: Australia's Cricket Captains*, Wakefield Press, Adelaide, 1996, p. 81.

months. After passing the administration desk, guests would experience a spacious court with a glass roof and masses of greenery with lounges and tables creating a paradise amid mid-city bustle. Beyond the court were wide, well-carpeted passages and tiers of handsomely furnished apartments, the entrance to which could be gained from a quiet back street adjacent to a square where bands would often play in the evenings. Residing in such a place for rest on Sundays must have made it difficult for the cricketers to stir themselves to undertake longer or shorter rail journeys all over the country for county and Test matches. As the hotel management also provided a commodious common room, it was there that team manager Wardill and the team could enjoy a well-earned break.[11]

On this occasion, however, the team's late arrival meant they were in no condition to play a few hours later. Lack of sleep found them half dead when they took the field and though Jones captured an early wicket he could hardly raise a gallop thereafter. Thus, it was hardly a surprise that Grace's team ran up a score of 431 with Alec Hearne and Len Braund making centuries and Australia had to rely on Frank Iredale's first innings hundred to help secure a draw. The side lost only its second game of the tour in the following match against Surrey at The Oval where fast bowlers Bill Lockwood and Tom Richardson were in devastating form but would have been in slightly better spirits responding to Sussex's score of 414 with 4 for 624 declared at Hove. Darling passed fifty for the first time in ten innings but would have been even more delighted in sharing the crease with Trumper when the young man reached 300 not out. For six hours he played perfect cricket, taking 130 minutes to reach his century, gaining his second hundred in 85 minutes, and the third in two and three-quarter hours. Whether driving, pulling or glancing to leg he revealed the most aesthetic style and a terrific variety of stroke play. Perhaps bearing witness to that innings lifted his own form, as Darling brought up his third tour century in a nine wicket win in a second match against the MCC at Lord's.

Victor Trumper was the first Australian to reach a triple-century on an English tour.

Interestingly, it could have been that game to which Hugh Trumble referred in 1934 in an article for the Melbourne *Herald*:

> We were playing at Lord's where the crowds are different from the others. They are more aristocratic than those of the industrial centres, more conservative, and on the whole, more sedate; but they are nonetheless prone to display their feelings on occasions. I remember on one occasion at Lord's when Joe Darling went into bat, a bit lame. He was suffering from a bruised heel and he played carefully—and so very slow for Joe Darling.

---

11 *Observer* 23 September 1899, p. 19.

> The crowd did not like this from such a dashing batsman. Presently someone began to whistle 'Poor Old Joe' and the crowd took it up and you could hear the tune all round the ground. Then the whistling leader started up 'We Won't Go Home Till Morning,' and the crowd responded again. Finally they whistled the 'Dead March in Saul.'
>
> Well, poor old Joe got all worked up over this demonstration. However, it must have done him good for he finished up with something over the century not out [128], and one hopes that the whistlers were as pleased as we were.[12]

The reason for the qualifier 'could' above in relation to the quotation is that memories (and especially cricketers' memories) frequently play false. A little over a year earlier, Clem Hill had also referred to the whistlers of the 'Dead March in Saul' while Darling was batting with a bruised heel. Hill (like Trumble) placed the incident at Lord's but connected it with a three hour innings of 39 instead of a century — Darling's 39 had been at Manchester.

England could only tie the series at The Oval, yet a crowd of 20,000 attended the first day and must have proved an inspiration to their team which reached 4-435 following an opening partnership by Tom Hayward and Jackson who each scored centuries on the way to 576 and an object of bowling Australia out twice. At 4-120 there was some chance of this, but Darling now played his most important innings of the series. As the afternoon wore on, the light became dull and soon after Gregory's arrival the batsman who decided it was too dark to play appealed against the light although it improved after a short interval. When play resumed, Darling was free in his stroke play and on one occasion lifted the ball into the crowd. At 178, Townsend was tried with his leg-breaks, but to no purpose. It was only when Darling miscued and was caught by Fry at third man that the break came after an even 100 run partnership at 5-220. Darling had batted for just over two and a half hours for his 71 and gave a faultless display hitting eight fours and a five. An early breakthrough on the final day might have given England a chance, but 117 by Gregory was chiefly responsible for an eventual total of 352 and half-centuries by Worrall — his second for the match — McLeod and Noble saw them to safety for the loss of five wickets.

Six games remained after the final Test, and Darling then scored heavily. The Test series had been hard fought and it might have been difficult to recognise the genial-looking broad shouldered young man who sat on the right hand side of the Earl of Jersey at the farewell banquet on the Australian's last night as the ordinarily stern-visaged Joe Darling.

The penultimate game at Scarborough saw the second use of sawdust. The match was also memorable because Rhodes took 9 wickets for 24 on a sticky wicket in the second innings. In the second innings of the Englishmen, Jones bowling at three-quarter pace in order to ensure his footing, was deadly and took all of the seven wickets to fall. Play was stopped for a shower, and Darling then took his chance of doing what Richardson had done with the umpire's assistance for Surrey. Jackson, who was captaining Thornton's Eleven, thought this was incorrect but Darling

---

12 Melbourne *Herald* 25 May 1934 cited in Darling, *Test Tussles*, pp. 65-6.

pointed out that he was following an English custom and looking after the interests of his team. Although Jackson threatened to bring the attention of the MCC for unsporting behaviour the outcome of the incident resulted in the following paragraph being included in instructions to umpires in the Laws: 'There is no objection to the bowler's footholes being filled up with sawdust, though the game be not actually in progress.'

Perhaps it was not until the last day of the final tour match against South of England at Hastings that he gave uninhibited rein to his batting in a brilliant innings of 167 in three and a half hours with 28 boundaries.[13] Earlier, the cares and worries of leadership had weighed him down, and in significant parts of the tour he had not done himself justice. His Test match return of 232 runs at 25.77 was below his, and probably his team's, expectations. The pressure lifted after the Manchester Test when the Ashes (only then beginning to be popularised as a concept) could no longer be forfeited. From then on, his prowess shone and is testified by the fact that in 21 matches ending at Old Trafford he scored 954 runs while in 14 games after he contributed 987. In the end, his tour total of 1941 runs at 41.29 from 56 innings with five centuries was the highest ever recorded by an Australian player.

As a captain, however, he won praise and there could be no argument with his stamina as he played in all 35 tour matches. Apart from his judgment in handling the bowling, his skill in settling upon a batsman's weak spots and placing the field accordingly was masterful, but his best feature was his selflessness. When games demanded defence he blocked, yet when runs were wanted, he forced the pace without caring about his batting average in order to win matches. One of the problems was arranging the batting order. At first Iredale was tried opening the innings with Darling himself but that failed, then he lost form, then Worrall took over, Trumble promoted from eight to the head of the list, and finally McLeod's improved form demanded a lift in the order.

When the team left Adelaide in March, conflicting opinions were held concerning the ability of the team. At the end of the tour, Australians could readily welcome their team home with 'See the conquering heroes come' as they had filled the highest expectations by expressing soundness in all departments of the game which had never before been excelled. The best batsman was Hill, who missed the second half of the tour owing to illness, while Noble, Worrall, Trumper, Iredale, Trumble and Gregory all joined their captain in passing 1000

Three Australians were chosen as Wisden's Five Cricketers of the Year — Joe Darling, Monty Noble and Clem Hill.

---

13 *Observer* 9 September 1899, p. 20.

runs. While the attack revolved around Trumble, Howell and Jones, who each took over 100 wickets, Noble and McLeod offered significant support with more than 80 wickets apiece. One disappointment for Darling as leader was the partisanship of English crowds. On only three occasions had the team been enthusiastically cheered and that was after matches in which they had suffered defeat. As their total record was 16 wins three losses and 16 draws applause was scant on the field and virtually none was forthcoming at the end of play.[14]

---
14 *Observer* 23 September 1899, p. 19.

Advertisers are ever ready to take commercial opportunities.

NEW DIRECTIONS 1899-1902

Darling continued his aggressive Hastings form in his first club innings for East Torrens at the Alberton Oval over two Saturdays on 4 and 11 November. On the opening day, the seaside team was disposed of for 88 and their opponents had reached 103 runs without loss with Lyons 65 and Darling 36. Lyons took the attack to the bowlers from the start and reached 117 before departing at 1-201 with Darling 82, but after the second and third wickets fell cheaply, Darling totally dominated play for the rest of the afternoon as the total reached 6-450 at the close. Darling's innings contained plenty of flaws as when he was 104 he gave three successive chances off Jones' bowling, another at 131 off Sidoli, and a fifth at 220 off Williams. While the bowlers, and no doubt some of the spectators, were horrified by the misses, others in the crowd appreciated his big hitting, which saw him record 27 fours and 4 fives in his 259 not out as he reached his highest score in any class of cricket, surpassing the 252 he had made as a boy for Prince Alfred College against St Peter's in 1885.[1] The following week he was also in fine touch on a bad wicket against Sturt at Unley Oval in scoring 76. There were hopes that this form would be translated into the first-class arena.

Not so. Cricket can be a humbling game, and Darling's two failures in late November, opening the batting for scores of 9 and 5 against Victoria at Adelaide Oval where the match was lost by 248 runs, were disappointing. Darling was probably hoping for a decent club innings on 9 December against North Adelaide to regain his touch, but found himself dismissed to a running catch by Edwin Kekwick off Ernie Jones for a first ball duck.[2] And the rot continued a week later, with another home game thrashing by New South Wales, when the winning margin for the visitors was an innings and 392 runs. Batting at number four, Darling was dismissed for 4 out of 155 and dropped out of the match with influenza at the end of the second day when the NSW scorecard read 4-446 on the way to reaching 807 in nine and a quarter hours. Victor Trumper (165), Monty Noble (200) and Syd Gregory (176) all weighed in with big centuries while leaving some sorry bowling analyses on the other side of the ledger. Tireless veteran Giffen probably took some satisfaction out of his 8 for 287 from 77.1 overs, but fast man Jones would have wished he was elsewhere after capturing just 1 for 210 from 50 overs.

---

1 *Observer* 18 November 1899, p. 19.

2 *Observer* 16 December 1899, p. 19.

Darling made 40 and 16 in intense heat in a match in Melbourne played over New Year which the Victorians won comfortably before effecting a marvellous turnaround in form with a six wicket win against NSW at the Sydney Cricket Ground. In the latter game, rain washed out the first two days play which raised doubts about the quality of the pitch. The scores of 214 to 197 were close after the first innings when Darling (47), batting at first drop, enjoyed the only sizeable South Australian partnership of 85 for the second wicket with Fred Hack. An even batting performance by New South Wales of 317 on the fifth day left SA with the large task of scoring 334 runs for victory. In triumphing by six wickets, it proved to be a heroic accomplishment and Darling played a major role after the second wicket fell for 9, although it must be admitted that sloppy fielding contributed to the result. Darling hit his first delivery hard back to leg-spinner Leslie Pye who failed to take it and when Hack was 59 he gave an easy chance to Donnan at mid-on off Bert Hopkins which was grassed. The batsmen remained together at lunch at 2-117 but then scored rapidly taking 47 runs in half an hour, the highlight of which was Darling striking Victor Trumper into the Smokers' Pavilion and Hack liberally taking fours from any bowler who faced him to reach his century in two and three quarter hours. Darling passed his half-century and was taking control of the game when Howell came on causing him to sky a ball on the off side where Alex Mackenzie took a magnificent catch running in the same direction as the ball. Darling's 55 had occupied 72 minutes with nine fours and a five but more importantly his third wicket partnership of 101 for the third wicket with Hack had placed his side in a strong position which they did not surrender. Hack continued unconquered to 158 in a fraction over five hours and a hard-hitting 55 from all-rounder Jack Reedman (an identical score to that of Darling) put the issue beyond doubt with another century stand before the two Freds — Jarvis and Hack — knocked off the winning runs, the final hit coming from a cut from Noble which Iredale allowed to roll on to the asphalt bicycle track.[3]

With the Sheffield Shield contests behind him, Darling returned to club cricket and, batting in dry conditions, was in splendid form scoring 93 with 14 fours in East Torrens' three wicket win over East Adelaide.[4]

A final first-class match staged in early February at the SCG was headed in the Sydney sporting newspaper, the *Referee*, as 'Test Match in aid of the War Fund'. It was not a Test match, but a game organised for the Australian Bushmen's Contingent and New South Wales Patriotic Funds for the Boer War and thus represented an early connection between sport and war. Pitting an Australian Eleven against The Rest, each side was captained by a South Australian as Darling led the Australian team and Reedman their opponents. Batting first for the Eleven, only Trumper and Noble revealed any sign of form and Darling with 4 was among the failures as the first innings ended at 237. It looked as though The Rest would forge a substantial lead when they passed 250 with only five wickets down, but a late collapse saw them succumb for 281 and a lead of 44.

---

3   *Observer* 20 January 1900, p. 19.
4   *Observer* 3 February 1900, p. 19.

A gratifying feature was the strong patronage at the match with about 9000 people present on the second day. A popular interlude was the entrance of a detachment of 100 members of the Bushmen's Contingent at 4 o'clock who marched around the ground and met with tremendous bursts of cheering as they passed the main grandstands.[5]

The Eleven rattled on the runs in the second innings with a consistent batting display by the top order such that four of the top five batsman reached half-centuries and Trumper was just one run short. Darling entered at 3-197 and might have been caught first ball when he lofted Tasmanian all-rounder Edward Windsor to long-off where Stuckey first dashed and then pulled up to take the ball on the bounce suggesting that he might have been deliberately generous to the Australian captain. From then on Darling plundered the bowling while enjoying a couple more lives to score 72 in 76 minutes and the Eleven's second innings of 400 enabled it to gain an easy win. The Rest, however, performed creditably and certainly threatened to take the honours at various points. Financially the match was a success with £512 taken at the gates and £120 contributed by members to collecting boxes as well as an expected contribution of £50 from the New South Wales Cricket Association under whose auspices the game was played. As expenses were light the combined funds were likely to profit by around £550.[6]

Darling's remaining cricket was for East Torrens in the tightly contested electorate competition and he struck a rich vein of form. Weather conditions were difficult at Alberton Oval on 17 February as a vigorous wind produced blinding showers of dust which upset batsmen and the field and might have had something to do with a tardy beginning to his innings. However, he peppered the boundaries later in reaching 147 not out at stumps and declaring the following week to gain a win over Port Adelaide against whom he had now scored 406 runs for the season without being dismissed.[7] A fortnight later he hit with terrific force in an innings of 41 against West Torrens at the Neutral Ground[8] and at the same venue brought up another century (103) against West Adelaide when he quickly collared the bowling and was unlucky to be caught from a stroke which many spectators reckoned had cleared the boundary.[9]

It was an unlucky end to a season which saw him combine a disappointing 252 runs at 28.00 at first-class level with a superlative 722 runs at 144.40 (including four centuries) in club games. Despite his terrific scoring for East Torrens, however, the club had to settle for second place on the premiership ladder behind East Adelaide for whom that other brilliant left-hander Clem Hill returned figures of 545 runs at 136.25.[10]

---

5 *Referee* 10 February 1900, p. 8.
6 Adelaide *Chronicle* 10 February 1900, p. 33.
7 *Observer* 24 February 1900, p. 19.
8 *Observer* 10 March 1900, p. 19.
9 *Chronicle* 24 March 1900, p. 33.
10 *Observer* 14 April 1900, p. 19.

Stonehenge. Photo by Graeme Ryan

Intermission – Stonehenge

The purchase of the Stonehenge estate in the Tasmanian Midlands in mid-1900 indicated a change of direction and location in Joe Darling's life and an intention to follow agricultural and pastoral pursuits. Evidently, however, it was a well-kept secret. Seeing a large amount of luggage leaving Darling's house a neighbour said, 'Hello, Joe, where are you off?' Darling merely replied, 'To get my hair cut.' Very few people knew of his intention to leave South Australia, and they only knew about it a day or two before he left.[11]

At the same time his cricket retirement was mooted.[12] With a view to clearing away any doubt on the matter the *South Australian Register* telegraphed him to enquire whether he intended to play club cricket and be available for international matches and received the following reply: 'May play cricket in Tasmania; undecided about internationals.' The newspaper hoped Darling would be ready when the opportunity arrived to lead Australia against the next English team due to visit in 1901-02 and suggested that the Tasmanians would welcome his services and that he could maintain his form on the excellent turf pitches in Launceston.[13]

The Stonehenge property was plagued with rabbits on his arrival and Joe Darling enlarged on the problem in the early years in a letter to the Hobart *Mercury* in 1916, stated that at the beginning the property was 'simply alive with rabbits, and the trappers used to take off 20,000 a year, and then leave a lot behind'.[14]

Faced with problems of this magnitude it is easy to understand why he played no cricket in the 1900-01 season and, in fact, one of his few contacts with the game that summer came when on a return to Adelaide in January 1901 he was afforded a belated farewell social by the East Torrens

---

11 Incident recalled in the *Critic* 22 February 1905, p. 12.
12 *Tasmanian News* 14 July 1900, p. 4.
13 *South Australian Register* 18 July 1900, p. 4.
14 Hobart *Mercury* 19 December 1916, p. 2.

Electorate Cricket Club at the Norwood Town Hall. This function, which was described as a 'very quiet affair' was attended by leading South Australian Cricket Association (SACA) officials such as Mostyn Evan and John Hill, and former Test team-mates George Giffen and Jack Lyons, with Sydney Talbot Smith acting as master of ceremonies, but there was criticism of the club for not using the Adelaide Town Hall and opening invitations to the wider cricketing public. A mere sixty people paying their respects was an insultingly low number. Smith offered the main toast to the 'health and continued prosperity' of the guest of honour and in response Darling said that while his future home would be Tasmania he would be 'bound by the strongest ties to the state of South Australia', and would always follow their welfare on the cricket field.[15]

Return to cricket 1901-02

An early intimation of Darling's return to cricket came when he replied to a letter from Major Wardill of 17 September enquiring about his availability in the coming summer's Test matches. In his own correspondence, dated 27 September, he discussed the balance of Archie MacLaren's English touring side and concluded that they had 'got together a rattling good side that will take a lot of beating on Australian wickets'. He added:

> After due consideration I am prepared to play in the first three test matches if required, and will see about the other two later on. Owing to shearing not being finished until about November 20, it will not be possible for me to play in Adelaide on November 9 against the Englishmen. All being well I could arrive in Melbourne by December 1, and so have a fortnight's hard practice to get in form for the first test match in Sydney.[16]

To modern eyes such a request and reply seems ridiculous, but it has to be remembered that the Melbourne Cricket Club was still acting in its entrepreneurial role as an international tour promoter and the Australian Eleven remained much like a club. Within that framework, Darling's status remained high, indeed so high that complete lack of match practice was seen as no impediment to his return.

Darling makes reference to not being available to play in Adelaide which would have meant him turning out for South Australia. Evidently this followed the New South Wales Cricket Association stating early in the season that it would not object to Darling playing interstate matches for his old state even though he had been resident in Tasmania for more than a year. But work on his farm ruled out that possibility as well in the first games beginning in late November. Getting into form was thus left to net practice, and at least one journalist was convinced that Joe

---

15 *Advertiser* 15 January 1901, p. 6; *Critic* 19 January 1901, p. 10.
16 *Register* 5 October 1901, p. 5.

Packed crowd at the Sydney Cricket Ground on the first day of the first Test on 13 December 1901.
State Library of New South Wales Collection

would remain a 'tower of strength to Australia' and 'shine once again with all his old splendour' simply because he had been living the outdoor life and was feeling in good trim.[17]

Writing a week before the first Test, 'Felix' (Tom Horan) in the *Australasian* commented that 'nearly every cricketer and lover of cricket whom I have met' had picked a team for the match and some had left Darling out because they were under the impression that he would not play. However, he had arrived bearded from Tasmania on the 31 November and was hard at work at the Melbourne Cricket Ground nets on 3 December. He quickly trimmed his beard, quipping that the price of wool had gone up, and then made his way to Sydney on 7 December. The prediction was that the selectors Hugh Trumble, Clem Hill and Monty Noble would as near as possible stick with the old guard of the Australian Eleven of 1899. Any claims of new men such as batsman Leslie Poidevin who had scored a second innings 151 not out, and Belgian-born leg-spinner GRC Clarke who had taken career-best figures of 10 wickets for 231 against MacLaren's Eleven for New South Wales were certainly ignored as was that of veteran George Giffen who had captured 13 wickets for 93 runs in the tourists opening game against South Australia. As it turned out, 'Felix' had predicted the side to a man — Gregory, Trumper, Hill, Noble, Darling, McLeod, Kelly,

---

17   Sydney *Sportsman* 3 December 1901, p. 8.

Howell, Laver, Trumble and Jones — he may as well have been sole selector. It was obvious that in dragging his gear from Tasmania to Sydney, Darling was not going to be omitted.[18]

In fact, he captained the Australian side and it was no glorious resumption as England reversed their poor form in the lead-up matches by winning by an innings and 124 runs. An opening partnership of 154 between MacLaren and Tom Hayward was the basis of a first innings score of 464 runs in even time in which the *Referee's* 'Not Out' (JC Davis) remarked as follows on the bowling changes:

> In the first innings of England, Jones and Noble opened the bowling and no fewer than 24 changes were made before the innings was brought to a close. There were six changes before the first wicket fell and Trumble, who got the wicket, did not go on until 115 runs were made. On the first day 272 runs were made for six wickets, 11 changes being made; on Saturday 192 runs were added, and 13 changes made. Jones and Noble were each tried five times, McLeod, Howell and Trumble each four times, Laver three times and Trumper once. Howell went on first at 33, was taken off at 70, and did not bowl again until 257 runs were on the board. Jones did not take a wicket until his fifth trial.[19]

Was this a criticism of Darling's leadership?

When Australia batted, the inexperienced attack of Sydney Barnes right-arm fast medium, Len Braund's leg breaks and Colin Blythe's left-arm orthodox spin shared the wickets almost equally with respective match figures of 6 for 139, 7 for 101 and 7 for 56 as the home side was disposed of for 168. In Australia's first innings, Gregory and Hill provided the only substantial partnership of 86 for the second wicket, but after four wickets fell at 112 only Darling (batting at eight) with 39 in an hour and a quarter supplied any significant number of lower order runs. Once or twice he appeared in difficulties but without showing his best he shaped well enough to suggest that with practice his form would be as sound as ever. Whether this gave him undue confidence, or whether he simply thought in view of a deficit of 296 runs he needed to lead from the front, Darling promoted himself to open with Trumper in the second innings, but was caught for 3 when he half-hit Braund to square leg and Jessop jumping high took an astonishing one-handed catch.

Australia made a couple of changes to its side for the second Test beginning in Melbourne on New Year's Day. Charlie McLeod, who had dreamt of making a pair in Sydney and duly did so, was dropped despite being the most effective bowler with four wickets, as was his Victorian team-mate Frank Laver, and into their places came two members of the younger brigade, New South Wales middle-order batsman Reg Duff and Victorian all-rounder Warwick Armstrong.

Test honours were even after Australia won by 229 runs following an extraordinary first day on which 25 wickets fell for 221 runs. Rain the day before the match and on the first morning

---

18 *Australasian* 7 December 1901, p. 21.
19 *Referee* 18 December 1901, p. 8.

influenced MacLaren to send Australia in to bat and the decision appeared well justified when Trumper fell second ball of the match and the whole side was removed for 112 by Barnes (6 for 42) and Blythe (4 for 64) with only Duff's 32 offering much opposition. Few observers, however, would have imagined that the Englishmen would last barely an hour as only quick swinging from Jessop (27 in 20 minutes) enabled them to reach 61 as Noble (7 for 17) and Trumble (3 for 38) ran through the rest. Even so, when Australia had lost 5-48 in its second innings the Englishmen were again in a splendid position. However, Darling's brilliant captaincy in holding back Hill to bat at seven with Trumper, Noble, Duff and Armstrong to follow paid rich dividends on an improving pitch to reach 353. The recovery was a triumph for the home side and while Hill's 99 provided the middle order sustenance, Duff (who scored 104) and Armstrong (45 not out) revealed their mettle and quality as batsmen in a last-wicket stand of 120 to set a victory target of 405 which proved way out of reach.[20]

Panoramic photograph taken from north mound looking towards the western grandstands at Adelaide Oval during the third Test in January 1902. Photo by Ernest Gall, SLSA B7539

In looking at the bald figures of the match, Darling's innings of 19 and 23 might appear insignificant and there was a body of opinion that he should have been omitted from the second game. However, his batting in Sydney had been satisfactory and in almost unplayable conditions on the first day in Melbourne was exemplary. While his captaincy in Sydney had revealed weaknesses, it was undoubtedly due to his two years rusticating in Tasmania. Now his thinking was sharp and his perception of his opponent's weaknesses was as sound as ever.

The third Test match would begin in Adelaide in mid-January, but in between South Australia was to host a Sheffield Shield match against New South Wales at the ground and this appeared to be an excellent opportunity for Darling to get much-needed match practice. Darling made himself available and a special meeting of the cricket committee of the SACA was held to consider the issue. One section strongly supported his inclusion because of national interests and that he had a perfect right to take part in the game as a native-born player. Conversely other members

---

20 *Referee* 8 January 1902, p. 8; Webster, *First-Class Cricket*, p. 292.

contended that as he had left to reside permanently in Tasmania his services 'could not with due regard to the dignity of the state be utilized' and argued in favour of blooding promising junior players. As this group had the numbers, the state selectors were asked not to choose Darling, a decision which was regarded with incredulity in other parts of the country.[21]

The rubber was tied when the combatants reached Adelaide for the third Test. Under energetic secretary John Creswell, the SACA prepared for a profitable Test. Creswell even covered the pitch with galvanised iron to protect it, a highly unorthodox action but justified by the fact that the association had control until play began. The Adelaide Oval could accommodate 40,000 spectators and did for near that number for the Royal tour of the Duke and Duchess of Windsor (later King George V and Queen Mary) on 11 July of the previous year. Creswell placed an extra 2000 chairs in the members' reserve and catering booths and tents were erected around the ground.

The weather was glorious for the opening day and Darling was welcomed home with the Oval resplendent with flags and banners. Streamers hung from grandstand roofs, and over the smokers' stand floated the Commonwealth flag and a large green and gold ensign with the word 'Australia' emblazoned in gold letters. The front of the vice-regal box was decorated with the Union Jack and a display of cricketing colours: the green and gold of Australia; red, white and blue of England; red, yellow and black of South Australia; dark blue of Victoria and light blue of New South Wales. England had maintained faith with their players from Melbourne but the Australian selectors had replaced local hero Ernie Jones with Charlie McLeod. Jones's omission was not a surprise as he had lacked penetration in Sydney and was hardly used in Melbourne, yet SA supporters would have preferred the inclusion of slow left-armer Joe Travers.

Syd Barnes' injury was a crucial loss to England.

Darling lost the toss, and MacLaren and Hayward controlled the early part of the game with a stand of 149 until two run outs in mid-afternoon and three quick strikes by Trumble reduced the innings to 5-186 before a recovery by Billy Quaife and Braund (103 not out) took the score to 388 just after lunch on the second day. The crowd was tense as Darling and Trumper opened for Australia, groaned when the captain quickly fell to an over-pitched ball by Blythe, but quickly rejoiced in a virtuoso batting display by Trumper and Hill who added a second-wicket partnership of 137 in 94 minutes. During this partnership disaster befell England when champion bowler Barnes, who had taken 19 wickets in the first two Tests, broke down with a twisted knee and played no further part in the series.

At 2-173 Australia was in a strong position on Monday morning with Hill on 83 but when he reached 98 he attempted to bring up his century with a big hit off Braund, lifted the ball long

---

21 *Referee* 8 January 1902, p. 8; *Register* 9 January 1902, p. 4.

and high, but saw it fall straight into the hands of Johnny Tyldesley standing on the asphalt bicycle track which surrounded the playing field. On many grounds the stroke would have given Hill five runs and achieved his century. Local supporters yelled 'Not out!' but the local rule did not favour the batsman. The dismissal also signalled a collapse by Australia which lost its last seven wickets for 92 runs to trail by 67. England made another strong start through their openers and after a wild storm interrupted play on the fourth day eventually set the Australians a sizeable fourth innings total of 314 with the pitch bearing an ugly worn patch at the northern end.

Darling perhaps revealed his genius by promoting Duff to open with Trumper. It was the first time the great duo would open in a Test but although it failed at the first attempt it would prove beneficial in the future. Hill then became the backbone of the innings, enjoying productive stands with Trumper and Gregory in reaching 3-98 when Darling came to the crease he would play his last and most significant innings of the series.

Hugh Trumble

The two great left-handers made the bowlers work hard. At 138 MacLaren introduced Hayward's medium-paced off-breaks which the batsmen appreciated as they took 28 runs from four overs. Then Jessop was swung into the attack with his pace and his fourth ball brought a powerful appeal when he struck Hill's pads for no result. However, it might have unsettled the batsman as two balls later he attempted to leg glance and was bowled off his pads for 97 to end the infamous trio of scores following those of 99 and 98. At 4-194 the partnership had been worth 96 runs and 121 runs were needed.

On the sixth and final day, Darling and Trumble batted doggedly to bring Australia victory. Batting with extreme caution, only one run came in the first five overs but no one complained. Darling raised his fifty with a late cut to the boundary and gave a splendid exhibition of defence mixed with fine stroke play. By the time Hayward caught him at mid-on off Jessop for 69 right on lunch, the score was 5-255 and just 60 runs were required. Trumble remained resolute to remain 62 not out to go with match figures of 9 for 198, which would have won any man of the match awards, and victory was achieved with four wickets in hand.[22]

With Australia leading 2-1, Darling returned to his farm and surprisingly there was almost no comment in Australia about his absence. It seems merely to have been understood. The following remarks came, instead, from the English magazine, *Cricket: A Weekly Record of the Game*:

> It has been a bit of hard luck for the Australians to lose the valuable help of such a judicious captain, putting aside his great ability as a cricketer, as J Darling in the last two of the test matches. Domestic affairs, in conjunction with the heavy responsibilities of a sheep station, called him back to Stonehenge, in Tasmania, immediately after the conclusion of the third test match at Adelaide

---

22 Whimpress and Hart, *Adelaide Oval Test Cricket*, pp. 26-31.

on January 23rd. It is, indeed, quite on the cards that he may not be able to come to England with the Australian team who are to leave Adelaide on March 20th. What his loss must mean to the Australians in these last test matches may be judged from the fact that it was his masterly innings of three hours and a half, in conjunction with Hugh Trumble at the end of the third test, that gave the Australians their well earned victory by four wickets.[23]

To make matters worse in the match immediately preceding the fourth Test, however, MacLaren's team ran up the huge score of 769 and gained an innings victory over New South Wales at the Sydney Cricket Ground where the next match would be played. What adverse criticism there was of the selectors related to Aboriginal fast bowler Jack Marsh being ignored despite taking 39 wickets at 9.18 in Sydney electorate cricket and 24 wickets at 22.37 in the previous summer's first-class season. He was also said to have altered his action so that many of those who believed he threw the ball now held that he was above suspicion.[24]

In Darling's absence, Trumble took over the leadership, gaining a surprise victory in Sydney to win the series when the Englishmen collapsed in their second innings for 99 on a good wicket against Noble and debutant, left-arm spinner Jack Saunders, after holding a first innings lead. The final game in Melbourne was also won narrowly when the visitors were caught on a difficult fourth innings wicket resulting in a 4-1 victory margin which probably flattered the Australians.

Darling's role in the series was problematic. As a batsman, his 154 runs at 25.66 were far from imposing, and his captaincy was rusty in the first match. However, his generalship was regarded as instrumental in the successes of the second and third matches. In the second Test at Melbourne, although Australia led by 51 runs on the first innings, Darling realised the danger posed by Barnes and opened himself with Trumble. The pair survived for an hour and a half and even though Barnes took four wickets late in the day, Darling regarded his innings of 23 as one of his most valuable. As has been noted, his 69 in the second innings of the third Test provided vital support to Hill and Trumble. With the series being won, he had no difficulty gaining support to lead the Australian Eleven to England for the second time.[25]

---

23 *Cricket: A Weekly Record of the Game*, 27 February 1902.
24 *Referee* 15 February 1902, p. 20.
25 Whimpress, *On Our Selection*, p. 59.

Australian Coat of Arms from Joe Darling blazer pocket (top). Joe Darling (right). Little girl batting against Australian players probably in gardens at the rear of the Inns of Court Hotel (below).

THIRD ENGLISH TOUR 1902

Australian Cricket Team 1902. Back row: JJ Kelly, JV Saunders, H Trumble, WW Armstrong, MA Noble, WP Howell, BJ Wardill (manager). Seated: C Hill, RA Duff, J Darling (captain) VT Trumper, E Jones. Front: AJY Hopkins, H Carter, SE Gregory. Melbourne Cricket Club Collection.

Major Wardill again managed the eleventh Australian team so that there was further continuity with 1899. Because of the duration of the 1901-02 Test series, the team was not chosen until early March, and when it was there might have been some grumbles about the omission of Charles Eady and Travers who had appeared in the fifth Test in Melbourne and received little opportunity with the ball. Back into the side came Darling as captain with Trumper, Duff, Gregory, Noble, Hopkins, Kelly, Carter and Howell from New South Wales; Trumble, Armstrong and Saunders from Victoria; and Hill and Jones from South Australia. As if to remind the selectors of the gravity of their error in leaving him out, Eady rolled out an innings of 566 for Break o'Day against Wellington at Hobart's TCA Ground over 15 and 22 March and 5 April, a total that remains the highest score in adult cricket throughout the world.

The party sailed from Adelaide on the *Omrah* on 20 March carrying not only the Australians, but also MacLaren's team who had completed their tour with a six wicket win over South Australia just two days before. As Gideon Haigh reminds us:

A spirit of cricketing brotherhood prevailed. On-field rivalries were forgotten, shared Britishness celebrated in rounds of bullboard and deck billiards … Two teams of cricketers were, in different senses, on their way 'home'.[1]

Among other travellers were Joe Darling's wife Alice and the wives of manager Wardill, and fellow players Gregory and Kelly, former Australian Test hero Frederick Spofforth, one-Test wonder and perennial cricket tourist Dr Rowley Pope, and Leslie Poidevin who but for finger injuries at the wrong time was likely to have been a member of the side. Poidevin had been twelfth man in the first Test in Sydney in December and was travelling to Britain to study medicine. Nine of the team arrived in London prematurely on 21 April, having left the ship in Marseilles and travelled overland but changed their minds about spending time in Paris, while the rest of the team continued the voyage with their manager.

SS Omrah on which the Australian team and English teams that had just completed the 1901-02 Test series sailed together to renew acquaintances in England.

Unlike 1899, which had been a dry English summer, the start of the 1902 cricket season was bitterly cold, wet and miserable, resulting in so many players suffering from influenza that Pope, who travelled with the team as an honorary medical adviser, had to make up the eleven against Cambridge University. Despite their ills, the Australians performed well in seven matches before the first Test, winning four (three by an innings) with three games drawn. While the main blow to the side was Hugh Trumble dislocating the thumb on his bowling hand at practice before matches

---

1   Gideon Haigh, *The Big Ship: Warwick Armstrong and the Making of Modern Cricket*, Text Publishing, Melbourne, 2001, p. 47.

began, and missing the first month of play, others found form. In conditions favouring the bowlers, Armstrong had second innings figures of 8 for 47 against Nottinghamshire in the second match, Howell a match analysis of 11 for 56 against Surrey, Noble 12 for 69 against Leicestershire, Trumper a five wicket bag against Essex, and Saunders second innings figures of 7 for 67 against Oxford University. The batsmen were not as successful but Hill scored a century at Leyton and Trumper back-to-back hundreds at Oxford and against the MCC at Lord's.[2]

Joe Darling, 1902

Darling opened the tour strongly with scores of 26 and 92 against WG Graces's London County in the first match at Crystal Palace and followed with 128 at Trent Bridge. Each had their distinctive character. Of his 92 it certainly could be described as cavalier as he batted for just 100 minutes and treated the spectators to an exhibition of superb driving including lifting leg-spinner Braund out of the ground for six. By contrast, in the game against Nottinghamshire, Darling gave a roundheaded display of determined batting, his innings lasting four hours and 50 minutes, combining wonderful patience with strong driving when the occasion offered, and was a great factor in his side's first win of the tour.[3] Thereafter his string of scores showed him getting starts for 19, 7, 25, 22 not out, 5 not out and 28 batting (with one exception) at number five.[4]

When the series got underway at Edgbaston, England had the best of the first day in reaching 9-351, but it should not have been that easy, especially after being 3-35 and despite a minor recovery through a resolute half-century from Stanley Jackson they were still in trouble at 5-121. Lax fielding gave Johnny Tyldesley no less than three let offs at 43, after which he settled down to reach 138. Following heavy rain overnight, the innings was resumed mid-afternoon on the second day with Lockwood and Rhodes continuing an unbeaten partnership when MacLaren declared at 376. It proved to be perfect timing as the pitch was now drying and both sticky and tricky. Australia's miserable reply was just 36 with Trumper scoring half that total. Darling's contribution was 3 as the wretched wicket proved ideal for Rhodes who captured 7 for 17 and his Yorkshire partner Hirst took the remaining three wickets.

Trailing by 340 and forced to follow on, Trumper and Duff had added only eight runs when rain stopped play. It continued heavily during the night and the ground was almost under water the following morning. The turf was so sloppy that play hardly seemed possible, but with the sun shining, the crowd swelled until it grew to 14,000 who began demanding admission. The umpires

---

2 Cricinfo season archive 1902
3 *Observer 17 May 1902*, p. 18.
4 Cricinfo season archive 1902.

Joe Darling — Cricketer, Farmer, Politician and Family Man

Horse drawn brake — Australian XI leaving Hotel Birmingham, 1902

inspected the pitch several times but it was not until 5 o'clock that they agreed to play. Long before that the crowd had got out of hand, several hundred rushed the gates causing a number of men and women to be knocked down and it was fortunate there were no fatalities. Eventually at 5.15, Trumper and Duff resumed on a soft pitch determined to play for a draw. Although both lost their wickets, the score was 2-46 when play ended.[5]

Bleak weather conditions prevailed when the Australians moved north to Leeds for their next county match where they recorded their lowest ever score of 23 in the second innings of a five wicket loss to Yorkshire. On this occasion Rhodes the destroyer did not even get the ball in his hand as Hirst (5 for 9) and Jackson (5 for 12) completed the win. The tourists got into batting form against Lancashire at Old Trafford by scoring 7-356 on the first day, but the rest of the game was washed out and all-rounder Bert Hopkins achieved the startling analysis of 7 for 10 in an innings win over Cambridge University. Darling's last three innings were 3, 1 and 9 but he could claim illness as an excuse as entering the Lord's Test he, Howell and Noble were all suffering from influenza and Saunders had tonsillitis.

The second Test was delayed by appalling weather until 2.45 on the opening day when the loss of Fry and Ranjitsinhji without a run being scored recalled the Birmingham match. In Hopkins' first over Fry made a weak stroke to a well-pitched up ball on his legs and then Ranji was completely defeated by the same bowler. The dismissals brought the following comment from Darling:

The weather was bitterly cold and several of the Australians felt it so badly that they wore their

---

5   *Observer* 7 June 1902, p. 19.

blazers under ther cricket sweaters. Ernie Jones opened the attack and bowled the first over to MacLaren which was a maiden. As Trumble and Howell were both unfit to bowl, I did not know who to put on at the other end, and in desperation I tossed the ball to Hopkins who was only a fair bowler. He bowled CB Fry a very bad ball which Fry should have hit for four but being the first ball he received he played it softly to Clem Hill at square leg and England had lost one for 0.

Ranjitsinhji then came in and in the same over Hopkins bowled him off his pads for a duck, and England had lost two for 0. No one was more surprised than Hopkins, as neither of the balls really deserved a wicket but that is where the glorious uncertainty of the game comes in.[6]

JOE DARLING LEADING HIS FAMOUS 1902 TEAM ONTO THE FIELD AT LORDS
Left to Right: J. Darling, E. Jones, H. Trumble, V. Trumper, R. Duff, C. Hill, J. Kelly (Wicketkeeper).

As in the previous match, Jackson was called upon to save the side and after one streaky stroke through the slips he did so along with MacLaren to reach 2-102 before rain washed out play for the day and the match. A curious feature of the Australian attack was that Darling employed six bowlers to deliver 38 overs in 105 minutes. Perhaps he was simply trying to keep everyone warm.

With the weather cruelling the first two Test matches, the rubber did not come alive until the third game amid the smokestacks of Bramall Lane, Sheffield where Victorian off-spinner Trumble returned to the side and proved a vital component with 26 wickets in the next three contests. The Australians had four wins in succession leading into the game, but Darling must have been concerned with his own form which saw him make a pair of ducks in consecutive

---

6   Darling, *Test Tussles*, 44-5

first-class matches against an England Eleven at Bradford as well as the Test with an innings of 1 in a non-first-class match against Scotland at Edinburgh sandwiched in between. His figures of 0, 0, 1, 0, 0 were not a great series.[7]

When play was under way in the third Test, Darling was annoyed to find that the wicket was tampered with twice. After winning the toss, the Australians were dismissed on a fairly good wicket for 194 and England lost 5-102 when stumps were drawn at the end of the first day. Rain fell during the night and when the pitch was inspected the following morning it was discovered that it had been illegally rolled at 9 o'clock on the second morning. There was nothing that could be done but the Australians realised that if they could dismiss the rest of the Englishmen cheaply the extra rolling could work to their advantage.

And that is what occurred as the last five wickets fell for 43 runs, giving the Australians a 49-run lead on the first innings. Thus, the wicket had three rollings before lunch: the illegal one, a second and legitimate one at 11 o'clock and the third just before the Australians started their second innings which eventually totalled 289 with England set 339 to win.

At stumps England had reached 1-73 with Jessop 33 not out and the game in an interesting stage. Darling stated that he and wicket-keeper Kelly rushed to the ground early on the third day in hope of catching the groundsmen rolling the wicket but were too late as it had already been done. The Australians could have complained but played on and won the low scoring match on the strength of Hill's second innings century and Noble's 11 wickets for 103 runs. A second pleasure was that when the groundsman visited the team's dressing room door expecting a two guinea tip, he was not only refused, but tipped through the door by the scruff of the neck.[8]

Darling finally gathered some runs with 37 against Warwickshire followed by scores of 9, 13 not out (batting at seven in a total of 5-545 declared against Gloucestershire), 20 versus Somerset and 32 against Surrey, before one of the most historic Test matches of all time and the one which would make his name because it sealed the series win for Australia.

The fourth match at Old Trafford has been most widely reported, following Neville Cardus, as Fred Tate's tragedy, but without wanting to downplay the importance of the romance of storytelling, great sporting contests have many ebbs and flows before reaching their climax. A second telling is of Victor Trumper establishing Australia's victory with a century (104) before lunch on the first day, but a 3 run win involves many what-ifs and other heroes include fast bowler Lockwood with 11 wickets for 76 and Jackson with a first innings of 128 for the losers, and Trumble with 10 wicket for 128 for the winners. Darling himself played a major role with the bat as well as his cool captaincy at the finish.

Australia certainly got off to a brilliant start with Trumper and Duff raising the 100 in 57 minutes, and when Duff was dismissed for 54 the total was 135 in 78 minutes. At lunch it was a dominant 1-173 but the impetus was lost when Rhodes removed Trumper, Noble and Gregory

---

7   Cricinfo season archive 1902.
8   Darling, *Test Tussles*, p. 32.

in a four over spell. Enter Darling at 4-183 to mount a recovery which he and Hill did in slashing style by adding 73 runs in three quarters of an hour. Darling hit Rhodes twice out of the ground for six at the Warwick Road end, the first sixes recorded in England to go with the first six he had hit to bring up his century in the Adelaide Test of 1898, plus three fours which carried into the crowd and would have been awarded six runs under later rules. It was a blazing innings of 51, but the Australian tail fell quickly and 299 was a poor result although it started to assume gigantic proportions as the first five English wickets tumbled for 44 runs and a small recovery to 70 at the end of a spellbinding first day. The first session of the second day belonged to England as Jackson and Braund extended a sixth wicket partnership to 141 and Jackson provided the backbone of the innings of 262.

Thirty-seven runs was only a slim lead and the great probability was that Darling would close the Australian innings late on the third day in the remote possibility of an English collapse. This would not happen as Lockwood made a severe dent in the innings by removing Trumper, Duff and Hill in quick order to leave the score at 3-10. Darling had promoted himself to number four and the wreckage of the innings might have been worse when he lofted Braund to deep square leg and was dropped by Tate at 16. For many commentators this was the turning point of the match, but why Tate was blamed to that extent is unclear. Darling hit Braund out of the ground in his next over and added a vital 54 run partnership with Gregory as he top scored with 37, a sterling hand marked by fine hitting, but the innings total of 86 and target of 124 seemed well within England's reach when they went to lunch on at 0-36, just 88 runs to get with all wickets intact. History, of course, revealed that the Australians would triumph, but Darling provided a

Victor Trumper's brilliant century before lunch on the first day was a highlight of the exciting Old Trafford Test.

more meaningful turning point than Tate's miss, stating rather that it was when MacLaren was magnificently caught for 35 in the outfield by Duff:

This was one of the finest catches that I have ever seen, as Duff had to run a long way and just caught the ball at his toes when running at full speed. If Duff had missed that catch it would have been all over as far as Australia was concerned.[9]

MacLaren's departure at 3-72 gave the Australians a sniff of victory but when Ranjitsinhji and Abel were at the crease 20 runs later their prospects were dim. Instead, Trumble and Saunders applied the screws and the fall of wickets read 4-92 (Ranji), 5-97 (Abel), 6-107 (Jackson), 7-109 (Braund), 8-109 (Lockwood) and 9-116 (Lilley). So tense was the atmosphere that Australian manager Wardill's wife ran a needle through the palm of her hand as she crocheted while watching.[10]

Eight runs remained with one wicket to fall, but before Tate reached the pitch it began raining and the players left for the dressing room. Forty-five minutes later they resumed. Saunders to Tate and the first ball he played between Duff's legs, the ball beating Armstrong running from slip to the boundary. To the second ball Tate played an adequate forward defensive stroke and he survived the third. The fourth ball bowled him off stump. In some accounts it was described as a 'shooter', in others as Saunders 'quicker ball' which in view of various doubts about his action might have been a euphemism for something else. For Darling, however, it was a moment to savour and he recalled the match with absolute delight in a letter to his father:

At Manchester yesterday was finished the greatest cricket match ever known, when we defeated All England by the very small margin of only three runs. Talk about keenness and excitement. In all my cricketing career I have never seen anything to approach it. When it got near the end, and they wanted eight runs to win and only one wicket to fall, as the bowler started to bowl you could not hear a sound from the 12,000 spectators on the ground. As the ball was played, or missed, there was a tremendous cheer, and when Tate, the last man in snicked a fluky four runs just past his leg stump, the roar went up and the cheering etc. were simply deafening.

Three balls later the end came. As Saunders knocked Tate's off stump clean out of the ground with a fast ball and the stump turned over three or four times in the air, then our players simply lost our heads, and started waving our caps and cheering as we ran to the pavilion. It was a great match and glorious win, and if our team had not stuck to it and played right through to the finish with *nil desperandum* as our motto we must certainly have been defeated as nearly all through it looked odds on England winning.

Too much praise can not be given to the boys for the grand way they played and stuck to the

---

9   Darling, *Test Tussles*, p. 28.
10 Haigh, *Big Ship*, p. 68.

game, and thus ended the greatest cricket match ever played, or likely to be played for many years to come in the cricket field. This win puts us in the grand position of winning the rubber and returning with the ashes to Australia.

Every time I woke up last night I imagined I could see the last ball bowled and the off stump flying through the air. Whilst playing we did not feel the strain too much but after the match we were all simply done to the world, and as long as I live I never want another match like it.[11]

In fact, the next match was very much like it — another heart-stopper — although with the difference that the series was decided and thus it had not the same significance. Nevertheless, as an individual contest, it produced excitement galore with Jessop entering at 5-48 chasing 263 and playing one of the most astonishing innings of all time, reaching the identical score of 104 to Trumper at Manchester, and doing so while adding 109 with Jackson in 65 minutes before the latter was caught and bowled by Trumble. The loss of his partner did not stop Jessop who went on hitting, so that when his innings concluded he had been batting for a mere hour and a quarter, made his runs out of 139, including 17 fours and a five in his own total.

Gilbert Jessop's batting fireworks enabled a thrilling English victory at The Oval by 1 wicket.

Jessop's innings remains part of the romance of cricket, but in Hill's 1933 reminiscences he offers an interesting perspective on Darling's leadership in the context of the match:

> Darling was a great captain, but we thought he was in error in this match. The only way Jessop could play Trumble was by jumping out and hitting him. One end of Kennington Oval is longer than the other. Trumble was bowling from the short end, known as the pavilion end, with the result that Jessop was hitting him into the grandstand. If he had been on at the long end, and Jessop had continued making the same lusty hits, he would have been caught in the outfield.[12]

However, memory can play strange tricks and Hill was caught out by the fact that only one of Jessop's hits cleared the grandstand. It is always easy to be a tactical genius with the benefit of hindsight and another theory advanced was that Darling was placing too much reliance on Saunders and should have introduced Noble into the attack because determination characterised his cricket and his heady approach to the game would have been invaluable.[13]

Of course, there was still work to be done and with one wicket in hand Hirst and Rhodes saw

---

11 Printed in the *Express & Telegraph* 4 September 1902, p. 3.
12 Hill, *Reminiscences*, p. 70.
13 Sydney *Sun 8 July 1919*, p. 3.

Joe Darling toasting England at a formal dinner in London, 1902.

England home with the mythological comment 'We'll get them in singles', a statement proved by the statistical pedants who have checked the scorecard to have been just that.

Darling's team won 23 drew 12 and lost only two of its 37 first-class matches. In the first Test at Birmingham, England put one of its greatest sides into the field in MacLaren, Fry, Ranjitsinhji, Jackson, Johnny Tyldesley, Lilley, Hirst, Jessop, Braund, Lockwood and Rhodes yet the sides were marvellously balanced. Although the Australians escaped after being dismissed for 36 in their first innings they went on to win the series 2-1 against a team Darling rightly called 'All England'. It also underlined the 1902 side as one of the great Australian teams and which bears comparison with its successors in Armstrong's 1921 team, Bradman's 1948 Invincibles and Steve Waugh's 2001 combination.

Over the tour as a whole, Trumper was the outstanding batsman and despite the wet weather scored 2570 runs at 48.49 with 11 centuries thus putting Darling's 1899 total of 1941 runs and five hundreds completely in the shade. Other batsmen had their moments of glory and especially Noble (284) and Armstrong (172 not out) with their sixth wicket partnership of 428 against Sussex at Hove, and Hill's hundred in the Sheffield Test. In all, seven batsmen — Trumper, Hill, Duff, Noble, Darling, Hopkins and Armstrong — passed the 1000 run mark. The wickets were also spread more evenly among the bowlers with Trumble and Saunders topping 100 wickets with Noble a near miss and Armstrong, Howell and Jones passing 60 wickets. Of his own form, Darling might have been disappointed with 1112 runs at 24.71 with just two centuries, and especially the run drought mid-tour and his 109 Test runs at 15.57. However, the compensation would come from his leadership, backing up his 1899 English tour success and his part in the previous Australian summer with a third consecutive series win. As *Wisden* commented in its 1903 edition:

> The Australians last season started with the advantage of being splendidly equipped at every point, but owed a great deal to the fact that except where illness lay some of them aside, they were always physically fit to do their best. Good conditions helped to make their ground fielding a marvel of sustained energy and enabled them to go through an exhausting tour with scarcely a trace of staleness. In this all-important matter of physical well being, they undoubtedly owed much to the precept example of their captain. In his own sphere of action Darling is a born leader. When he comes to England, he comes simply and solely to play cricket and he has the rare power of being able to keep a whole team up to something approaching his own standard. He has immense concentration of purpose and under his guidance the players were just as keen at the end of three month's cricket as they had been at the beginning of their tour.[14]

Where would he go from here?

The short answer was that the team would depart from Waterloo Station in a saloon car laden with flowers. Team members would net between £500 and £550 as their share of the proceeds of the trip to England, Wales and Scotland but they had also packed their trunks with merchandise among which were some curious items. Howell packed 30 bats for his friends and dozens of Sheffield razors, Darling's stock contained a lot of cricket material for he still owned his Adelaide sports store, Saunders' taste led him to acquire extensive purchases of Royal Worcester china, Hill

SS Dunvegan Castle which transported the Australian team from England to South Africa at the end of the 1902 tour.

---

14 *Wisden Cricketers' Almanack 1903*, pp. 242-3.

and Trumble bought sporting guns and golf clubs, and Gregory (who admired London tailoring) bought enough suits to last him a generation.

The party left Southampton on 20 September aboard the *Dunvegan Castle* bound for South Africa where they would play three Test matches on the way home. South Australian mining magnate Abe Bailey had guaranteed a minimum of £2000 and the team had readily accepted the invitation to play.[15] While Darling's team won the series 2-0 on matting wickets, the local side was far from disgraced, scoring 454 in the first drawn match at the Old Wanderers Ground in Johannesburg and taking a solid first innings lead in the same arena a week later. Hill led the batting aggregate and averages, Armstrong carried his bat for 159 not out in the second Test while Saunders (15 for 176) and Trumble (14 for 174) made merry in two matches apiece. For the home team the outstanding figures were by two all-rounders, Charlie Llewellyn with 25 wicket at 17.92 and Jimmy Sinclair who hit centuries in the second and third games as well as taking nine wickets. The one player who missed out was Darling who in five innings made 25 runs with a top score of 14.

Australian leading players during Joe Darling's second interval from Test cricket — Monty Noble who took over as Test captain, star batsman Victor Trumper and all-rounder Warwick Armstrong.

---

15 Haigh, *Big Ship*, p. 69.

SECOND INTERVAL AND AFTER 1903-05

The short answer to Joe Darling's cricket future was that he went back to his sheep station at Stonehenge and did not handle a bat again until 1904 when he returned to Adelaide and again took up cricket. He played no cricket in the summer of 1902-03 nor 1903-04 when the next English Test side led by Pelham Warner toured Australia.

The game, however, had not lost interest in him, nor he it, as he was disposed to give an interview to the Adelaide *Register* expressing his opinions on English cricketers and Warner's team. It was an early occasion when given a voice by the press and he would provide trenchant criticisms about a range of cricket subjects down the years. Now he offered:

> The only players that are not coming with Mr Warner's team that would have strengthened the side are MacLaren, Jackson, Ranji, and perhaps Lockwood, but in the latter's case, it would have been very risky to have brought him on account of his being strained. I do not think Fry or Jessop would have strengthened the side, as Fry has never performed well against Australian bowlers in the past. And as regards Jessop, the wickets are too fast for his style of hitting, which was clearly proved when he was out with the last English Eleven.
>
> The side that is coming, in my opinion, is quite as good as, if not better than, the previous one and will take a lot of beating in the test matches. Although some of the names are new to Australia, most of the members of Warner's team have played on more than one occasion against the last Australian Eleven that visited England, and performed well.
>
> In picking an all-England eleven, after the first five or six men have been selected, there are at least 30 or 40 players that have very strong claims to be included in the team and this applies to most of the members of the visiting team that have not already taken part in a test match. If Australia wants to retain the ashes she will have to play up to her best form in the forthcoming test matches, as the team that she will have to meet is a very strong, all-round side.[1]

Perhaps the newspapers were loath to regard Darling as a pastoralist although a short report on his visit to Adelaide in January 1904 suggests that they might have begun to move in that

---

1 *Evening News* 5 November 1903, p. 2.

Caricature of Joe Darling in civilian clothes, 1904. Express & Telegraph, 16 January 1904

direction as 'the famous cricketer' was described as having grown a beard and looking 'more like a squatter than an everyday cricketer'. The journalist continued, that in conversation with Darling, he was given to understand that managing a station and playing cricket did not combine easily, so that he had decided to 'abandon the game altogether'. The report then ends ruefully: 'Thus the cricketing world loses one of the best batsmen that ever faced a bowler.'[2]

At that point there was no mention of Darling returning to Adelaide, but three months later there was a strong rumour that he would return to the city and permanently settle in South Australia with a manager to look after Stonehenge. There was no mention of cricket at that time, but six months later he was back in creams.

1904-05

Darling was quickly into his stride in a pre-season match on a matting wicket for his new electorate club Sturt against Adelaide and Suburban Association team Bankville by scoring 108. As he intended settling in the district, the ambition of the club to gain the association premiership seemed likely to be realised.[3] Darling was listed as an importer in the Sands & McDougall directory for 1905, although whether that meant sporting equipment or sheep is not specified and took up residence in Austral Terrace, Malvern.

Darling made his first senior appearance for the double-blues on 1 October against West Torrens at Unley Oval and lost his off stump after just four runs but was in much better batting humour at the same ground in the following round with an innings of 83.[4]

At a time when the selection of the next Australian Eleven for England was an early season topic of conversation, the annual engagement between the states was regarded with especial interest. But in the South Australia–Victoria game at Adelaide Oval in mid-November there was also an added curiosity in that former Australian captains Harry Trott and Darling were each included in their teams after an absence, but played under the leadership of Laver and Hill respectively. Hill was the only batsman to counter the Victorian bowling with a century and half-century in each innings, but while Darling made starts for 16 and 19, he failed to convert them to sizeable scores in a nine wicket defeat.[5]

Back in club cricket, Darling was in grand form, following a hard-hitting 58 against Port Adelaide with a smashing 137 not out in the middle order against West Adelaide at Unley Oval in which at one point he and opening batsman Bert Bailey (123) added 205 runs in 23 overs at

---

2 *The Clipper* 12 January 1904, p. 4.
3 *Observer* 24 September 1904, p. 19.
4 *Observer* 8 October 1904, p. 19; 22 October 1904, p. 17.
5 *Observer* 19 November 1904, p. 17.

A Victorian villa in the Adelaide suburb of Malvern was a comfortable home for Joe Darling and his young family. Photo by Bernard Whimpress.

nearly nine runs per over. Darling was in rare fettle, reaching his century in even time and his total innings was made in 133 minutes in a magnificent display of powerful strokes. Three times the ball flew over the picket fence and 20 times it reached the boundary.[6] Darling found some touch in the first-class arena with 67 in the first innings of the game against New South Wales at Adelaide Oval, but since he was the only local player to pass fifty for the match and South Australia was beaten by an innings, it would have been small satisfaction. There would have been no satisfaction with a duck in the second innings.[7]

Towards the end of December, Darling was interviewed regarding the manager of the forthcoming twelfth Australian side and answered in a direct manner:

> It is a matter for the players to decide. I don't see that it concerns the associations at all. The English trip is a financial speculation on the part of the players, who entrust their manager with their business and hold him responsible for all accounts. If they lose money on the trip the associations will not recoup them. The players have just as much right to appoint their own manager as I have to appoint the manager of my business. The associations have no right to interfere.[8]

---

6 *Observer* 19 November 1904, p. 17; 3 December 1904, p. 17.
7 *Observer* 24 December 1904, p. 19.
8 *Barrier Miner* 24 December 1904, p. 4.

South Australia fared better with an innings victory over Victoria at the MCG over New Year courtesy of a brilliant 170 by Algy Gehrs opening the batting, and veteran Jack Reedman taking advantage of a spiteful wicket in capturing 13 wickets for 149 in a career-best performance. Darling's own contribution of 35 was modest, and it would appear he was not doing enough to win a place in the touring side.

The Australian selectors in Noble, Bob McLeod and Darling himself reverted to the old habit of picking the team in batches and chose the first ten players to visit England on 2 January. These were Noble, Trumper, Duff, Gregory, Hopkins and Kelly from New South Wales, Armstrong from Victoria, and Hill, Gehrs and Philip Newland from South Australia. The reason for the early selection was because the team was due to depart on 1 February. Two Sheffield Shield matches remained — a clash between SA and NSW in Sydney at the end of the week, and the major confrontation between NSW and Victoria also in Sydney at the end of January. An initial criticism of the side was that it lacked a hitter of the Hugh Massie, George Bonnor, Jack Lyons mould and it was felt that the remaining players would be either bowlers or all-rounders.

Chronicle cartoon of 14 November 1905 showing the four South Australian members of the Australian team which had toured England: Joe Darling (with bat), Algy Gehrs, Clem Hill and Phil Newland (with wicket-keeping gloves).

Darling might have been waiting for a substantial score before submitting his own name. Despite missing out twice in his state's seven wicket loss at the SCG to give him a season's total of 159 runs at 22.71 in first-class games, he was one of the four players added a week later along with Howell, Cotter and Charles McLeod.

As for the mechanics of the selection, however, it appears that Darling was the last man chosen. The selectors met in the pavilion at the Sydney Cricket Ground at the end of the interstate match and the consultation lasted about an hour with reason to believe there were some difficulties made in arriving at the final decision. At first things went smoothly for Howell and Cotter were picked without hesitation. This left two positions to be filled, and there were grave differences of opinion with Noble wanting two more bowlers, but being overruled by his colleagues who argued that manager Frank Laver could be called upon on occasions. Eventually after further discussion, McLeod and Darling were chosen, and according to a statement by one of the selectors, the selection of McLeod was unanimous.[9]

With the full team to examine the *Referee's* 'Not Out', one of the most astute observers of Australian cricket, made a number of remarks. He thought the loss in bowling strength was

---

9   *Chronicle* 14 January 1905, p. 19.

obvious in that Noble and Howell were no longer the force they were, and there was a sameness about the attack with the lack of a left-arm bowler and slow man. All the bowlers were right arm, five about the same pace breaking from the off with just Cotter (pace) and Armstrong (medium-pace leg-spin) offering variation.

However, his most devastating comments were passed on Darling's selection which he regarded as an experiment:

Joe Darling was the last man selected for the 1905 English tour.

> He has stood out of first-class cricket for so long; in 1902 he showed nothing like his form of five years back, and he has since done nothing at all in important cricket. If Darling were as great a batsman as he was in his prime he would add material strength to the side on bad wickets. In the latest interstate match his form was not good. Indeed, if a young player got out as he did to Cotter it would be forever quoted against him. Darling, of course, is not yet 35 years of age and he is one of those men who is always at his best physically. If he strikes form he will be of very great assistance on bowlers' wickets against the left-handers. But will he strike form? Probably not. Another debatable point about Darling's selection is that he takes the place which should be occupied by a bowler. If Darling is worthy of selection, one of the other batsmen should not have been picked. Australian bowling as represented by those who have taken part in this season's first-class cricket is not strong and no matter who was picked from those players the combination would not be a great one. Nevertheless one believes that the bowling of the team, as now selected, could be improved in both quality and variety.

'Not Out' continued that he was one who admired the cricket 'and the heroic pluck of the South Australian' before ending with an ominous ring:

> I sincerely hope that he will vastly improve on the form he has shown in Australian cricket since 1900, both for the sake of Australian cricket and for that of those who are responsible for his re-entry into international cricket, to the exclusion of younger and more successful performers in current Australian cricket.[10]

These observations would certainly give Darling something to chew over, as were the attempts to draft other players into the side. On 15 January, cricket and politics began to mix when Laver received an intimation from Senator Keating to the effect that Tasmanian cricket supporters who believed all-rounder Windsor would strengthen the team, were willing to pay his expenses to be

---

10 *Referee* 11 January 1905, p. 8.

taken to England as an extra man.[11] Five days later, the Carlton Cricket Club held an extraordinary meeting in support of Jack Saunders being sent to England under the patronage of the club.[12]

In England there was speculation about who would lead the Australians, and discussion of the respective merits of Darling and Noble. While Darling was described as 'a born leader of men' with captaincy 'writ all over his dark, hollow-cheeked face' and 'his expression was testimony to courage and confidence'. Noble was fashioned in a different mould, lacking Darling's fire and passion but possessing 'the judicial mind, the equable temperament, the intelligent observation, the indomitable patience — all qualities which go to make the successful skipper'.[13]

The election of the team captain, however, had not been decided at the time of departure and the original intention was for it to take place on the way to New Zealand where the team was playing several matches and Noble was expected to defeat Darling by eight votes to six.[14]

As the summer was drawing to a close, however, there were some interesting curiosities. The

Sturt CC premiership team 1904-05. Back: J Smith (scorer), W Giffen, G Hutton, H Chinner, P Stuart, P Hutton. Sitting: W Hewer, H Hay, J Darling (captain), F Hack, R Bailey. Front: P Rofe, P Leak, W Buchanan. Sturt Cricket Club courtesy of John Lysikatos.

Australian team left Sydney on 1 February by the *Manauka* for Auckland, but the New South Wales–Victoria Sheffield Shield game in which 10 of the tourists plus the manager were playing did not end until 1 o'clock that day. No official send-off for the party was given by the New South

11 *Chronicle* 21 January 1905, p. 19.
12 *Chronicle* 28 January 1905, p. 19.
13 *Register* 7 February 1905, p. 4.
14 *Referee* 1 February 1905, p. 8.

Wales Cricket Association, although it had been proposed to do so at either the Australia Hotel or in the pavilion at the ground. But the idea was abandoned at the suggestion of Noble for reasons best known to himself.

Because Darling elected to skip the New Zealand matches, and neither he nor Newland would be present on the Tasman Sea crossing, the vote on the captaincy was deferred until the team's arrival in England. While this made sense, a stranger decision was the election of Hill to captain the matches in New Zealand, and as vice-captain of the tour. Did all this confusion suggest some division in the ranks?

It is presumed that Darling remained in Adelaide to tidy up business affairs, but he also turned out in club matches for Sturt. By scoring 100 retired out against East Torrens at the Norwood Oval on 18 February and 49 against North Adelaide a week later, he took his season's total to 431 runs

Bricknell's Café on the south (right hand) side of Rundle Street in the early 1890s. It was a popular unlicensed dining venue and where Joe Darling received a warm send-off from members of the Prince Alfred College Old Scholars Association before his departure for England on the 1905 cricket tour. The top levels of the building are still present in today's Rundle Mall opposite the Myer Centre. SLSA B 73225

at 86.20 in electorate cricket matches and provided vital assistance to his club in winning the premiership.[15]

Darling would not leave for England until 23 March (seven weeks after his team-mates) but did receive a farewell send-off from members of the Prince Alfred College Old Collegians' Association at Bricknell's Café in Adelaide on 20 March. It was appropriate that his former schoolmates who would wish him bon voyage, as it was his 252 for his college that had first brought his name to prominence as a cricketer.[16]

---

15 *Observer* 25 February 1905, p. 18; 4 March 1905, p. 18.
16 *Register* 23 March 1905, p. 5.

1　　2 3　　4　　5 6 7　　　　　　　　8　　　　9　　　　　　　　10　11

THE AUSTRALIAN TEAM ENTERING THE CRICKET GROUND, CRYSTAL PALACE,
FOR THEIR FIRST MATCH, MAY 4th 1905.

THE NAMES ARE: 1. R. A. DUFF 2. J. J. KELLY, 3. C. HILL. 4. A. COTTER, 5. W. W. ARMSTRONG, 6. S. E. GREGORY, 7. A. J. HOPKINS, 8. V. TRUMPER, 9. C. E. MC LEOD, 10. M. A. NOBLE (VICE-CAPTAIN), 11. J. DARLING (CAPTAIN).

DARLING　　　　　JACKSON.

ENGLAND
v
AUSTRALIA.

THE
RIVAL CAPTAINS
RETURNING AFTER
THE TOSS.

THE FIRST TEST MATCH AT TRENT BRIDGE, NOTTM 1905.

FOURTH ENGLISH TOUR 1905

Australian Cricket Team 1905

The Australian team's visit to New Zealand was the fifth occasion it had done so, though in most instances it was on the return trip from England. The first team to tour was Dave Gregory's pioneer combination of 1878 and they were succeeded by the 1880, 1886 and 1896 sides.[1] Not surprisingly, the party was far too strong for its opponents, winning three and drawing one of the odds matches played against Auckland, Wellington, Canterbury and Otago, and then drawing and defeating New Zealand Elevens at Christchurch and Wellington.

Of the matches on even terms, the draw at Lancaster Park flattered the home team as the Australians had powered to 533 with centuries to Hill and Armstrong and then dismissed NZ for

---

1 *Observer* 4 March 1905, p. 18.

Clem Hill and Monty Noble skipping with their wives on board ship. Photo by Frank Laver.

Albert Cotter in goat cart. Frank Laver Collection, National Sports Museum

138 and had them 7-112 in their second innings when fading light ended play. The Australians were then even more ruthless in the final match at the Basin Reserve as the New Zealanders were put out for 94, fielded helplessly as Trumper and Hill with further hundreds smashed the attack to all parts of the ground on the way to 9-593, and were disposed of for 154 to be beaten by an innings and 345 runs.[2]

The tourists departed on 15 March and sailed across the Pacific, winning a single innings match against Eighteen of Fiji at Suva twelve days later before travelling overland through Canada and the United States and arriving in Liverpool on 26 April. Travelling in the other direction on the *Marmora*, Joe Darling was interviewed by the *Morning Herald* of Perth. When asked about the team's prospects, he considered they were strong in batting, exceptionally

---

2   Chris Harte, *A History of Australian Cricket,* Andre Deutsch, London, p. 223; Australasian 18 March 1905, p. 21; 25 March 1905, p. 21.

SS Marmora on which Joe Darling travelled to England separately from his team.

strong in fielding, and not as weak in bowling as supposed. He praised McLeod's bowling in English conditions, but admitted that the unknown quantity was Cotter. Referring to the fast bowler he wittily remarked, 'At times he sends down a ball that would be a good-pitched ball if bowled from the other end.'[3]

Joe Darling had the misfortune to be in transit to England when his father, John, died in Adelaide on 11 April.[4] When he eventually joined the rest of the team he was elected captain with Noble as his deputy. Several of the leading New South Wales players favoured Darling and that decided the issue even if other opinions supported Noble because he had been intimately associated with Australian cricket and its leadership since 1901 whereas Darling had practically been a retired player. Only results would determine the wisdom of the decision.[5]

Seven matches were played before the first Test beginning with three draws against the Gentlemen of England, Nottinghamshire and Surrey followed by wins over Oxford University, a second match with the Gentlemen, Yorkshire and Lancashire. The Australians had not met the Gentlemen since Percy McDonnell's team in 1888 but now they faced them in the opening

---

3   *Observer* 15 April 1905, p. 18.

4   The will of John Darling senior was sworn at £67,500 and although Joe was a fellow trustee with his elder brother, John, he did not receive a bequest whereas John received £8000, and other siblings received amounts ranging down from £7000 to third son, Charles, to £4000 for only daughter, Isabella. Joe's exclusion was probably because he had been set up with the holding at Stonehenge. *Register* 5 June 1905, p. 6

5   *Referee* 3 May 1905, p. 8.

Joe Darling

game in which the 57-year-old WG Grace led the side at Crystal Palace. While Grace made a quick exit in his only innings the match produced 1081 runs, 796 of them by the Australians. In the second innings, in particular, they destroyed the attack to the tune of 526 runs in 112 overs with Noble reaching the first century of the tour (162) and Hill and Darling compiling half-centuries. Lancashire fast bowler Walter Brearley, who would make his mark late in the Test series and had taken 5 for 87 in the first innings, achieved the best figures of 4 for 141 while Middlesex all-rounder George Beldam, a pioneer of action photography who would capture the famous image of Victor Trumper jumping out to drive later in the tour, took 4 to 207 from slow medium deliveries the batsmen enjoyed.[6]

In the early games the attack exceeded expectations, but the outstanding bowling performances came from the manager Laver with innings figures of 5 for 61 at The Oval, and match figures of 13 for 133 at Oxford, and 12 for 101 at Sheffield. Darling's own form was solid, batting at six with scores of 23, 65, 29, 20 not out, 17, 12, 117 not out, 54 and 22 for 367 runs at 40.77, the highlight coming in the innings victory over the Gentlemen at Lord's where in his century he partnered Warwick Armstrong (248 not out) in an undefeated sixth wicket stand of 273 out of 6-555 declared. The partnership came at a wonderful rate, occupying just two hours and 40 minutes, and Darling's innings included 18 fours and one five.[7]

The turnaround in the first Test thus must have provided a shock. Several shocks. First, on winning the toss the Englishmen would have expected a score above 300 on a good wicket, but were soon in trouble at 5-47 against medium-pacer Laver who finished with figures of 7 for 64 and their total of 196 was sub-par. Then the back strain suffered by Trumper, which caused him to retire at 13 (and put him out of the match), was a blow although the situation was being retrieved by half-centuries to Hill and Noble when Jackson, who bowled a mixture of fast-medium and off-cutters, struck with his famous over in which he had Noble caught behind from his first ball, bowled Hill with his fourth, and had Darling caught by Bosanquet with his sixth. Australia's 221 gave them a small lead on the second day but when MacLaren and Hayward were opening with a brilliant stand of 145 at a run a minute came another shock. Darling tossed the ball to Armstrong who bowled 30 overs of leg-spin pitched outside the leg-stump for 50 runs as the score increased from 110 to 301. While not naming Darling directly, *Wisden* observed, 'It was something quite new to see the Australians on the second afternoon of a Test match playing for a draw rather

---

6   *Observer* 13 May 1905, p. 20.
7   *Chronicle* 27 May 1905, p. 19.

than a win.' In the end it might have been expected that the tourists could save the game when England declared at 4-426 with just four and a half hours remaining. But even though Darling promoted himself to open with Duff, and they added 62 for the first wicket, the rest of the side was flummoxed by Bosanquet's leg-spin as he achieved his best-Test figures of 8 for 107 on a firm pitch to produce a 213 run win.[8]

An interesting aspect of the end of this match, however, was Darling's display of sportsmanship. With an hour to play, McLeod went in as last man in poor light, but Darling instructed him not to appeal. After a further quarter of an hour, McLeod signalled to his captain who went on to the field. He told McLeod to continue batting as he did not want to prevent England winning by appealing and having the match a draw.

Owing to the injury to Trumper, Darling moved himself back to opening in the next four games and although he didn't get a substantial score, his innings of 38, 16, 19, 2, 0 not out (when Australia faced only one ball in its match against the MCC at Lord's) and 19 showed that he was at least getting starts. A win over Cambridge University and draws in a second match against Yorkshire, the MCC and Leicestershire were the results in the lead-up to the second Test at Lord's which was also undecided.[9]

England's 282 was enough to give it a strong lead as Australia replied with 181 when caught on a soft pitch following overnight rain. Darling entered at 3-95 before a crowd of 28,000 and contributed a disciplined innings of 41 in an hour and three quarters, but following his dismissal, caught low down by Haigh at deep mid-off at 7-175, the innings quickly dissolved. As the home team reached 5-151 at stumps they were the only side in position to force a win, but rain began to fall at 3.30 on the final day, the wicket was converted into a mud heap, the rain continued and the game was abandoned.[10]

Darling opened again in Australia's second loss of the tour in a low scoring game against Essex at Leyton, but dropped down the order and contributed successive half-centuries in an innings win over Warwickshire and a draw against Gloucestershire.

The third Test was the first staged at the Headingley ground in Leeds and was another game drawn, but heavily in the home side's favour. The Australians went into the field on a cool, cloudy morning but again it was curious that they seemed intent on not losing the game by using Armstrong from one end bowling his leg breaks with seven men on the leg side. After an opening partnership of 51, the complexion of the game quickly changed to 4-64 and England's 301 was chiefly due to the vital innings of their captain, Jackson, who carried his bat for 144. When Australia's response was 195 and England again scored freely to reach 5-295 in its second innings and a lead of 402, all Australia could hope to do on the last afternoon was play out time. This they managed to achieve but not without wobbles as they lost seven wickets in the process.

---

8 Match report of first Test at Trent Bridge, *Wisden Cricketers' Almanack 1906* included in Benny Green (ed.) *Wisden Anthology 1900-1940*, p. 38.

9 Cricinfo season archive 1905.

10 *Chronicle* 24 June 1905, p. 19.

Warwick Armstrong became the second Australian batsman to record a triple-century in England.

Darling had a poor match, scarcely troubling the scorers with innings of 2 and 5. At this point in the series the Australians had been outplayed and supporters would have had to be blindly optimistic to anticipate the Ashes coming home. In the three matches completed the Englishmen had scored 1640 runs at an average of 36.57 runs per wicket compared to the Australians 1009 runs at 24.42.[11]

Darling rested for only his second match against Hampshire at Southampton where the Australians recorded 620 with three century-makers (Hill, Armstrong and Gregory) on the way to an innings win but returned for a win over Derbyshire, and draws against Somerset and Scotland. In these games his form was solid with totals of 38, 35, 49 not out, 49 and 3. It must be said that he was unlucky in the middle of those hands at Bath as he batted at number six in a total of 4-609 declared after Armstrong with 303 not out reached the highest score of his career.[12]

The Australians needed to win the final two Test matches but instead the series was lost at Manchester as they slipped to an innings defeat by lunch on the final day. Once again the English batting was impressive with a second century to Jackson and half-centuries to Hayward and Spooner in reaching 446 but rain during the night meant deterioration of the wicket and the Australians struggled from the outset as three wickets fell for 27. Darling attempted to stop the rot by bold hitting and his 73 in 85 minutes with 13 fours was recognised by the crowd as full of merit, but it was a lone hand and the team was obliged to follow on. Batting a second time the wicket had rolled out well, Trumper and Duff added 65 in 40 minutes, and Duff and Hill maintained their places at 1-118 to trail by 131 runs at the close of play. It might have been expected that the tourists would save the game, but bad luck again befell them with morning rain and on a difficult wicket the last nine wickets tumbled for 48 runs. Darling did not repeat his first innings success as he was caught second ball low down in the slips by Rhodes off Brearley who captured four wickets in each innings of his Test debut.[13]

Twenty-four tour matches had now been completed, but 14 remained. If it was imagined that the Australians had lost their incentive to win, such thoughts would have been wrong as they experienced no further defeats. Wins came against Surrey and Sussex, a draw against

---

11 *Chronicle* 8 July 1905, p. 21; *Referee* 12 July 1905, p. 6.
12 Cricinfo season archive 1905.
13 *Australasian* 29 July 1905, p. 23.

Worcestershire in the third game Darling missed, and another win over Middlesex before the final Test match.

The game against Surrey from 27 to 29 July was the most exciting contest with the victory margin of 22 runs achieved after Clem Hill top-scored in each innings for the Australians and Tom Hayward doing likewise for the county. Of more significance in the history of cricket and aesthetics was that it was the time when photographer George Beldam's created his famous image of Victor Trumper jumping out to drive. Beldam took photographs of many batsmen making such a move (mostly front-on to the camera) and on 1 May he had photographed Trumper and other Australian players at Lord's.[14] On that occasion Joe Darling had been among his subjects but unfortunately Beldam did him no favours by photographing the left-hander from behind thus creating an ugly shambling pose. If lighting was an issue, one is left to wonder why the photographer did not ask Darling to take strike at the other end of the pitch.

Darling's absence at Worcester might have caused the other players to be less attentive than otherwise and as Hill recalls, he and Trumper did not sit patiently in the grandstand after they were dismissed about 3 o'clock:

> It seemed reasonable to suppose that as only three wickets were down the other batsmen would stay in for the day, so we strolled off, called for our wives at the hotel, and went to buy antique furniture.
>
> We were passing a critical eye over a table when we were startled by a newspaper boy calling out 'Collapse of the Australians'. We bought a paper. Yes, it was true, they were all out. Hurrying to the ground in a cab, we found that our mates were out on the field and hustling the umpires to make a start. The scoundrels, out of devilment, wanted to have a ball bowled so that we would be fined for being absent.
>
> Then down came the rain. It was never more welcome. The players scurried to the dressing room and by that time we had jumped into our flannels and thrown a sweater over our shirt. We escaped the fine, which by the terms of our agreement, we would have been called upon to pay by being late.[15]

In these games Darling's form was middling although his 93 supported Noble on his way to 267 out of 556 in the innings victory at Hove.

The fifth Test at The Oval in fine weather on a perfect pitch was always likely to be drawn in a match restricted to three days and it was with England scoring 430 and 6-261 courtesy of centuries by Fry and Tyledesley against Australia's 363 and the loss of four second innings wickets when time ran out. Cotter appreciated being given extended use of the ball to capture first innings figures of 7 for 148 while Duff's 146 enabled him to become the first player to score centuries in

---

14 Gideon Haigh, *Stroke of Genius: Victor Trumper and the shot that changed cricket*, Penguin, Melbourne, 2016, p. 131.
15 Hill, *Reminiscences*, p. 76.

Joe Darling — Cricketer, Farmer, Politician and Family Man

Joe Darling's version of jumping out to drive. Photo by George Beldam

Victor Trumper jumping out to drive, 1905. Photo by George Beldam

his first and last Tests for his country. Darling entered at 4-218 to support Duff, but his partner did not last long, so that his 57 in an hour was merely a boost to the tail and his 12 not out in the second innings gave him the satisfaction of being there at the end.[16]

After the game it was reported that Darling refused an interview with a journalist from one of the London daily newspapers on the pretext that he did not approve of cricketers writing for papers as he thought they were providing unfair competition for professional journalists. It had never stopped him giving interviews previously, nor would it would prevent him doing so in the future.

In the remaining games the Australians completed four wins and four draws, three innings victories coming in consecutive games against Northamptonshire where yet another score of 600 plus was attained, Lancashire and Kent. The side was certainly threatened with a loss when it edged home with a one wicket win over an England Eleven at Bournemouth, but was unlucky not to avenge an earlier loss to Essex who squeaked to a draw with one wicket in hand. The other drawn games were adversely affected by the weather. As he had done on the 1899 tour, Darling struck his most consistent run-getting towards the end of the campaign. At Canterbury he passed three figures for just the second time while his 99 when opening the innings on the Cheltenham College Ground in the return game against Gloucestershire was a frustrating miss in that marvellous aesthetic setting.[17]

English captain Stanley Jackson was definitely man of the series.

When Darling arrived home on the brig HMS *China* in mid-October, a journalist quipped that he was looking for the Ashes to which Darling made a quick rejoinder that unfortunately they had been left behind. He did, however, point out that his side lost only three of 35 first-class matches against 15 wins and 17 draws which was a good record. He also remarked on the team's bad luck losing Trumper in the first Test when the side was in a winning position and batting on difficult wickets at Lord's and Old Trafford.[18]

On the tour, Noble topped 2000 runs and five other batsmen (Armstrong, Darling, Hill, Trumper and Duff) reached four figures with Hopkins finishing just four runs short, while Laver, Armstrong and Cotter all passed 100 wickets. Unfortunately Cotter did not find his best form until late and for long periods Armstrong bowled in a defensive mode. Darling's performance of scoring 1694 runs at 39.39 probably surpassed expectations. In the Tests, however, while five Englishmen aggregated more than 300 runs and there were six century-makers only one Australian (Duff) reached these marks. As *Wisden* noted:

---

16 *Observer* 19 August 1905, p. 22.
17 Cricinfo season archive 1905; *Truth* 30 September 1905, p. 6.
18 Perth *Daily News* 17 October 1905, p. 12.

Trumper furnished the most striking example of failure when big innings meant so much, his highest score in the five Test matches being 31. Leaving aside Duff's score at The Oval (146), Darling was the finest batsman in the side in the Test games, playing superb cricket under very trying conditions. Nothing more remarkable than his hitting at Manchester was seen during the whole series. He scored 73 runs in 80 minutes on a sticky wicket.[19]

In the end perhaps in summarising Test series, it simply came down to the toss. Darling lost all spins of the coin and yet by the most peculiar of coincidences the man who opposed him Stanley Jackson who finished both top of the batting and bowling averages with 492 runs at 70.28 and took 13 wickets at 15.46 was born on the exact same day, 21 November 1870. Now there's a conundrum for the astrologers when predicting fortune. Was it simply a matter of hemispheres?

PORT SAID, 1905. M. NOBLE, F. LAVER, J. DARLING, J. KELLY

Stop over at Port Said on return trip.

---

19 *Wisden Cricketers' Almanack 1906*, p. 2.

TOWARDS THE PAVILION 1905-08

Joe Darling's first-class cricket career was drawing to a close, yet was not finished and he remained active in Adelaide club cricket for the next three years. Unfortunately he had no opportunity for a club appearance before the opening Sheffield Shield game of the 1905-06 season against Victoria on Adelaide Oval on 11 November when he made just 11 and the top score of 36 in an innings defeat.

An innings of 83 for Sturt against Adelaide a week later opened his club account and he continued with scores of 39 and 20 before completing the rest of the interstate program over the next three weeks. A further innings defeat by New South Wales was disheartening, and the only highlight was SA's 120 run win in Melbourne before another thrashing at the hands of NSW in Sydney. At that point of the season Darling must have wondered why he was still playing as in eight innings he failed to register a half-century and his batting aggregate was just 148 runs at 18.50. The one bright spot from a personal viewpoint was his good form for the Australian Eleven against New South Wales in Jim Kelly's benefit match in which he scored 66 and 73 and led the Eleven to a 79 run victory. In Adelaide district cricket he had a decent season with 228 runs at 45.60.

During the summer there was also news in the *Mount Barker Courier* that Darling had purchased Sir James Boucaut's Dalmeney Park Estate at the base of the mountain, 35 kilometres south-east of Adelaide, for the likely purpose of sheep breeding.[1] A week later the same newspaper was effusive in its praise of the property changing hands and congratulated the people of Mount Barker on acquiring such an 'eligible citizen' as Joe Darling. Famous all over the world as a cricketer, he had (according to the reporter) 'just the traits of character which render him such an excellent leader, more particularly when playing an uphill game, which form his excellent equipment in respect to the ordinary avocations of life'. He had 'energy, courage and brains, which, added to capital' would enable him to 'win success anywhere'. The paper went on to say that the estate's previous owner had won fame in England for his wheat which won a gold medal at the Crystal Palace Exhibition in 1951 and made the nice point that Darling had achieved equal distinction in cricket performances on the Crystal Palace ground. The hope now was that he would once more lift the prestige of Dalmeney Park as a producer of good grain or pasturage for high-class stock.[2]

---

1   *Mount Barker Courier* 23 February 1906, p. 2.
2   *Mount Barker Courier* 2 March 1906, p. 3.

In September 1906 Darling was off to a slow pre-season following a compulsory spell owing to a severe kick to his shin and ankle by a horse which confined him to bed for several days and meant he could only move about with pain.[3] Perhaps it was during his enforced convalescence that he determined on a new direction regarding Dalmeney Park as the estate was subdivided and offered for sale in blocks in early October.[4]

1906-07

Darling missed the opening round of district cricket, but made his first appearance for Sturt against North Adelaide at Unley Oval on 20 October when opening the batting he made 22 alongside Clem Hill who recorded a century on debut for the club.[5] He followed this with 68 against Port Adelaide at Alberton Oval on 3 November which put him in good touch for the first Sheffield Shield game against Victoria.[6]

Joe Darling, Sturt CC captain 1904-08. South Australian Cricket Association Collection

As it turned out, this game played in mid-November would be Darling's only first-class encounter for the summer. Despite making 77 runs in 86 minutes, an innings described as 'rousing the enthusiasm of the spectators by magnificent play which brought to mind his great innings of 178 in a Test match' it was not to be repeated.[7] In the second innings he made 14 before absenting himself for several weeks by visiting Stonehenge in Tasmania and missing both South Australia's next home game against New South Wales and the eastern states tour. Since Hill was also unavailable for the tour it was expected that a severely depleted side led by Norrie Claxton would be thrashed in both games. Instead, SA triumphed by 319 runs in Melbourne but lost by an innings to NSW in Sydney.[8]

Darling returned to club cricket action in early January with 22 against West Torrens at Unley Oval and maintained remarkable consistency for the rest of the season including a century against Port Adelaide and half centuries against North Adelaide, Adelaide and East Torrens. With 509 runs at 50.90 he finished fourth in the district averages behind team-mates Clem Hill and Fred Hack and the trio's heavy run-scoring was a big factor in Sturt's third premiership success in five years. As the *Observer* recorded:

---

3   *Observer* 8 September 1906, p. 21.
4   *Mount Barker Courier* 12 October 1906, p. 2.
5   *Observer* 27 October 1906, p. 21.
6   *Chronicle* 10 November 1906, p. 24.
7   *Observer* 17 November 1906, p. 21.
8   Webster, *First-Class Cricket*, pp. 370-1.

The Sturt players have won the premiership and their performances in such departments of the game merit their position this season. Their first step toward climbing to the premiership was winning three matches in succession by their fielding. Narrow margins of 6, 29 and 13 runs were in their favour. All through the season, the support given by the fieldsmen to the attack has been a remarkable feature of the play and their captaincy by the leader of the Australian Eleven has had much to do with their coming out top. Darling himself has had a remarkably successful batting season and he did not miss double figures on any of the ten occasions when he went to the wickets.[9]

If Darling had a regret during the summer it was missing the New South Wales versus The Rest match at the Sydney Cricket Ground which was arranged as a benefit for Syd Gregory and from which the player eventually received £630.[10] In a long letter to Victor Trumper, Darling explained that nobody was more anxious than himself that the little Waverley man should have a sterling benefit. However, he was unable to play in the match due to the manager of his South Australian business having left him at short notice and nobody was available to take his place.[11]

1907-08

When the new season rolled around it was reported that the Sturt club would probably have a much changed team. International cricket would claim Hill and Darling suggesting that both would be available for the summer's Ashes series.[12]

In district cricket, Darling began with innings of 9 and 44 against West Torrens and Port Adelaide before leading South Australia against the MCC team captained by Arthur Jones.[13]

Miniature diary inscribed 'Joe', 1908

Glorious weather prevailed for the opening of the match against the Englishmen and Charlie Checkett prepared his customary perfect batting wicket. The SACA also deserved praise for the manner in which they had terraced the lawn in front of the members' reserve providing seats for many hundreds of people who previously would have had to stand or, if seated, had difficulty viewing the play. When Darling won the toss he took advantage of the wicket and the weather by batting. Hill's century represented stirling cricket and backed by future Test batsman Claude Jennings and Claxton saw the South Australian side post 343 runs on the second day. Then came the tourists reply, and although they opened cautiously, their total grew and grew until it represented their highest

---

9 *Observer* 20 April 1907, p. 22. John Lysikatos, *108 Not Out: The history of the Sturt Cricket Club*, Sturt District Cricket Club, 2005, p. 73.
10 Webster, *First-Class Cricket*, p. 373.
11 *Australian Star* 7 February 1907, p. 5.
12 *Observer* 12 October 1907, p. 20.
13 *Chronicle* 19 October 1907, p. 20; 26 October 1907, p. 15; *Observer* 9 November 1907, p. 15.

total of 8-660 declared including four century-makers — Jones, Joe Hardstaff, Braund (who had previous experience of Australian conditions) and 20-year-old all-rounder Jack Crawford whose century in 54 minutes and including 18 fours and 3 sixes was the fastest in Australian first-class cricket history at the time. The Englishmen had a train to catch to Melbourne at 4.30 pm on the fourth day but dismissed SA cheaply in their second innings with Hill making nearly half the team total of 134. As a player Darling's performance was poor as he was out for 11 and 2, both times to Sydney Barnes. Although there was no mention of retirement, he might have realised his time had come as it proved to be his final first-class match.[14]

Darling scored 13 against East Torrens at the end of November so that it was a lean start to the season. He and Hill had both been selected on South Australia's eastern states tour even though Hill would be unavailable for the first match in Melbourne and Darling for the second in Sydney.[15] In fact, neither man played against Victoria in which the home side made 699 runs to win by an innings. Darling also missed a famous match at the SCG which was the first in Australia to enter the sixth playing day, and resulted in such a turnaround in form that SA won by 20 runs after dismissing NSW for the astonishing total of 572 in the fourth innings.[16]

No mention was made of Darling's absence in the press from the first encounter, yet it is noteworthy that he turned out for Sturt on the same weekend and scored 50 against North Adelaide.[17] For the rest of the season his cricket was restricted to club duties and he performed at a high level with innings of 79, 83, 85, and 28 against Adelaide, West Torrens, Port Adelaide and East Torrens but missed some late season matches to finish with a total of 386 runs at 48.25.[18] A curiosity also attended to Darling in the rare form as a bowler. With his side thin on resources, Darling caused amusement and then ire by bowling full tosses at the top of the stumps and secured two wickets clean bowled after going on as a last resort. The ball delivered in this way was regarded as exasperating to the batsman who in attempting to avoid concussion found the ball falling on to his wicket. While fairly delivered, the practice was regarded as unconventional and more inclined to have been pursued with mischief by the likes of WG Grace than the former Australian captain.[19]

---

14 *Chronicle* 16 November 1907, p. 23; *Observer* 16 November 1907, p. 22.
15 *Observer* 30 November, p. 21.
16 Webster, *First-Class Cricket*, p. 385.
17 *Observer* 7 December 1907, p. 21.
18 *Observer* 28 December 1907, p. 19; 25 January 1908, p. 22; 8 February 1908, p. 18; *Chronicle* 22 February 1908, p. 19.
19 Perth *Daily News* 10 March 1908, p. 7.

END OF PLAY AND RETURN

Joe Darling's announcement of retirement from top-class cricket came in September 1908 when he determined to leave South Australia and settle back at Stonehenge in Tasmania. In swapping the life of a cricketer for a farmer it was suggested that he could relive wondrous games which had made his name a household word in the cricket world and recall his influence on the Australian game for the previous 15 years.

While his batting figures had been eclipsed by others, he was an extraordinary combination of defence and defiance. He was able play an ordinary, colourless innings or to hit with tremendous power and corresponding skill if the occasion called for it. He would be remembered as a bulldog fighter against the odds as well as the most scientific hitter of his time. Perception, caution and grit were three qualities which had carried him to the top of the ladder. Also, he frequently either carried his side to victory or saved it from defeat when the likelihood of achieving those aims seemed far away.

Darling was first a boy and then a man for the big occasion.

Public attention was first attracted to Darling by his score of 252 in the annual intercollegiate match for Prince Alfred College against St Peter's in 1885, but he came under adult notice in the 1893-94 season with scores of 63 not out, 87 and 24 against Victoria and once he got his foot on the ladder there was no stopping his climb to the top. The century with which he opened operations on the English bowling during Andrew Stoddart's tour the following year marked him for national honours.

In the ordeal of his first Test match at Sydney in December 1894 he made a well-struck top score of 53 in the second innings after having made a duck in the first. Then in the final Test of the 1897-98 series (also at the SCG), he led Australia to a six wicket victory by thumping a brilliant innings of 160 in which he belted Tom Richardson, a veritable king among fast bowlers, to every corner of the field.

His last Test innings in Australia was a splendid 69 on the Adelaide Oval in January 1902 when, assisted by Hugh Trumble, he guided his side to a four wicket win. For Adelaide cricket watchers his magnificent 178 on his home ground in 1898 was an innings to remember and especially the six which carried him from 98 to 104. How the spectators cheered as the ball sailed away over the trees and out of the ground and little Johnny Briggs who had delivered it could merely give a shrug and join the applause.

Clem Hill

Four times he crossed to England, initially on the 1896 tour as a player and then on the next three (1899, 1902 and 1905) as captain, and each time he made 1000 runs and twice brought home the Ashes. On the 1899 tour his batting figures surpassed those of all his predecessors although they were eclipsed by Victor Trumper in 1902.

In South Australian cricket he was a big force as a player and administrator and at meetings of the Ground and Finance Committee of the South Australian Cricket Association (on which he briefly served) his opinions carried heavy weight. Players regarded him as their champion because he recognised many of the difficulties of those who made great sacrifices to play the first-class game.[1]

One assessment which used to dog Darling, both during his playing days and after, was comparison with his fellow left-hander and South Australian team-mate Clem Hill so that it is of interest to recall the words of *Referee* writer JC Davis in 1914, pointing to the strengths of each man:

Joe Darling, with his unsurpassable power and self control as batsman, his leadership, and his severe and exemplary ideas on life and conduct, was a personality of striking influence on the cricket of his time. But with all his sterling qualities, he was not the run-getting force year in and year out on Australian wickets that Clem Hill has been. Darling's was the exaltation of orthodox methods; Clem Hill was an original. He had the genius to carry out with almost mechanical precision strikingly daring shots even to the most dangerous of bowlers. And his courage matched that of Darling. He and Darling were contemporaries in first-class cricket, though the latter is seven years his senior. I suppose no State will ever again possess two such striking left-handers at the same period. Though they were contemporaries it is very difficult to compare the two as batsmen. They had certain essentials in common, but, otherwise were so different. Darling could do what Clem Hill could not do, and Clem could do lots of things Darling could not do. Their greatness, ran in different directions but toward the one goal. On Australian wickets, however, I subscribe to the general opinion that Clem Hill is the greatest batsman this hemisphere has produced.[2]

A Second Cricket Life

In 1919, Joe and Alice Darling purchased Claremont House about 13 kilometres north of Hobart leaving their eldest son, Gordon, to manage Stonehenge. Claremont had a rich history and was

---

1 *Register* 25 September 1908, p. 5.
2 *Referee* 18 November 1914, p. 1.

a grand mansion located on top of a hill overlooking extensive gardens, farmland and orchards with a large staff to run the property and household. However, the family did not move into the house until 1920 because of worries about the influenza epidemic in nearby urban areas.[3]

The visit of Johnny Douglas's English team to Australia and a letter to the *Mercury* on 1 November 1920 might have persuaded Darling to come out of cricket retirement. The letter ran:

> Sir
>
> This team will be here in January. In most contests a coach is appointed to train the contestants. I would suggest that Mr Joe Darling be asked to do this. He has already expressed his willingness to do so; with a little pressure he might be induced to play. For his captaincy alone he would be worth a place. Judging from the play on the association ground on Saturday our fellows require a lot of coaching. The batting was very slow, no risks were taken, only one or two showing aggressive play. The scoring board should also be properly attended to. Someone should be appointed by each club to see to this interesting feature of the game. Yours, etc,
>
> ONLOOKER

One outcome was that Darling emerged from 13 years of retirement in a match played at Claremont on New Year's Day, 1921. The feature was a hard-hit century by him compiled in an hour and included 13 fours and three sixes. In one over he scored 29 runs as Claremont declared at 7-241 and Glenorchy lost nine wickets for 117 runs.[4] Five weeks later he proved the performance was no fluke by scoring 103 retired against Molesworth in a chanceless exhibition which lasted 100 minutes, and included 11 fours and three sixes.[5]

At the end of the same season he also captained the Country side in a match between Town and Country; and played for the South in the return North versus South match in Hobart. Being a pastoralist made Darling eligible for Country in the first match and although he was not the Darling of old his innings of 12 and 19 revealed some evidence of the skill which made him famous, but left him on the losing side.[6] In the second game he scored 10 and 14 in a five wicket win.[7]

Darling captained Country against Town again in 1922 and the match opened dramatically when W Ellis took a hat-trick with the first three balls of the match. However, Country recovered to 322 and Darling showing all his old ability for an uphill fight made 38 as his side eventually triumphed by 71 runs.[8]

He also began to play matches with the Break O'Day club in Hobart and began scoring well except for a brief return to A grade in the 1921-22 season when he accumulated just 23

---

3   Claremont House Conservation Plan, pp. 10, 14.
4   *Referee* 12 January 1921, p. 5.
5   *Referee* 23 February 1921, p. 8.
6   *Sun* 1 March 1921, p. 8.
7   *Referee* 6 April 1921, p. 12.
8   *Sportsman* 11 January 1922, p. 5.

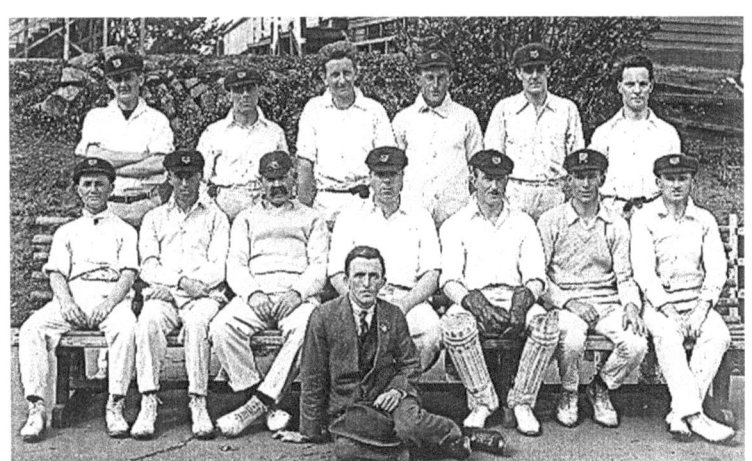

Return to cricket with Break O'Day 1922-23. Joe Darling is third from left front row. Tasmanian Cricket Museum.

runs in four innings. The Tasmanian Cricket Association (TCA) at that time only comprised three clubs with Wellington and Derwent being the other two. In a B Grade pennant match on 13 January 1923, Darling went in first in the second innings with an hour and a half to make 203 runs to win. Batting on they reached 6-219 with Darling carrying his bat for 133, hitting 12 fours and seven sixes in his first three-figure score for 16 years.[9]

District cricket was first introduced in the 1923-24 season and Darling joined the New Town District Club, captaining the B grade team as well as coaching young players. He topped the TCA B Grade batting averages several times and in 1926 won the bowling average taking 43 wickets at 11.07 runs per wicket, but hopefully without dropping the ball on top of the wicket. He played five consecutive seasons with New Town B grade and won the batting average each season with figures of 50, 49, 51, 34 and 38.[10]

After celebrating his 54th birthday in 1924 he showed that he was far from being a back number by contributing 100 not out for New Town as one of his sons knocked up 27 in the same innings before being run out. Despite heavy calls on his time, Darling remained willing to give up a leisurely hour to coach young cricketers and his work with his club and his wider interest in cricket was appreciated.[11]

The 1924-25 season proved an interesting one, but it ended sensationally and then controversially. In February, Darling captained the Tasmanian Pastoralists against the New South Wales Graziers in their last match in the southern part of the state and top-scored with 71 out of 8-201 to their opponent's 7-150. The following week he made 44 for New Town against Eastern

Joe Darling as a member of a Pastoralists team 1925 seated second from left back row. Tasmanian Cricket Museum.

---

9   *Referee* 24 January 1923, p. 12.
10 Darling, *Test Tussles*, p. 19.
11 *Mercury* 28 November 1924, p. 12.

Suburbs, but hardly left the crease as his runs included four boundaries and three hits over the fence.[12]

However, the match between New Town and South Hobart was remarkable in many ways. On the first day's play, New Town was dismissed for 78 and South Hobart was 3-109 when stumps were drawn. When this total was carried to 151 everyone thought the match was over, but New Town hit up a quick 5-161 in the second innings when the closure was applied. Requiring 89 to win, and with ample time to make them, South Hobart commenced their second innings. With five wickets still in hand, and only 23 runs to make, a sensational ending came about with all the wickets falling without the addition of a run. Joe Darling was the destructive agent by taking three wickets in one over. In the next over, two wickets fell to A Brownwell. In so doing, New Town secured the outright win and the B grade premiership.

It was just as well that New Town pulled the match out of the fire, as North-West Hobart were close behind and ready to snap up the premiership if they had been defeated. New Town had been several times in perilous positions but had generally found their way out of trouble which made their win all the more meritorious.[13]

The controversy lay in the matter of the TCA having the following week to deal with charges against Darling and members of his team for alleged time wasting in their match against North-West on 31 March. The committee found that Darling acted in accordance with the laws of the game in appealing against the light, but that it was inadvisable of him to persist since he had already received an intimation from the umpire that the decision did not rest with him. With reference to the charges by umpire Lonergan and the North-West club against Darling and his team for deliberately wasting time, the committee found that these were not proven and therefore New Town's win in that game (and the premiership) were allowed to stand.[14]

Douglas Darling has written that he played under his father's captaincy in 1926 and 1927 in the New Town B grade side and could visualise what had been written about Joe's captaincy and batting:

> When batting with him one never attempted to back up, because his straight driving was so terrific it was dangerous to start moving until he had hit the ball. On the New Town ground I saw him hit a ball that went no more than four feet above the bowler's head and it landed over the fence for six. I have never seen any other batsman do so as to hit a six a batsman usually lofts the ball. On two occasions I saw him hit a ball at the TCA oval clean out of the ground and onto the Domain, one being right over the top of the TCA Pavilion. As I was born in 1905, I did not see him play any first-class cricket. However, at age 57 I would say that there were few, if any, better batsmen in

---

12 *Referee* 25 February 1925, p. 13, 4 March, p. 13.
13 Adelaide *News* 9 April 1925, p. 3.
14 *Referee* 15 April 1925, p. 12.

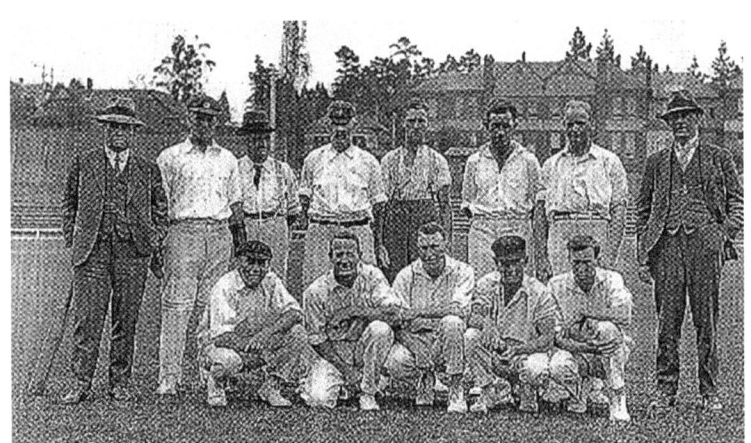
New Town B grade team 1927–28

southern Tasmania. As a fieldsman what he lacked in speed he more than made up for with anticipation and safe pair of hands.[15]

In his final season he made a score of 94 in January 1928 and playing in the premiership match against South Hobart made 32 to assist his club to an innings win and a hat-trick of premierships in all three grades.[16]

From 1921, when he was elected as a Member of Parliament until the beginning of World War II, Darling generally donned the flannels for the annual cricket match between Parliament and the Press and in 1924 he provided one of his most explosive innings. After the legislators were outpointed in the first innings by 113 runs to 35 (of which he made 12) they took a second knock and reached 5-94. On this occasion, Darling got into his stride instantly and made 59 not out with seven fours and two sixes.[17] The following year, however, saw the politicians on top as they scored 6-200 to defeat the Press with 103. The Parliament could, of course, boast a second international cricketer in Charles Eady but it was Darling who led the scoring with 48 while Premier Joe Lyons took two wickets for 13.[18]

A memorial

In recognition of his services to Australian cricket, the Tasmanian Cricket Association hung an enlarged photograph of him in the pavilion at the Tasmanian Cricket Association Ground in Hobart. The photograph was unveiled on Saturday 15 March 1930 during the luncheon adjournment of the match between the Australian team and Tasmania by TCA president Eady, who had toured England with Darling on one occasion.

Eady mentioned not only Darling's contribution to Australian cricket as a player and captain, but of his role in inaugurating benefit matches for George Giffen and Bill Howell and heading the subscription lists on each occasion. He stated that the TCA was glad Tasmania had taken the opportunity of honouring him because he had received no recognition in his home state of South Australia other than being made a life member of the South Australian Cricket Association.

When Darling responded he spoke of being born and playing practically all his cricket in South Australia, but that the SACA had not honoured him in any way. When he was a small

---

15 Darling, *Test Tussles*, pp. 19-20.
16 Melbourne *Sporting Globe* 25 January 1928, p. 8; *Referee* 18 April 1928, p. 11; *Mercury* 23 April 1928, p. 12.
17 *Referee* 17 December 1924, p. 13.
18 *Sun* 11 December 1925, p. 10.

boy, he was fond of the game, and had loved it all his life. During his time he said the Australian cricketers were handicapped in one respect compared to the Englishmen as they were self taught. This was one of the reasons he had done what he could to help young players in Tasmanian club cricket. He also pointed to the fact that he had given advice to Clem Hill when he was a young man and to Vic Richardson when he was a lad at college, and how he now (as vice-captain of the 1930 team) was 'a great batsman and brilliant fieldsman'.

Addressing himself to the younger members of Bill Woodfull's team, Darling said that 11 of them would be playing in England for the first time and they would find conditions differed considerably from Australia, particularly during a wet summer. At times they would face wet wickets, but suggested that these were not necessarily bad and he preferred an English wet wicket to a sticky pitch at the Melbourne Cricket Ground.

In stating that he wanted to see the Australian team return with the Ashes, he said that the captain had a difficult task and needed every assistance from his team. He said there were frequent occasions when it was necessary to take risks and make experiments and he wished the side the best of luck and 'to uphold the honour of this country, both on and off the field'.

Joe Darling memorial photograph

Australian cricketers in seaboard pose, 1905. Frank Laver Collection, National Sports Museum

Frank Laver as motorist, 1905. Frank Laver Collection, National Sports Museum

PLAYERS

Joe Darling left a number of opinions and stories on the cricketers he played with and against.

WG Grace

'The greatest all-round cricketer of all time and the greatest batsman there has ever been on all wickets' was his view. Darling first encountered Grace, then aged 48, in the first match of the 1896 Australian tour at Sheffield Park and he was out for 49 and 26 caught off Ernie Jones in both innings. Darling recalls that this was the first match for both him and Jones in England and that the first two balls that Jones bowled hit Grace hard on the body. He explains that he then looked to see what would happen next as a lot of young batsmen would have pulled away from the next delivery near the body. 'Not so with Dr Grace. It was a ball on the wicket, bowled rather short and chest high and he gracefully guided it through the slips for four.'

As a bowler, Darling described Grace as deceptive and tricky and generally dismissed most young players the first time he met them but was wary against hitters. He could always worry some of Australia's best batsmen such as Iredale and Gregory and the tail end were 'always a gift to the old man'.

Grace was also cunning and played to win. Before playing against him, Darling says the Australians were warned by old players not to give him half a chance of appealing for slight breaches of the rules. And, a batsman should never pick up and throw the ball to the bowler as Grace was notorious for appealing for handling the ball.

Although Grace never missed a point on the cricket field, Darling regarded him as a great friend to Australian cricketers off the field. 'He had the natural gift and temperament to play cricket. Keen eyesight, good judgment, plenty of pluck and he absolutely lived for the game'. During the winter months he often went into winter training, including cross-country running — he had been a champion athlete in his youth — which enabled him to play first-class cricket to a late age.

On Darling's last tour of England in 1905 they met Grace, then 57 years of age in the first match at Crystal Palace. Australia batted first and were dismissed 20 minutes before stumps which allowed the English 10 minutes to bat before stumps, always a difficult task for the opening batsmen who have been in the field and then have to face the fast bowlers with the light fading.

Joe Darling and WG Grace

The only object was to play out time and Darling was surprised that Grace would come in first to face fast bowler Tibby Cotter. Cotter was as quick as Ernie Jones but more erratic and therefore likely to knock a batsman about. He struck Grace over the heart which brought an appeal against the light and ended play, and the following morning Grace called Darling into the dressing room to show him the bruise which was the size of a saucer. His decision in coming in to bat in those conditions showed admirable courage.[1]

---

1 *News* 4 December 1924, p. 5.

George Giffen

'The reason why I consider that Dr Grace was a better all-round cricketer than either George Giffen or Noble is that he was a far better batsman than either of the other two on bad wickets particularly when playing against good left-hand bowling. Both Giffen and Noble were in trouble as soon as the bowler could turn the ball from leg and keep pegging away on the blind spot on or about the leg stump, and breaking away.

George Giffen on Australian wickets, and with Australian conditions, was a better cricketer than both Dr Grace or Noble, but Grace beat Giffen on all kinds of wickets, and in this respect he was better than Noble also. There is another great factor in Giffen's favour, namely that he was always playing for the weakest of all the states in Sheffield Shield matches, whereas Noble was playing with the strongest, and had more assistance from the other players than Giffen.

George Giffen

No cricketer has done as much for South Australian and Australian cricket as Giffen, for he had a lot to do with persuading New South Wales and Victoria to play home and home matches against South Australia. If it had not been for this fact it is more than likely that Jones, Hill, myself, and others may never have been heard of in the cricketing world, as we had thus the opportunity of proving ourselves. But for Giffen, South Australian cricket might have remained in the same position as we find Tasmania and Western Australian cricket today.

George Giffen had his faults, and one great fault was that being absolutely the best bowler on the South Australian side, he overlooked the fact that the batsmen could get set against him, and that a change of bowlers, even if not as good, was advisable.

Giffen was not too popular, particularly in Melbourne, and I can well remember that in the first match that I played in Melbourne in 1894, the crowd behind the bowler rose and hooted Giffen just as Carlton, the bowler, was about to deliver the first ball to him, in the hope, no doubt, of putting Giffen off. If the crowd only knew Giffen as well as I did, they would have saved their breath as this in itself would only tend to make Giffen more determined than ever.

A lot of Giffen's unpopularity was brought about because he selected his brother Walter to go to England in 1893. Knowing Walter Giffen as well as I do, I say without fear of contradiction that he was one of the finest type of men that I have ever had the pleasure of playing with or against, and he was most unassuming. If Walter Giffen had not been George Giffen's brother, he would have forced himself into an Australian Eleven, irrespective of George Giffen, as he was a born cricketer and a fine athlete in every sense of the word.[2]

George Giffen was a great man to fight, or box, and he could use his fists if the occasion warranted it, but Walter Giffen was his master. I say that George Giffen was a man who was not properly appreciated. He had his faults, but I would like to meet the man who has not. He was outspoken, would call a spade a spade, and would not cringe to anyone. Just to show the readers of this article what George Giffen was at heart, I will here state what he told me himself one day. He was then more than 40 years of age, and I jokingly said to him that it was about time that he got married, and he replied, "Look here, Joe, I cannot get married, as there is no one to keep my poor old father and mother."

George, like Grace, absolutely lived for the game and trained very hard. He used to put a sweater on and run two or three miles before breakfast, have a bath and rub down, go in for a lot of boxing before the season started, so as to keep himself always fit, and then as soon as the cricket season started he would bowl at the nets two and three nights a week for a stretch so as to give the young, promising players test match bowling, at the practice nets. Again I say unhesitatingly that he had a lot to do with making both Hill and myself great batsmen.

There has been a lot of controversy as to which Australian was the best all-round cricketer. and I think it has been narrowed down to Giffen and Noble. As I have played a lot of cricket both with and against these two great cricketers, I have no hesitation in awarding the palm to George Giffen, although there is not much to choose between them. They were both plucky and determined cricketers, with Noble the better of the two against fast bowling and on all wickets. As a batsman on all wickets I would give the palm to Noble, although there was not much between him and Giffen.

Bowling on all wickets they were about equal, and the same thing applies as regards their fielding. Noble was fine at point and good at fielding close in on the leg side, but he was a poor field anywhere else whereas Giffen could field anywhere, being a far more active man than Noble in every sense of the word. Taking their cricketing abilities alone. I am inclined.to give the palm to Noble, but where Giffen beat him hollow was in stamina. Giffen could bowl and bat for a week but Noble had to be nursed and saved as much as possible, as his stamina was much inferior to Giffen's in every conceivable way.

Giffen was a powerful man. He was a great footballer in his day, but Noble was much hampered by his feet, and herein lay his great weakness. In all other respects Noble was a finely made man, but his feet were far too large for any ordinary man, to say nothing about an athlete. These feet made Noble slow in his movements, and he tired much quicker than most other cricketers because of it. If he had not fielded at point, thus being saved much running about when fielding he would have been a tired cricketer, and his performances would have suffered much in consequence. If

---

2 Darling's judgement is open to question as Walter Giffen's 20 year first-class career failed to yield a century. In 55 innings for South Australia he scored 943 runs at an average of 18.49 with a top score of 89.

Noble made a tall score he could not do much bowling in the same match, and he had to be nursed a lot when bowling so as not to tire him too much for his batting.

Just compare him with Giffen. Whereas Noble had to be nursed by fielding him at point, and so on, you could not kill Giffen with an axe. As far as batting and bowling were concerned, he was like, the brook, and could keep going for ever. As regards stamina, strength, and determination he was a perfect marvel. Against Victoria in Melbourne when playing for South Australia, he scored 237 runs and took I think, 16 wickets in the same match. He followed this by scoring 271 against Victoria in the next match, in which game he also captured a good number of wickets. This is where Giffen was superior to Noble. Whereas Giffen, could do the double in the same match, Noble could not stand the strain. Noble could, and did make large scores and took a lot of wickets in his time, but I cannot recollect on any one occasion Noble doing the double in the one and same match; yet it was common for Giffen to do it.[3]

I well remember an instance when we were playing against New South Wales at Sydney. Giffen and Jones got New South Wales all out about 5 o'clock, Giffen bowling from one end all the time. Giffen then went in first and was not out when stumps were drawn. Thus he bowled and batted all day. I would like to see Noble or anyone else do it. This only goes to show the stamina of Giffen.[4]

Syd Gregory

Gregory was a player Darling admired because he never considered his own average but tried to win matches every time. During the first match of the 1896 tour of England, Darling gives the example of Gregory being run out in the second innings for a duck. When he went in to bat the side was in trouble but captain Harry Trott was about 40 not out. Before facing a ball there was a misunderstanding between the two batsmen when going for a run and when Gregory saw that one of them would be run out he made for that wicket purposely to save Trott. This selflessness was because Trott was well set and more likely to make a good score whereas Gregory had yet to get started.

By contrast Darling compared this action with that of a young player who thought he should have been selected for an English tour but was overlooked. South Australia had played Victoria and this player had scored well over 100 not out in Melbourne when

Syd Gregory

---

3   Darling's memory is slightly at fault here in the South Australian games against Victoria. In January 1891 he scored 237 and then took match figures of 12 for 192 at the Melbourne Cricket Ground. In then next match against the same opponents in November 1891 he scored 271 and took 16 wickets for 166 runs. When Darling mentions a 'double' he is referring to a player scoring a century and taking 10 wickets in a match.

4   *News* 15 January 1925, p. 8.

opening the batting. Against New South Wales in Sydney he was again sent in first but there was a difference. When he scored heavily against Victoria they had no fast bowler, whereas NSW had Cotter then at his best. The batsman failed in the first innings and when it was time to bat a second time he asked Darling to drop him down the order and for Darling himself to go in first as he did not like batting against Cotter. Darling pointed out that the player was then in his prime at 27 years of age.[5]

Victor Trumper

Victor Trumper

'Victor Trumper, a lad of under 20 in 1899, was making a lot of runs in club cricket in Sydney but practically nothing in interstate matches, and failed on every occasion against South Australia.[6] I was one of the selectors who helped choose the Australian XI to visit England and from what I had seen of Trumper in big cricket I could not select him. That fine judge of cricketers, Hughie Trumble, also agreed with me. Syd Gregory was the selector representing New South Wales and he was so enamoured with Trumper and the way he was making runs in Sydney he wanted Trumper selected. But Trumble and I could not agree with him owing to persistent repeated failures in Sheffield Shield matches. Before the 1899 team sailed for England, it was decided to play three matches against the Rest of Australia, one each in Sydney, Melbourne and Adelaide. Trumper played for the Rest of Australia in these three matches. He did only fairly in Melbourne or Sydney and did not impress Trumble or myself as a coming champion. Yet in the match in Adelaide he played a superb innings of 75 against the Australian XI. It was

---

5   *News* 11 December 1924, p. 5.

6   Darling has made a couple of errors here as Trumper was born on 20 November 1877 and it was not true to say that he had done practically nothing in interstate matches. He had not achieved much in Sheffield Shield games but he had made scores of 292 not out against Tasmania in December 1898 and 253 against New Zealand in February 1899.

one of the finest innings played against the Australians in their trial matches. Trumble and I were then convinced that Trumper was the coming champion and we had made a mistake in not selecting him, owing to the fact that he had not given us a chance of seeing him bat at his best.

Before the team sailed, a meeting was called and we decided to take an extra man—Trumper was included in the team two days before the ship sailed. Trumper may never have been heard of as a cricketer if he had not gone to England in 1899.

In 1902, Trumper astonished the cricket world by his wonderful performances in England during a wet season. He proved himself to be the best batsman in the world on all wickets. Unfortunately, he inherited a weak constitution which eventually led to his death when only a young man in 1915.

I am absolutely certain that if Trumper had been a strong man he would have stood alone as the champion batsman that the world has known, even surpassing that champion of champions, the late Dr WG Grace.

In 1899, Trumper scored 300 not out against Sussex at Brighton. Towards the latter part of this innings I was batting and scored 60 not out in my best form; yet he made me feel as if I could not play the game and on reaching the dressing room I told some of the players that we could not play the game in comparison with Trumper.[7]

Unfortunately, owing to the fact that he did not enjoy the best of health, Trumper had many bad days, but when fit and well there was only one cricketer in it as a champion of the world, and that was Trumper.

Trumper, after scoring this beautiful 300 not out against Sussex, did practically nothing for the next three weeks, as this big innings had sapped his strength. He was a general favourite with all with whom he came in contact and was a man who took great care of himself in every way, being a strict teetotaller and a non-smoker.

Trumper was a good fast bowler but his services in this respect could not be availed of as I nursed him for his batting. What a great all-rounder he would have been if only he were a stronger man. He would take three strides only and could throw the cricket ball 115 yards without field. He was a fine slip field, and one of the best outfields Australia has ever had. Champion batsman and a good bowler, yet Australia lost his valuable services owing to his weak constitution.

At times I was forced to put him on to bowl and he invariably brought about a much-needed separation when two batsmen were well set. During the 1902 tour Trumper bowled 152 overs taking 20 wickets at an average of 20.75 per wicket.'[8]

---

7   Darling actually made 49 not out in the Sussex match.
8   Darling, *Test Tussles*, pp. 26-7.

KS Ranjitsinhji

KS Ranjitsinhji

'I can well remember the first Test match that Ranjitsinhji played in and against us. It was in 1896. He did not play in the first Test at Lord's as the authorities had grave doubt as to whether it was fair for him to be allowed to play for All England when he was not an Englishman. Ranji was making so many runs in England that, as he was living in England and playing for Sussex, he was eligible to play. The authorities wrote and asked us if we had any objection to Ranjitsinhji playing in the Test matches. We immediately wrote back and stated that we would be only too pleased to allow Ranji to play.

On winning the toss we had no hesitation in batting first on a good wicket and made 400 runs and England was forced to follow on. When stumps were drawn at the end of the second day's play, England had lost five of her best batsmen and was still more than 100 runs behind. It looked like a foregone conclusion and all interest was lost in the match. Very few spectators witnessed the play on Saturday, the last day of the match and they missed the treat of their lives.

Ranji got going and made 154 not out and made our bowlers look like a lot of schoolboys. We required 124 runs to win and scraped home by three wickets. At one stage we were 7 down for 97. The excitement was so intense that Trott, our captain, could not stand the strain and went for a drive in a cab. Ranji always gave us a lot of trouble in 1896 and 1899 and also when in Australia as a member of Stoddart's English side.

We tried all kinds of devices to check this brilliant Indian juggler, including off theory. When facing off theory, Ranjitsinhji used to step across very quickly and pull a ball pitched well out on the off side and hit it to leg. I am firmly convinced that he had far quicker eyesight than an ordinary cricketer, and this being the case, he was able to see the ball sooner, and as all cricketers know, the eye practically telegraphs to the brain, and everything is done so to speak, simultaneously. He was able to bring off the most risky shots and strokes that I, in my prime, would never have attempted. In fact, the only cricketer that I have seen approach Ranjitsinhji in making these impossible shots was Victor Trumper.

Many a time in my spare moments I tried to work out some plan in which to block this juggler, as that is what Ranjitsinhji really was. He was a past master in placing the ball on the leg side, and invariably beat the fieldsmen stationed at short leg and mid-on. I noticed that he very often hit a ball very hard on the leg side about six inches to one foot in height, but owing to the quickness of movement he made the stroke safely.

In desperation, after consulting with my leading bowlers, I placed an entirely different field to what we had ever used before for Ranjitsinhji. I weakened the off field and put two and sometimes three extra men on the leg side. Two men were stationed about 10 yards from Ranji, one being nearly square and the other fine leg. Behind these two legs, really 'silly legs', was stationed a man on the leg boundary to save four; also at times a man on pull on the boundary and the usual mid-on. The bowlers were instructed to peg away at Ranji's leg stump and pads.

Syd Gregory was absolutely the finest fieldsman on our side and whereas he always fielded at cover point I purposely took him away from that position and put him 'silly' fine leg and field 'silly' square leg myself.

Ranji always used to have a look where we were both fielding before the bowler started to deliver the ball and as soon as he had his last look and the bowler was actually on the point of delivering the ball, we generally shifted our positions a few yards, sometimes one way and sometimes the other and occasionally only one would move or we would not move at all. Ranji never knew where we were actually fielding when he was about to make a stroke and this eventually put him clean off his game.

On one occasion he made a beautiful stroke on the leg side, the ball travelling at great pace only a few inches off the ground and to all intents and purposes right between the two men stationed at 'silly' leg, but Gregory had shifted and brought off a fine catch, much to the disgust of Ranji. From that day Ranji was never again the same batsman. The reason was that we got on his nerves and this worried him and eventually led to his being left out of the England side.

I well remember the English captain Archie MacLaren coming into our dressing room after we had beaten England by only 3 runs, at Manchester in 1902, to congratulate us on our win. MacLaren was a great favourite with the Australian players as he was a great captain, and one of the finest sportsmen that I have ever met. On this occasion he told me that Ranji was in such a 'blue funk' that he was nearly sending him in last.

Hughie Trumble made three appeals against Ranji for lbw in the one over and got him out with the last. I will never forget when Ranjitsinhji came in to bat. If it was possible for a black man to be white, Ranji was the nearest approach to it.

Ranjitsinhji was a wonderful cricketer. He played in 15 Tests for England and made 989 runs at an average of 44.95. His highest score in a Test match was 175 runs.'[9]

Ernie Jones

'I consider that Ernie Jones (known as Jonah) was a better fast bowler than Larwood, as the latter had to be spelled after bowling four or five overs whereas Jones could bowl for an hour stretch without losing pace. As the wickets were rougher and not prepared as well in my day, I am firmly convinced that if Jones had bowled like Larwood did with a packed leg field, then someone would have been killed.

---

9 Darling, *Test Tussles*, pp. 32–4

Ernie Jones

There were plenty of good fast bowlers every bit as fast as Larwood. They used to bowl a ball every now and then at the batsmen just as Larwood did, but not frequently and with only one man on the leg side, whereas Larwood had eight men fielding on the leg side.

During a tour of England, G Jessop was deliberately bowling at the Australian batsmen and hit several of us on a fiery wicket. Jones retaliated, with the result that a batsman named HL Taylor was carried off the field and confined to bed for two weeks. Jones had only two men on the on side and goodness knows what would have happened if he had been told to bowl the same as Larwood did to a packed leg field.

Once when Australia was playing Gloucestershire and Charlie Townsend came in to bat (he afterwards played for England), I commented that he was the thinnest man I had ever seen, being well over six feet tall and as fine as a match. When Townsend was taking strike to Jones the latter came up to me and said, "Joe, I do not like bowling to this man," and when asked why not, Jones replied, "I am frightened that if I hit him the ball will go right through him."

Jones was a fine sport and did not want to hurt the batsman. He had a wonderful physique and as a fieldsman at mid-off had no superior. However, in many ways Jonah was a bit of a boy. During one of the matches he had been bowling a fair amount on a very hot day and afer he had had a rest and was brought on again, he was not bowling at his fastest. As the two batsmen were well set and it all depended on separating them as to whether Australia would win or not, without saying anything to Jones, I went up and spoke to Jim Kelly the wicket-keeper and said, "Go up close to the wickets to Jonah." Kelly asked, "What for?" to which I replied, "I want to make Jonah bowl his fastest." As both Jones and I hailed from South Australia I knew what the result would be as Jones always used to boast that there was not a wicket-keeper who would dare stand up close to his bowling … As soon as Jonah saw Kelly come up to the wickets he took it as an insult, just as I wanted him to do. Jonah said, "Alright, Jim, I will soon shift you." He sent the ball down for all his worth, not so much as to bowl the batsman but to shift Kelly. Fortunately he got a really good ball in, and being so fast he took the batsman by surprise and clean bowled him. From then onwards, when Jonah was not bowling at his top speed, Kelly would stand up close to the wickets and this would always have the desired result.

On another occasion in a Test match, Jonah was bowling, and when a certain batsman was coming in I went up to Jonah and told him that the incoming batsman reckoned he was only a medium fast bowler. It was quite amusing to see the pace that Jonah raised when bowling to this batsman, with the result that before long he secured his wicket. As soon as Jonah got him he came up to me and said, "That will show him whether I can bowl fast or not."'[10]

---
10 Darling, *Test Tussles*, pp. 37-8

BATTLES WITH THE BOARD

Joe Darling was a South Australian delegate on the Australasian Cricket Council (ACC) from 1897 to 1900, the Australian Board of Control from 1907 to 1908 and the Tasmanian delegate on the Board in 1924. That did not stop him from being a critic of both bodies, from within and without, during his playing career and in retirement. It can be well argued that Darling was a player's man. He grew up in cricket with the Australian players organising their own tours and he did not readily brook interference from administrative bodies. When the Board of Control for Australian Cricket was formed in 1905, and began to flex its muscles relating to the operation of Test tours, it was not surprising that he should remain in favour of the status quo and generally opposed the Board in the years ahead.

While captaining the Australian side during their 1905 tour of England, for example, Darling sent a letter dated 11 June, to South Australian Cricket Association secretary John Creswell stating that the game's governing body, the Marylebone Cricket Club (MCC), would not recognise the Board unless it fully represented the interests of Australian cricket. He added that the Australian Eleven players would not agree to the constitution which had the support of the Victorian and New South Wales associations. Furthermore, he stated that at the request of the MCC, the Australian team had sent four representatives to meet them to discuss difficulties in Australia.[1]

South Australian Cricket Association secretary John Creswell with whom Joe Darling corresponded over recognition of the Australian Board of Control.

In October 1905, Darling was accused of attacking those who held different views from himself and particularly board members who had 'no practical experience as cricketers'. He thought the Board of Control was 'a very excellent idea if the delegates were thoroughly capable men, possessing the confidence of the cricket community and ready to sink interstate jealousies' but maintained his allegiance to the role of the Melbourne Cricket Club as the promoter of international cricket tours. Referring back to the Board's predecessor, the Australian Cricket Council (ACC) in the 1890s, he thought it had achieved nothing beneficial. The argument against Darling's attitude was that he had been a

---

1 *Express & Telegraph* 17 July 1905, p. 1.

member of the defunct council together with other celebrated cricketers, but that their ability as players did not indicate that they possessed any extraordinary cricket legislative ability in order to administer the game.[2]

Revolution could clearly be seen to be brewing.

By the middle of 1906, as the battle for control of Australian cricket continued, Darling reflected on the 1893 and 1896 Australian touring teams which were under the control of the ACC, when some players did not receive full shares of team profits. Although it was his first tour, Darling was a member of an executive committee of five which conducted business on behalf of the team. The manager was one representative and another player was appointed by the council which meant they had two votes. In 1899, 1902 and 1905, however, on the tours Darling led, the players were in total control and considered all to be equal partners. In supporting player control, Darling stated:

> The manager's books are always audited by two auditors appointed by the team, and every player receives at the end of the tour a detailed account and statement, showing the total receipts and expenditure of the matches so that there is nothing underhanded at all. The team always arranges its affairs on a business-like footing. The manager has to produce vouchers of expenditure and every player who received advances from the manager has to give him a receipt for them, and have it checked by an auditor. It is like an ordinary company.[3]

As a player/member of the Board of Control, Darling could sometimes support that body as he did a year later in a front-page interview with the Sydney *Sun*, stating that he was 'agreeably surprised' about the prospect of 'formulating a proper controlling body' and placed much of a supposed conflict between players and board down to 'press imaginings'.[4]

Board of control secretary William McElhone

Darling was recognised as a strong champion of the rights of players and was proud of the fact that South Australia treated its players better than the other state associations and particularly New South Wales. The NSWCA was certainly niggardly and in 1907 he claimed that he tried to get a resolution passed that the financial arrangements of the next Australian Eleven would be the same as in the past. That was not adopted, but he had the assurance from several delegates, including Board of Control secretary William McElhone, that it would be all right. On the strength of that assurance, Darling stated that he was able to get the players to appear in the 1907-08 Test series, but knew that if some board delegates had interfered with arrangements the team would have been put in jeopardy and the sooner the board was 'smashed up the better'.[5] The comment about assurances,

---

2   *Referee* 25 October 1905, p. 8.
3   *Evening Star* 8 June 1906, p. 3.
4   *Sun* 11 August 1907, p. 1.
5   *Northern Miner* 29 September 1908, p. 4.

however, was immediately denied by McElhone who said that the players should be 'treated in a liberal manner'.[6]

Background to the 1912 fiasco

At a public meeting at the Hobart Town Hall in March 1912, Joe Darling was the principal speaker in support of the Big Six — Victor Trumper, Clem Hill, Warwick Armstrong, Vernon Ransford, Tibby Cotter and Hanson Carter — in their withdrawal from the 1912 Australian team to tour England to take part in the first Triangular Test series with England and South Africa. He dealt with cricket history and the selection of players for England, beginning with a meeting held in Sydney in January 1902 to consider the advisability of forming a Board of Control and how he had recommended having cricketers represented on it, but that this had been objected to by McElhone who he described as 'causing all the present trouble'. The meeting then passed three resolutions: the first in favour of choosing a thoroughly representative Australian Eleven; the second entering an emphatic protest against the action of the Board of Control in not submitting answers of the six players to a full meeting of the board and their uncompromising attitude against the players; and the third asking the chairman of the Board of Control to resign in view of the fact that he had lost the confidence of the cricket loving public and the cricketers of Australia to reach an amicable settlement between the board and the players.[7]

In August 1926, Darling wrote a much longer article in which he outlined the Board of Control's formation, conduct and victimisation which led to the 1912 fiasco and enables some of his views to be put in context:

His 1905 Australian Eleven was the last Australian to tour England under the old system in which the players appointed their own captain and manager and also managed their own affairs. In the same year, a Board of Control for International Cricket in Australia was formed and when the Constitution was being drawn up he moved that the following clause be inserted, 'That the players of all future Australian Elevens to England or elsewhere appoint their own manager, subject to the approval of the Board only.'

This motion was carried unanimously and inserted into the Constitution accordingly (Rule 9). The reason behind the clause was that the manager had to have the respect and confidence of all players as they had to live, travel with and have implicit faith in him.

Darling pointed out that, as a delegate on the Board, he was disgusted with the way in which it operated, recalling that on one occasion when a letter was received from Fiji asking that a native team of cricketers be allowed to visit Australia and play matches in Sydney, Melbourne and Adelaide, the Board refused the application on account of the White Australia Policy. Yet by the time of the next meeting it had been approved, and the minutes were faked to show this.

---

6   *Evening News* 29 September 1908, p.
7   Sydney *Daily Telegraph* 7 March 1912, p. 7.

Monty Noble who found himself in conflict with the New South Wales Cricket Association because of his support for the Melbourne Cricket Club.

One of Darling's persistent criticisms was that very few of the Board delegates over 20 years had much experience of big cricket and he was appalled that cricketers such as Hughie Trumble, Warwick Armstrong and Vernon Ransford were consistently barred by the Victorian Cricket Association from being appointed as selectors on behalf of Victoria or Australia, because they were members of the Melbourne Cricket Club. He also referred to Monty Noble being similarly barred by the New South Wales Cricket Association. In Darling's view, no Board of Control for Australian cricket was a truly representative body acting in the best interests of Australian cricket when such men were overlooked.

Darling claimed to be a staunch supporter for one controlling body for cricket in Australia, but not of the set-up then in place. The Board only controlled international cricket insofar as visits of teams to Australia were concerned and visits of Australian teams overseas. The Victorian and New South Wales associations, took the gross proceeds of all matches, Tests or other, played in Melbourne and Sydney and controlled these games in every way, paying the expenses of both playing sides and pocketing the profits. The Board through its selectors, only selected the teams to represent Australia in Test matches. This Board of Control was a repetition of Federation he argued, over and over again, everything was for the big two states.

The Board of Control he envisaged would have absolute control of all financial aspects and pooling of profits of all matches played in Australia, with the profits divided on an equitable basis. This would then help the weaker states improve their cricket standards by providing finance to offset travelling expenses. As matters stood in 1926, before the Board of Control would allow a visiting English team to tour Tasmania, the governing bodies in that state had to guarantee to pay the expenses of the visiting side.

Regarding the appointment of a manager of Test teams on tour, Darling recalled that in his time the players appointed their own manager, and then appointed their captain and vice-captain. Finally, the players appointed three members to form an executive committee to act in conjunction with the manager and make major decisions. The team reserved the right to alter its captain and members of the executive at any time on tour. The manager, therefore, was not an autocrat as all important decisions were made by the executive of three players and the manager. On his four tours of England, not once was the position of captain ever questioned by the team nor were the members of the executive altered.

Darling argued that if the Board of Control wanted to maintain team harmony among its players on tour, it should at least consult them before appointing the manager, captain and vice-captain. He stated that Noble had offered his services as manager for the 1926 English tour, but was turned down with very little support. In his view this was because Noble (along with a number of old players) had supported the Melbourne Cricket Club which did much to foster cricket in Australia in the early days.

At times the Melbourne Cricket Club had lost heavily on early tours, but in conjunction with the trustees of the Sydney Cricket Ground, it brought out Stoddart's 1894-95, 1897-98 and AC MacLaren's 1901-02 teams to Australia. Big profits were made which more than covered earlier losses. However, it was then that the Board of Control was mooted and the New South Wales and Victorian cricket associations sought to take over control of Test tours. The NSWCA and the VCA wanted the plums without the risks and did a lot of underhand scheming to achieve their aims. The Board of Control was launched by these two associations and they induced Queensland to come in with a secret promise to take the Test match away from Adelaide and play it in Brisbane although 20 years later that promise had not been fulfilled.

As Darling explained, it was arranged that the Victorian, New South Wales and South Australian cricket associations should each have three delegates on the Board of Control. Queensland was to have two. Western Australia and the Melbourne Cricket Club were not represented. At the meetings he attended as one of the South Australian delegates, the Queensland delegates always voted absolutely with Victoria and New South Wales, or in other words, sold their votes in the hope of getting a Test match.

In his view, Tasmania had done more for Australian cricket than Queensland, as it had sent three players to England as members of Australian Elevens whereas Queensland had no representatives. Western Australia was denied even one delegate as the ruling clique was afraid their delegates might vote against them.

At the beginning, owing to the Board not being properly representative, South Australia refused to join. It was during the time when this so-called Board of Control sent an invitation to the Marylebone Cricket Club to send out an English team. The MCC quite rightly replied that until the Board was representative of Australian cricket it would not do so.

At that time Victoria was playing South Australia in a Sheffield Shield match in Adelaide, and on hearing of the MCC's refusal to send a team when a visit was due, Darling called a meeting of the leading South Australian and Victorian players. It was decided that if the leading players in New South Wales were also willing to sign a letter asking the Melbourne Cricket Club to bring out an English team, they would bind themselves to play for Australia.

In taking this action, the players felt they were acting in the best interests of Australian cricket, as the MCC had definitely declined the Board's invitation. In approaching the Melbourne Cricket Club, the cricketers were only asking the same body which had financed tours in the past.

As soon as the NSWCA discovered what had taken place, it disqualified all the NSW players who had signed the letter. When Clem Hill and Darling heard of this, they made it known that they would not play in Sydney until such time as the disqualifications were removed, and shortly afterwards they were lifted. However, this left a bitter taste in the mouths of the delegates of the New South Wales and Victorian associations, and 20 years later these men still controlled the

Board. In Darling's view the outcome was that the players in Victoria and New South Wales who signed the letter to the Melbourne Cricket Club had been tabooed from any appointments made by the Board of Control , such as selectors or managers of Australian Elevens.

When the partly-formed Board of Control knew it was beaten it backed down and allowed the Melbourne Cricket Club representation on the Board of Control. With the Melbourne Cricket Club agreeing to come in, so too did South Australia. The delegates on the Board which then took over the control of Australian cricket comprised—

New South Wales Cricket Association	3 delegates
Victorian Cricket Association	2 delegates
Melbourne Cricket Club	1 delegate
South Australian Cricket Association	3 delegates
Queensland Cricket Association	2 delegates
Tasmanian Cricket Association	1 delegate
Total	12 delegates

The Western Australian Cricket Association was not admitted until some years later.

Darling stated that as one of the SA delegates he was disgusted to find out that everything on the agenda for the meetings of the Board was discussed privately at a prior meeting of the delegates from Victoria, New South Wales and Queensland. This meant that in effect all the Board's business was done secretly, and when a vote was taken at the meeting it was just a formality as those three states had agreed and had seven out of the total of 12 votes between them. However, what he didn't explain was the voting of the Melbourne Cricket Club delegate. It might have been expected that he represented an independent voice rather than following in the path of his VCA colleagues.

According to Darling, Board delegates, particularly Bean and McElhone, openly boasted that they would not be satisfied until they drove out of the game all the players who had signed the letter to the Melbourne Cricket Club. Warwick Armstrong was the last, and attempts were made to prevent him captaining Australia against JWHT Douglas's team in 1920-21 and, even after a 5-0 series victory, to stop him leading his winning touring side of 1921.

The 1909 Australian Eleven, under Noble's captaincy, had gone to England under the control of the Board. Frank Laver was appointed manager and

Popular player/manager Frank Laver who was at the centre of the Big Six withdrawal from the 1912 Australian team to tour England.

Peter McAlister treasurer. These two men were on poor terms and this increased the friction which existed between the players and the Board of Control. As Darling observed, McAlister's appointment as vice-captain over the head of Victor Trumper added fuel to the fire.

Because Laver was a good cricketer, had proved a most competent manager for the 1905 and 1909 touring sides, and was well liked by the players, it was only natural that they wanted him as their manager for the 1912 tour. However, the Board had not forgiven him for signing the letter to the Melbourne Cricket Club and decided to appoint its own representative. In a last minute plea for a settlement, Victorian delegate Dr R Mailer suggested that the players' legal right to appoint their own manager should be respected, but when this was turned down the three South Australian delegates withdrew. In the ballot for the position the Queensland nominee, GS Crouch was selected. Upon the Board's refusal to appoint Laver as manager the six leading Australian players then refused to tour.[8]

A broken record

At times, Darling's attacks on the Board might have begun to sound like a broken record, and perhaps he pleads too strongly on behalf of the Melbourne Cricket Club, but this article certainly defines his position.

In 1920 he had emphasised that the greater number of delegates of the Board of Control had never been heard of as exponents of the game, queried whether they should have the power to appoint the captain of the Australian Test team, contrasted the position with the Marylebone Cricket Club which was mainly composed of old international players and ten years later he was saying the same thing.[9]

Among one of the better suggestions Darling made at the end of the 1920s was one in which he strongly advocated increasing the Board's power to absolutely control all interstate and international cricket played in Australia with the state associations to control only club cricket. A squabble between the Victorian and New South Wales associations revealed that the VCA controlled the game and with that end in view would not confine interstate matches to four days as requested by the NSWCA. And a further dispute occurred when Victoria objected to Bradman and Kippax playing for NSW in a Sheffield Shield game while their international representatives did not. Darling's view was that in the best interests of Australian cricket to deny leading players match practice so that they might be at their best for Test matches did more harm than good. 'Fifty runs well made in a match was worth more to a man than practice at the nets.'[10]

If it was thought that Darling was softening in his views towards the Board as he aged, however, it would be a mistake as he made a couple of his most caustic criticisms of that body in 1932 in

---

8   Darling, *Test Tussles*, pp. 52-8 passim
9   *Herald* 24 December 1920, p. 14; *Register* 5 July 1930, p. 26.
10 *Labor Daily* 28 February 1929, p. 3.

a letter to the Adelaide *Advertiser*. In opening he reiterated his attempts through the Board to start a fund to help old Australian international players who may meet with adversity and how nothing had been done. He was now writing at a time when Archie Jackson had contracted a serious illness and money and complete rest was urgently needed to assist his recovery. Instead, all he received from the Board was a vote of sympathy which was useless. Darling asserted that the Board of Control had never been fair to cricketers and before the members of the 1930 Australian team were allowed to undertake the trip to England they had to sign an unnecessary and unfair agreement. In citing the case of Alan Fairfax, who was out of work, Darling stated that the Board had made no effort to assist him and yet at the end of the tour it was trying to prevent him from making a living and bettering his future prospects, the result being that he left the country to pursue a professional cricketing career in England.[11]

A final shot at the administrative body came as a result of Bradman's dispute over his earnings from journalism at the beginning of the tumultuous 1932-33 season. 'Pay Bradman More' was Darling's solution when there was a threat that Bradman might not take part in the Ashes series.[12]

Former Australian Test players gathered at Fifth Test, Melbourne 1929.
From left: VS Ransford, C Hill, MA Noble, H Trumble, JM Gregory,
J Darling, J Worrall, WW Armstrong, PA McAlister.
Melbourne Cricket Club Collection.

---

11 *Advertiser* 26 January 1932, p. 12.
12 *Daily Telegraph* 1 October 1932, p. 1.

BEYOND THE BOUNDARY

Aside from his disputes with the Board of Control, Darling discussed a wide range of other issues (mainly during his retirement) in newpaper articles and lengthy letters to the press, particularly the Melbourne weekly newspaper, the *Australasian*.

Old Cricketers' Fund

Darling first mentioned the establishment of contributions to an old cricketers' fund as early as 1906, an issue which would absorb his interest in the future. In the benefit match held for Jim Kelly in Sydney in January 1906, he noted that the trustees of the Sydney Cricket Ground had offered the ground free and the Australian Eleven had paid their own expenses such as travelling, hotel and other outlays which showed that the players were willing to help any old cricketers in need. As a result, Kelly received the gross proceeds from the match which amounted to about £1500 and Darling was sure that all Australian Elevens would be pleased to give some of their takings in England to such a fund.[1]

In 1921 he again raised the issue of a fund for old cricketers in a forceful letter to the *Australasian* which is worth reprinting:

Jim Kelly

> Sir
>
> The Board of Control for Australian Cricket has made a lot of money out of the tour of the last English team and the visit to England and South Africa of the present Australian Eleven. This money was really made by the players themselves, and as they draw the crowds, I would like to suggest that a cricketers' fund be established to help old players that have played for Australia in their day, and that may at any time be in straitened circumstances. Very few people recognise what great sacrifices cricketers in Australia very often have to make to find the time to play first-class

---

1 *Evening Star* 8 June 1906, p. 3.

cricket. Most cricketers are jeopardising their prospects in life by playing cricket which is played in the busiest time in Australia, and no employer can give the most responsible billets, carrying the best salaries, to men who want to be away during the busiest time of the year. The result is that, in most cases, a first-class player, if he sticks to the game for any length of time, finds that before long he is a junior in position and pay to others who have not been employed so long in that particular business. In many cases a cricketer can only get a temporary position whilst playing cricket, and when he has finished playing the grand old game he finds himself stranded.

When I was a delegate to the present Board of Control I wanted a fund similar to this formed and I spoke to Messrs. Bean, McElhone and other delegates about it, and they rather favoured the scheme; but as I retired off the Board of Control when coming to live in Tasmania in 1908, that seems to have been the end of the scheme. I would like to suggest that the Board of Control set aside £3000 made during the last 12 months, and invest this amount in trustees, this amount to be added to from time to time, and old players to be helped out of this fund when deemed necessary. Personally I would like to see those two grand old players Jack Blackham and George Giffen receive an annuity. If it had not been for players like these in the early days of Australian cricket our cricket in Australia would never have reached the high standard that it is today.

Yours etc, JOE DARLING
Claremont, Tasmania[2]

Darling maintained his stand on the issue and pointed out that as the letter had made no impact he had written another to try and arrange two benefit matches to be played in the 1922-23 season. He had also started a subscription list through the *Register* newspaper in Adelaide for George Giffen who was reaching retirement age with the Post and Telegraph Department to provide for him in his old age.

Discussing Giffen, in particular, Darling said that he had jeopardised his prospects in life as he used to get leave of absence without pay in order to play and others were promoted over his head. If it had not been for Giffen, South Australia may never have played home and away matches with New South Wales and Victoria nor been admitted into the Sheffield Shield. Giffen's ability made South Australia into a team the other states had to recognise. If it had not been for Giffen, Darling himself might not have won promotion into the Test team in 1894, nor Clem Hill been selected on the English tour of 1896. The way that Giffen bowled to himself, Lyons, Hill and others at the practice nets did a lot to develop their latent cricket abilities. Few people, he added, realised Giffen's importance in encouraging young players by bowling and coaching them including those known as 'Early Risers' on the parklands.[3] He would have been pleased that the South Australian Cricket Association took up the suggestion of a benefit for Giffen and the proceeds of the South Australia–Victoria Sheffield Shield match of February 1923 were awarded

---

2 *Australasian* 26 November 1921, p. 27.
3 *Register* 3 December 1922, p. 3.

to the old champion. To assist fund-raising, Clem Hill returned to captain SA in his first match for four years and £2020 was raised.

A little over a year later Darling took up the cause of his old cricketing friend, Bill Howell, who was a fellow England tourist with the Australian Eleven on three occasions and was now crippled with rheumatism and had not been able to work for several years. In another long letter to the *Australasian*, Darling suggested that the source of Howell's illness was getting out of bed and playing in a match in England in 1902 when he was suffering with influenza and a temperature over 100 degrees Farenheit. As captain of that team, Darling would never have allowed Howell to play had he been able to ascertain such facts. As Howell, heading a family of seven, had to depend for his living on a small farm of 60 acres, and was not being able to employ labour, he was only able to scratch a bare living which led Darling to approach the New South Wales Cricket Association to stage a benefit match on his behalf. This game between New South Wales and an Australian Eleven was played in October 1924 and the 54-year-old Howell received £950 from the proceeds, a sum which represented around three and half year's wages for a working man. Unfortunately, however, Australian captain Warwick Armstrong was unable to captain the Australian team as the Victorian Cricket Association refused to take any part in the match and barred Victorian players from participating. Clem Hill came out of retirement once again to captain the Australian team in his final first-class match.[4]

Darling continued to push for the Old Players Fund in 1925 through the *Australasian* newspaper and by giving notice to the Board of Control that such a fund be established. Some delegates replied that the Board had no money but Darling's solution was to play two matches, one in Sydney and one in Melbourne, before all future Australian Elevens were selected, and the net proceeds from these matches be placed under trustees as a nucleus for the fund proposed. He also suggested that only eleven players to visit England be selected until after these matches were played thus keeping alive public interest in the players who might obtain the last three or four places. Again, this proposal fell on deaf ears.[5]

Selection

Darling served as an Australian cricket selector in 1897-98, 1905 and 1907-08 and as a South Australian selector from 1897 to 1900 and from 1904 to 1908. Down the years he was often asked his opinion on selection matters by the press and was generally forthright in his opinions.

At the end of the 1909 Australian tour of England led by Monty Noble he offered that young left-hand batsmen Warren Bardsley and Vernon Ransford were wonders and while Trumper was not the force of 1902 he had performed reasonably well. Overall, he was satisfied with the team.[6]

---

4   *Australasian* 2 August 1924, p. 29; Webster, *First-Class Cricket*, p. 615.
5   *Australasian* 27 June 1925, p. 33.
6   *Daily Post* 10 September 1909, p. 8.

Twelve years later, after watching Warwick Armstrong's side in England, he had the ring of the old-timer by stating that the great fast bowling pair Jack Gregory and Ted McDonald were not to be compared with Ernie Jones and Tibby Cotter. He also praised the Australians fielding which he thought was vastly superior to the Englishmen. But in making comparison between Armstrong's team and his own side of 1902, he stated that their opponents were nowhere near as strong owing to the great losses sustained by the England side during World War I with several prominent young players being killed in that conflict.[7]

Jack Hobbs ... criticism of his age backfired.

In January 1926, Darling was quick to denounce the Australian team selected to tour England as 15 per cent inferior to Armstrong's side, being much weaker in bowling. He thought that Charles Kelleway should have been included before Jack Ryder and Hunter Hendry, and that Hammy Love should have been picked ahead of Jack Ellis as second wicket-keeper.[8] A few days later he added fuel to the fire by saying that 'all cricketers are on the down grade after 35 years of age' and added that 'Jack Hobbs is nothing like the batsman he was in 1905'.[9] The issue might have died except the now 43-year-old Hobbs understandably took umbrage and replied that not only was Darling's comment 'absurd' but that he knew comparatively little about cricket in 1905 as it was his first season in first-class cricket.[10]

Darling certainly had to eat some of his words when the series was decided following the final Test at The Oval in August and he certainly paid tribute to the performance of Hobbs and Herbert Sutcliffe, pointing out that of the 716 runs made by England in the match 374 were scored by the opening pair and only 294 by the remaining batsmen with 48 sundries. He wondered what England would have done without those two players who were the best opening pair the world had seen. Australia did not have the bowlers to take advantage of the conditions and Mailey's 9 wickets had cost him 266 runs and Grimmett's 5 cost 182 runs while Macartney's left-arm orthodox spin and Arthur Richardson's off-spin proved negligible.[11]

Another series and too many stiff backs was Darling's opinion on the team selected to represent Australia in the second Test of the 1928-29 series. There was no fast bowler to replace Gregory and spin bowling was a thing of the past. Comparing the English and Australian attacks he stated that Harold Larwood and Maurice Tate were the two best bowlers in the world and Australia

---

7   Warwick *Daily News* 13 September 1921, p. 5.
8   *Evening News* 30 January 1926, p. 7.
9   *Sun* 5 February 1926, p. 7.
10 *Sporting Globe* 6 February 1926, p. 3.
11 *Launceston Examiner* 21 August 1926, p. 13.

had responded by picking the 46-year-old Don Blackie and 45-year-old Bert Ironmonger for the first time. The average of the Test team for the first match in Brisbane was 38 and it was the same for the second with most of the team past their prime.[12]

Three weeks later with the Ashes lost, Darling was again on the attack and damning the selectors for turning their backs on young players and the Board of Control for mismanagement, continuing (as he had said before) that Australia would rue the day the Board came into existence. Darling was irate about the role played by Board member (and selector) Ernest Bean congratulating the selectors on their one 'find' in Don Bradman. Instead, Darling thought it ridiculous that Bradman had been dropped for the second Test when he (along with the rest of the team) had failed in Brisbane. As he argued:

> If these selectors had chosen Bradman for the three Tests they could have congratulated themselves on their sound judgment. As it was they put an extra strain on Bradman as he must have known if he failed again he would have been left out for good. All the credit lies with Bradman himself in showing the cricket world that he has the right temperament for Test Cricket.[13]

Over time the impression gained is that newspapers turned to Darling because he offered controversial opinion. Certainly, there seemed to be no reason for gaining a long-range prediction of the 1930 tour of England nearly a year ahead of it taking place. Even so, he was ready to say that Tim Wall would need to bowl faster and Grimmett would be ineffective in a wet season. Discussing the batsmen, he thought Bradman and Archie Jackson would be in the team but did not entertain high hopes for the bowlers.[14] When the team was picked he regarded the omission of Jack Ryder as a grave mistake and by the selection of so many young players of the necessity that existed for a good proportion of old players going in order to 'stiffen the team'. Darling was becoming impossible to please. A little over a year before he complained about old men and stiff backs. Ryder was 40 years old. Four years earlier he had said players were over the hill at 35.

When the next Australian tour of England came around in 1934 Darling again thought the bowling was weak and that the team's best hopes of winning the Ashes rested with Bradman and O'Reilly or the result of the toss. Commenting on the selection, Darling preferred 20-year-old Tasmanian batsman Jack Badcock and 43-year-old Queensland all-rounder Rox Oxenham to 33-year-old Victorian batsman Bill Ponsford and his 26-year-old team-mate, left-arm wrist-spinner LO 'Chuck' Fleetwood-Smith. He expected that there would be a fair amount of fast bowling on the leg side and for that reason would have excluded Ponsford and perhaps Kippax. Fleetwood-Smith was erratic, and he doubted his capacity to take wickets in major matches. His selection along with that of Arthur Chipperfield were experiments. Badcock was a coming star who had

---

12 *Sun* 10 December 1928, p. 10.
13 *Labor Daily* 21 January 1929, p. 3.
14 *Evening News* 31 May 1929, p. 12.

eliminated a previous weakness of groping forward against slow leg-break bowlers, had recently made a century against Grimmett, had a fine defence and was strong all round the wicket.[15]

The trouble with Averages

Darling regarded averages as a curse, as newspapers in both England and Australia were forcing cricketers to play for their average which caused play to slow and spoil the game from the spectator's viewpoint. He asked readers to imagine a professional cricketer whose living depended on the game having a run of bad luck for a week or two and being compelled to bat for his average because of press criticism.

As a selector, Darling had ignored averages until he satisfied himself about the conditions and circumstances under which they were obtained. This was particularly important when considering players for English tours where matches were played to a time limit. Who would be the better choice — the player who had been making good scores in Australia and was likely to play for his average or the man who might not score as many runs but would aim to win matches?

To emphasise his point, Darling gave his own case before the start of the 1897-98 Test series when he was struck in the mouth at net practice through a ball returned hard by a spectator while he was bowling and still watching the batsman. The injury was followed by a bout of influenza with the result that when the Englishmen played South Australia in the first tour match he made 0 and 1 and fielded badly when he would have been better off in bed. This failure was followed by only 32 (run out) against Victoria and in consequence most newspapers and the public left him out of the Test team. However, Darling was selected for the first Test in Sydney but when the Englishmen had scored over 500 and he went in weary on the second day and was out for 7 the writing appeared to be on the wall. Fortunately, there was a second innings and a score of 101 was later to be followed by centuries in the third and fifth Tests for his best series ever.[16]

Covered pitches and defensive batting

Darling's criticisms often aimed at the general status of Australian cricket, and one of his repeated complaints was what he called the 'everlasting disgrace' of authorities 'covering the wickets in the interest of gate money rather than in the best interests of the sport'. He considered that it gave batsmen an unfair advantage over bowlers as they were able to bat on a paradise whereas bowlers often had a greasy ball and bad footholds to contend with. In this he was definitely running against the tide of opinion in the 1920s although he took the opportunity to predict that at some time in the future an Australian team would be beaten in England due to having no experience on wet wickets.

---

15 *Advertiser* 16 April 1934, p. 10.
16 *News* 11 December 1924, p. 5.

As he aged he became increasingly critical of modern approaches to cricket and claimed that young batsmen were 'afraid of hurting the ball'. Watching a district cricket semi-final in Melbourne in 1924 between St Kilda and Prahran, he noted that Clarrie Grimmett was bowling mainly slow balls but no batsmen had any idea of hitting the ball into the long field. He regretted he had not seen Bill Ponsford bat, but recalled that in the days of Lyons, Duff and Trumper a bowler like Grimmett would have had three men posted on the boundary. Darling had a preference for hitters and thought players were too conscious of averages. He would prefer a player who could make a quick 30 to win a game than another who might make a century and drag out the match to a tame draw.[17]

The wickets in the 1920s were better than in Darling's day, and he had never seen a wicket play better than that in Melbourne for the second Test in 1924-25 which only began to show signs of wearing on the sixth and seventh days. At the same time, he showed that he continued to live in the past by saying that the finger spin employed by Howell, Trumble or Noble would have got any side out for less than 200 runs. In discussing Arthur Gilligan's English team he thought too great a reliance was placed on Hobbs and Sutcliffe while Tate was the best bowler on either side. He also remarked on changes in field positions and that point, where Noble once fielded, was no longer used. The batsman of the present day had a tendency to dig themselves in and refuse to take risks, and he could not understand how Frank Woolley who started off in a characteristic free-flowing style by hitting 25 in his first half hour at the crease then took two hours to reach his half-century.

Umpiring

Darling was quick to defend Australian umpires in the wake of criticism by Lord Harris who described them as incompetent during the 1924-25 series in a complaint to the International Cricket Conference the following year. Darling agreed that the standard was not all that could have been desired but said that it compared favourably with that in England. He agreed that our umpires did not have the same amount of practice or experience as English officials standing six days a week but quoted Harris back to himself regarding good umpires having a good eye. He also quipped that many first-class umpires in England were old players who had been forced to retire from the game because of deteriorating eyesight. In the 1925 Adelaide Test match, which Arthur Gilligan's team had lost by 12 runs, it was true that Patsy Hendren and Roy Kilner were given out wrongly and the Australian team admitted this when he went into the dressing room after the match. He also reminded Harris of the notorious Barlow incidents from Trent Bridge in 1899 (earlier in this book) which had cost Australia that Test match. Darling expressed the view that one of the problems with English umpiring was that as professionals they depended on it for a living and as a result were frightened to give out players such as WG Grace and Stanley Jackson

---

17 *Barrier Miner* 29 April 1924, p. 1.

in his time. In his view Australia had produced three of the finest umpires in the world in Jim Phillips, Bob Crockett and Philip Argall whereas the only English umpire to be compared to them was Bob Thoms.[18]

Discrimination against professionals

Although he was born into money and attended a major private school, Darling despised the class division which separated amateurs and professionals in English cricket as full of hypocrisy. As he pointed out, the fact of amateurs and professionals having separate dressing rooms, dining at separate tables, and entering the field through separate gates was ugly enough but he was disgusted by the way some English captains spoke to their professionals as though they were dogs. Writing in 1926 he added:

Australian umpires Bob Crockett and Phil Argall who were highly rated as officials by Joe Darling.

> Cricket is only a game, and the best of all games, and I have always contended that whilst playing it all are equal. Some of my best cricketing friends are men who have had to work hard for their living, and I have always found that some of the best sportsmen I have played with and against have been professionals. Take Jack Hobbs, for instance. He is recognised as the best batsman in the world today, and one of the finest sportsmen who has ever played the game, and he is a professional.[19]

Other administrators

The Board of Control members were not the only cricket administrators Darling had in his sights. In his criticism of New South Wales authorities, Darling wrote that he would never forget the last interstate match he played in Sydney in 1907 when his team was doing a lot of leather hunting as the home state put together an innings of 573. The weather was extremely hot, but when the players adjourned at 4 o'clock they found their reserve occupied by administrators and hangers-on who rushed the afternoon tea and the waiters so busy the cricketers could not get a look in. It was time to take charge of the situation so that with the support of two mates he took possession of the tea urn and served the players first. As he pointed out the players were expected to return to the field promptly, so the rest could wait. It was only by taking a stand that they got a fair deal.[20]

---

18 *Launceston Examiner* 5 June 1926, p. 13.
19 Darling, *Test Tussles*, p. 37
20 Darling, *Test Tussles*, p. 39.

Eight ball overs and eight runs

The eight ball over had been introduced into Australian cricket after World War I and Darling did not like it. He thought it was a reasonable idea for Saturday afternoon cricket but was unfair to fast bowlers in first-class matches particularly during a heat wave. It had the effect of slowing the game down because bowlers sent down two or three of their deliveries simply to conserve energy and not to dismiss the batsman.[21]

Darling also made the suggestion to make the present six worth eight runs as a means of putting more life into cricket but the idea lacked support.[22]

Set teeth and Don't Funk

It was probably no surprise that Joe Darling had a solution to playing Bodyline as like a number of old players he reckoned he had seen it all before. So writing in the *Launceston Courier*, and reprinted in the Melbourne *Sporting Globe*, he recommended that batsman never lose sight of the ball. Interestingly however, the observations he was drawing upon at the time the first Test was beginning in Sydney were not from any cricket he had seen that summer, but from the final Test at Melbourne on Percy Chapman's tour four years before.

Watching Bill Woodfull facing Larwood from directly behind the wickets on that occasion, Darling had noticed him ducking from flying balls and losing sight of them. His advice was that, 'The right and only correct way to play the flying ball is not to duck or pull away but watch the ball all the way and just move your head or body out of the way. Sometimes you cannot avoid being hit and the only thing to is to set your teeth and not funk the situation.' It would have been interesting to know what the Australian players thought if they read this from a man who had not yet observed Douglas Jardine's employment of a fundamentally new tactic.[23]

Laws of Cricket

Darling had made a number of suggested alterations to the Laws during his playing days and did so again in 1936 after a long hiatus. In a letter to the Marylebone Cricket Club which was reprinted in the *Australasian* he proposed changes to the following:

1. Dealing with a run out off a no-ball.
2. As regards a batsman being given out run out or stumped.
3. A bowler should be debited with all no-balls or wides bowled.
4. Stumped off a wide.

---

21 *News* 14 January 1925, p. 11.
22 *Herald* 20 April 1932, p. 8.
23 *Sporting Globe* 3 December 1932, p. 6.

As regards No.1. This rule should be altered so as to read, 'when in the opinion of the umpires a batsman is attempting a run between the wickets'. At present let us a consider a batsman who touches the ball and is missed by the wicket-keeper, and the ball bounces off the keeper's hands on to the wicket, and the batsman is out of his ground. At present the batsman is given as run out off a no-ball when not even attempting to make a run. On the other hand, if the wicket-keeper had caught the ball or had stumped the batsman, he would be given not out off a no-ball. Again I have known a batsman to stop a yorker near his crease and be out of his ground with no idea of running, the wicket-keeper has picked up the ball and removed the bails before the batsman has recovered his crease and is given out, run out off a no-ball.

No.2. Here again the same thing occurs. A bowler beats a batsman, by enticing him out of his crease, and the batsman touches the ball, but the wicket-keeper misses the chance, and the ball rebounds on to the wicket and the bails fall off before the batsman recovers his crease, the batsman is given out, run out. In my opinion this should be out, stumped, as the bowler deserves the wicket just as much as he does when the ball rebounds off the wicket-keeper's pads to the wicket.

No. 3. A no-ball and wide both add at least one run to the batting side's score, and the fielding side is penalised. If two bowlers in the same innings take five wickets each for 50 runs scored off their bowling, and one of them bowls two no-balls and two wides, who is entitled to the better average? If the bowler's average was debited with no-balls or wides it would help to make the bowlers more careful about bowling wides or no-balls.

No. 4. At present a batsman can, I believe, still be given out stumped off a wide. A wide is a penalty ball just the same as a no-ball, and in each case the bowler has an extra ball. I have seen bowlers purposely bowl wide after wide to prevent the opposing side making runs against time. This happened in a final club match I played in at Adelaide many years ago, and one of our batsmen in endeavouring to score off a ball that had been called a wide by the umpire, slipped and fell down, and the wicket-keeper took the ball and ran over and knocked the wicket down before the batsman could get up and recover his crease. On an appeal being made to the umpire, the batsman was given not out. This led to a great deal of controversy and the matter was referred to your committee during the time Mr Lacey was secretary, and he replied that the batsman should have been given out. This decision, I feel sure, should be altered, as bowling purposely to prevent a batsman scoring quickly is not playing cricket as it should be played. No objection to bowling wide of the wicket as long as they are not 'wides' is all right. Here, again, in my opinion, a wide should be treated the same as a no-ball, and a batsman should not be given out, stumped off a wide for the reason herein given.

Joe Darling

These were eminently sensible suggestions and in closing his letter to the MCC, Darling reminded the committee that while Australian captain he had a great deal to do with the insertion of the following rules in cricket.

1. Declaration of innings at lunch and rolling of wicket during lunch interval. This match I referred to your committee for a ruling after the first Test match played at Nottingham in 1899.
2. Putting sawdust in the holes made by the bowlers during rain. The incident that led up to this rule took place in our match played at Scarborough in 1899.
3. Captains declaring teams before tossing. This I arranged with the English captain, FS Jackson before tossing at Nottingham in 1905.
4. Batsman being credited with six runs instead of four when hitting a ball over the fence. [24]

Darling had been outspoken for 30 years since his retirement, but while he had advocated some wise measures he sometimes appeared to be on the wrong track and raking up old history. As a player he stood for character and honesty, but as a critic he carried deep-rooted prejudices which made him blind to the virtues of some of those who opposed him.

---

24 *Australasian* 16 January 1937, p. 52.

Jack Creswell Secretary Cricket Association), Joe Darling (ex Australian Eleven Captain), and Harry Blinman (Chairman Cricket Committee).

FOOTBALLER 1885-95

'There was no massaging cricketers and footballers in my day' reflected Joe Darling at the Adelaide Oval when he was back in his old home town for the 1925 Ashes Test match. Players had to rub themselves down. The former captain of the Australian Eleven had, like some of his Test team-mates George Giffen, Jack Reedman, Ernie Jones, Clem Hill and Jack Worrall, played Australian Rules football at senior level.

Darling might have begun playing for North Parks in 1885 at the age of 14 as a 'J Darling' was mentioned in the North Parks line-up against Willunga in June of that year, and again in a match against West Torrens in August. North Parks comprised a large number of St Peter's, Prince Alfred and Whinham college boys and combined with the Adelaide Football Club for the purpose of entering a team in the major South Australian Football Association (SAFA) competition under the name of Adelaide while North Parks would play in the Adelaide and Suburban Football Association (ASFA).[1] It is possible that he also played for the ASFA Twenty-Threes and Twenty-Twos which were thrashed by visiting Victorian Football Association teams Hotham and South Melbourne in May and June. As no initial was given it could have been either Joe who turned out for Prince Alfred College in that year's intercollegiate game against St Peter's or his elder brother Charles (two years his senior) who represented Adelaide in one game.

Darling was certainly a college boy when Adelaide won the SAFA premiership for the first and only time the following year, and when he was described as having 'a strong kick' and being 'a good mark'. Adelaide largely represented North Adelaide which had previously been the district of the old Victorian club and one of the glories of the team was that every team member was South Australian born and bred. He kicked a goal in Princes loss to St Peter's in the intercollegiate match at Adelaide Oval on 17 June and made his association debut for Adelaide against Port Adelaide two days later at the Alberton Oval. Darling remained part of the team until the end of the season, with further games against Norwood, Port, Geelong, Port and Norwood. In the match against Norwood on 21 August which decided the premiership he kicked two of his team's six goals to nil victory. Overall, for the season he played five games and kicked six goals.[2]

Darling was absent for the final match of the 1886 season against South Adelaide on the

---

1 *Observer* 14 March 1885, p. 20.
2 *South Australian Weekly Chronicle* 28 August 1886, p. 14; 18 September 1886, p. 14.

Adelaide FC premiership team 1886. Bernard Whimpress Collection.

Adelaide Oval due to an accident and this was especially significant because he thus missed out on being pictured with the rest of the team in front of the grandstand in Adelaide's only premiership photograph. However, as a graphic report in the *South Australian Advertiser* indicates, the repercussions could have been much worse:

> A serious accident happened to Darling, of the Adelaides, during the week. He was riding home in company with his brother and a friend, and as the party were proceeding at a rapid rate along the Fullarton road they did not notice a wood cart, the light of which was very dim, until they were right on to it. The first man saw the cart in time to draw on to the side and pass the vehicle, and giving the alarm the second horseman followed suit, but Darling failed to see the dray until too late, and his pony rushing into the horse in the shafts was instantly killed. Darling was thrown with such force that he sustained concussion of the brain. For several days he remained unconscious, and was confined to bed for some days, but is now able to get about again.[3]

Fortunately, he made a quick recovery and in 1887, in his final year at Princes, Darling was a regular player for Adelaide, appearing in 14 games and kicking two goals. He began the season

---

3   *South Australian Advertiser* 28 August 1886 p. 3.

with a goal in a practice match against North Park and kicked a goal in the first SAFA game in a win over new club, Hotham, before playing in the drawn holiday game against Norwood on 24 May.[4]

Adelaide also visited Victoria in late May and early June, playing an astonishingly heavy schedule of six games in 10 days. Appearing before a crowd of 12,000 against Carlton at the Melbourne Cricket Ground on Saturday, 28 May the *Australasian's* pre-match report described Darling as a 'goal sneak, grand mark, very unselfish and a dead shot for goal'.[5] On the following Monday, Adelaide played against a Tasmanian representative side, against Fitzroy on Tuesday, St Kilda on Thursday, South Ballarat the following Saturday, and Geelong on Tuesday, 7 June.

Adelaide was a young fast side and considering the quality of opposition it might have been the time of 16-year-old Darling's football life, but it was a heavy work load and no doubt bruising would affect the team's pace as the matches continued. Adelaide began by leading Carlton at half-time, but went went down three goals to six, they were defeated heavily by Tasmania and Fitzroy, but thrashed St Kilda, narrowly defeated South Ballarat, and drew with Geelong for an

Adelaide FC 1887. Joe Darling is pictured to the left of captain Mostyn Evan (with ball). Evan became a prominent administrator, serving as both chairman of the Board of Control for Australian Cricket and president of the South Australian Cricket Association. South Australian National Football League Collection.

---

4   Research notes courtesy of Trevor Gyss.
5   *Australasian* 28 May 1887, p. 22.

overall creditable campaign.[6] It is not known how many of these games Darling took part in but since he was a regular for Adelaide throughout the SAFA season it is logical to suppose that he played most of them and he kicked a goal in the Geelong game.

Whether the matches took a toll on Adelaide's back-to-back premiership aspirations is a matter of conjecture, but the club dropped from first to third position. Darling played as a rover in a loss to Port Adelaide on his return from Victoria on 11 June and in a great win over the same club on 2 July. He kicked a goal and was prominent in Adelaide's wonderful victory over Carlton on 14 July, appeared in the drawn match against South Adelaide on 23 July and kicked a goal in a win over Norwood on 6 August.[7] At season's end, however, Darling was no longer seen as a sharp shooter but judged 'a warm forward who could not be trusted to kick goals'.[8]

The first part of Darling's football career was terminated and he did not feature in any newspaper reports of football. He then attended Roseworthy Agricultural College for whom he appeared in 1889 in at least three games, two in the first part of the season against Gawler and Gawler Centrals in which the college lost the first match at home by one goal to five but triumphed in the second playing away by six goals to three; and a third in August against Gawler which was drawn with four goals apiece.[9]

In some ways perhaps, the loss of the first match on 15 June was surprising given the perilous pre-match preparation experienced by the visiting side. All went well until the railway station was reached where the college four-in-hand hitched to a wagon waited. Then as the Gawler *Bunyip* reported, the fun started:

> All having mounted the vehicle was set in motion when suddenly hands, legs, feet, hats, pipes, umbrellas and men were mixed up and flew in all directions, those who kept their equilibrium dismounting with great alertness, the driver meanwhile performing some daring acrobatic feats, and to add to discomfort the rain seemed to fall quicker and harder. The sudden stoppage of the conveyance was due to the near side horse in the shafts kicking and falling on the railway crossing. When the horses were unhitched and set on all-fours the footballers had to lift the wagon off the line. The damages were happily summed up amounting to a few broken ribs of an umbrella, a piece of harness broken, and a damaged shaft. The two latter were soon put to rights, and the call to 'play on' was readily responded to … Owing to the late arrival 20 minutes was played each way and the interval dispensed with.

In the event the Gawler men were not put off their game and managed an easy win. For his

---

6 *South Australian Weekly Chronicle* 4 June 1887, pp. 15-16; *Observer* 11 June 1887, p. 19.
7 Trevor Gyss research notes.
8 *Observer* 17 September 1887, p. 18.
9 *Bunyip* 21 June 1889, p. 4; 28 June 1889, p. 4; 30 August 1889, p. 4.

part Darling, who had been in residence only a few weeks, was among the best college players who worked hard to avoid defeat.[10] In the third game he kicked two of his side's four goals.[11]

Gawler was in its third season maintaining a team in the SAFA competition, playing a reduced program of 11 matches compared to 17 by the city clubs, and finished fourth on the premiership table.[12] One of the difficulties the club faced was putting together a strong combination when travelling to away games as well as poor programming which meant that at one point there was a five-week gap between matches. The team had the basis of a good side but combined players of mediocre abilities with those of genuine football class. Darling played five games in the latter part of the season and kicked one goal.[13]

In 1890, Darling played one game with the Burra Football Club (known as the Navy Blues) as well as representing Adelaide against Norwood on 28 June. Burra was late getting started and played several scratch matches before meeting Terowie in an away game. In all they played only three matches, a second game at Clare and a return match at home against Terowie on 13 August. In this match which Burra won by 5 goals to 3 he kicked two of the goals and the Burra Band enlivened the event by playing musical selections during the intervals.[14] It has been suggested that Darling again played for Burra in 1891 but there is no mention of this in any of the four matches played by the club that season.[15] By 1892 there was a football club at Mundoora and he might have been a member of, and even captained, the team which had two wins (both home and away) against Koolunga as well as a victory over Port Broughton.[16]

He then returned to the city and joined the Norwood Football Club for whom he largely played in defence. In 1894, Darling played 20 matches for the Redlegs and was described as an 'excellent mark, good kick, short, stocky and a strong defender'. He was named in the best players on several occasions including the premiership decider against South Adelaide, making him a dual premiership player. As part of a strong back line which included Alf Grayson, Jim Thompson, JF Travers and Ern Peters, he was named in the back pocket for Adelaide *Observer's* Team of the Year.

Darling might have appeared in colonial colours at the Melbourne Cricket Ground on 21 July, but the South Australian team was without a Norwood representative on account of the club's

---

10 *Bunyip* 21 June 1889, p. 4.

11 *Bunyip* 30 August 1889, p. 4.

12 Gawler's four wins from 11 matches placed it above South Adelaide's six wins from 17 matches on the basis of having won 36.36 per cent of games compared to South's 35.29 per cent. Norwood and Port Adelaide actually contested 18 matches as a final game (won by Norwood) was played to decide the premiership and is regarded by some historians as the first grand final.

13 Trevor Gyss research notes.

14 *Burra Record* 19 August 1890, p. 3.

15 Selections and match reports checked in *Burra Record* 27 May 1891, p. 3; 24 June 1891, p. 3; 29 July 1891, p. 3; 26 August 1891, p. 3.

16 *South Australian Register* 27 June 1892, p. 6; 16 August 1892, p. 7; *Advertiser* 7 July 1892, p. 7; Trevor Gyss research notes; Robert Laidlaw article, 'Cricketer in Gawler before becoming Test Great', *Bunyip*.

Joe Darling — Cricketer, Farmer, Politician and Family Man

Norwood FC premiership team 1894. Joe Darling is third from right in second row. Norwood Football Club Museum.

objection to the side being asked to travel on the overnight train as second-class passengers.[17] Whether this had anything to do with SA's margin of defeat by 14 goals to nil is uncertain, but it proved a good game to miss. Instead, Darling turned out for a combined SAFA team against Yorke Peninsula on Adelaide Oval on 21 July and was a prominent player in the local team's win by five goals to four.[18]

After making his Test cricket debut during the summer, he planned to have the 1895 football season off but was convinced of the need to play in a couple of important matches against South Adelaide in May and August when he proved himself the mainstay of the attack.

He played no more football in the SAFA competition and toured England for the first time with an Australian cricket team in 1896. However, he did return to Mundoora at times and is recorded as living two miles west of the town and captaining the side in 1898, six months after his record-breaking cricket season of 1897-98.[19]

When Darling played football, pushing from behind was allowed which he considered unfair. Behinds were not counted during his playing days, but he thought their introduction was a good innovation in 1897. Jack Reedman, with whom he played many Sheffield Shield games for South

---

17 *Age* 21 July 1894, p. 5.
18 *South Australian Register* 23 July 1894, p. 7.
19 Kelly, *Mundoora Centenary 1874-1974*, p. 35.

Australia, was captain of South Adelaide when there were great battles between South and Norwood for premiership honours.

On a couple of occasions against South, Darling opposed Ernie Jones, the Australian fast bowler, who was a speedy player. He was a bit too fast for Darling who could keep his opponent down only by spoiling him in the air. He was also adept at kicking the ball with both feet which was a great advantage, for it enabled a man to get rid of the ball quickly.

Rules were different in the old days, and Darling thought the game had too much whistle in the 1920s. It favoured the player who staged for free kicks that he could not have obtained in

Mundoora Football Club c1898
Standing from left: Mark Haines, Bert Shearer, John Vanstone, Mr Dalby (secretary), Walt Vanstone, Charlie Button (vice-captain), Joe Darling (captain, holding ball), Bob Haines, Dick Francis, Fred Button, Joe Blake, Rhyne Dolling, Bob Windibank; Sitting from left: Harry Longmire, Jim Blake, Bert Meyers, Tim Carman, Harry Carter. Photo courtesy of Robert Laidlaw.

earlier times. On the other hand, boundary umpires had improved football and made it faster. There was no time for slow ruckmen as it was necessary to keep up with the ball.

Place kicking was a special skill in the 1890s and in this respect Albert Thurgood (Victoria), Aleck and Jack McKenzie, Dick Stephens, 'Bos' Daly, Charlie Woods and Percy Stewart were all excellent place kicks. Any kick within 50 yards from any angle was practically certain to go through the goal. There were 20 players a side and matches would start with a kick off from the centre. Opponents at the kick-off had to keep over the line and could not cross until the ball was in transit. However, bouncing of the ball in the centre improved the game as a spectacle.

Of all the footballers he had seen, Darling thought that there was no one to equal 'Bunny' Daly at his best. He was a wonderful judge of pace, with which he used to deceive a number of opponents.

Central umpires with the assistance of the boundary men had an easier time, than the umpire who figured alone. In the old times the umpire had to chase the ball over the boundary and to bounce it.

Darling kept in touch with football as he did with cricket and he witnessed the Australian Football Carnival held in Hobart in 1924 where one of the finest games was between Western Australia and South Australia. In his view, if South Australia had used less handball and their kicking for goal had been better, they would have won.[20]

---

20 *News* 25 January 1925, p. 9.

PASTORALIST AND PATRIARCH

Mention has already been made of the purchase of Stonehenge, the problem of rabbits and the clearing of timber on the property. Until 1912, as Douglas Darling has narrated, the ploughing and carting of wool to the railway siding at Andover (20 kilometres away) was done by bullocks. After the wool was unloaded groceries and provisions which had been ordered from Hobart and sent by rail to meet the bullock team were then reloaded. Flour and sugar were ordered by the ton and it was not until 1913 that horses replaced the bullocks and they in turn were replaced by trucks and tractors a decade later.

Merino rams were purchased from South Australia and Stonehenge became famous for its fleece. Described as having swapped his bat for a shepherd's crook, Joe Darling was seen as coining money when his clip at the Hobart sales in 1916 brought 22 pence and one farthing per pound, just a half-penny below the top of the market.[1] In 1919 the property produced 125 bales of wool branded 'JD Stonehenge' which became recognised for its quality overseas and particularly in Britain. In addition to sheep farming, Stonehenge carried several hundred head of Hereford cattle which were later superseded by the Black Angus breed. Joe introduced subterranean clover to Tasmania which revolutionised farming and turned medium-quality land into wonderful pastures and vastly increased the carrying capacity for stock.

Royal Show, Hobart 1920

Douglas Darling has described how Joe liked to keep physically fit and after he handed over the management of Stonehenge to his sons he helped at harvest and shearing times, continuing to do so into his seventies.[2]

Joe and Alice Darling had 15 children (nine boys and six girls) although three did not survive infancy. As a reminder of losses suffered by families in the Victorian era, son Ernest Sydney

---

1 *Inverell Times* 1 February 1916, p. 2.
2 Darling, *Test Tussles*, p. 70

died on 29 March 1897 aged 12 months and daughter Ethel Kathleen in November 1898 aged eight months. A testament to their brief lives is recorded on a headstone at Adelaide's Payneham Cemetery with the following poignant inscription.

Headstone of Ernest and Ethel Darling, infant children of Joe and Alice in Payneham Cemetery, Adelaide. Photo by Bernard Whimpress.

Two little lambs are gone
To dwell with Him who gave,
Two little darling babes
Are sheltered in the grave.

The third child to die young was Phyllis in December 1920 aged two years and she is buried along with her parents in Hobart.[3]

Deaths of children are always distressing to parents and even devout Christians sometimes found them difficult to accept. While those in the working classes had a higher proportion of victims than the middle and upper classes the latter were not immune, and it is likely that they stoically accepted the tragedy. At least for Alice, Joe was at home on those occasions although it must be said that after Ernest's death at Mundoora he boarded ship to take part in George Giffen's Goldfield's cricket tour in Western Australia just nine days later.

It was a man's world and Alice would have already had her first experience of soldiering on when raising her family for several months at a time. Joe and Alice's first child, Gordon Joseph Francis, was born in April 1894, taking two of his forenames from his father and his mother's family name, and was less than two years old when Joe undertook his first cricket tour of England and was away from home from March to December 1896. After the deaths of her second and third children, a fourth, Eileen Isabella, was born when Joe was on his second English tour in 1899. The couple's fifth child, Joseph Ronald, arrived when Joe was home in Stonehenge but a sixth, Lillian Jean, came in March 1902 just 12 days before Joe departed (with Alice) on his third English tour.

Several other player's wives accompanied their husbands on this tour along with the wife of manager Thomas Wardill. It is presumed, however, that Alice did not take the baby with her and this raises an interesting issue regarding Victorian (or Edwardian) child-rearing practices among the well-to-do. Was Lillian left with a wet nurse? And were seven-year-old Gordon, two and half-year-old Eileen, and Joseph (16 months) farmed out to relatives?

---

3   Darling family tree.

Victor Stafford, the seventh child named after Victor Trumper, was born while Joe was at home in October 1903, but Alice was pregnant with the eighth, Douglas Keith, during Joe's final English tour in 1905 and before giving birth in November that year. Alice bore seven more children between 1907 and 1918, making a 24-year birth cycle but at least Joe was home at for those births.[4]

It is assumed that Joe was honoured and obeyed as head of his household, but Alice was a practical woman and in Douglas Darling's account she saved the life of a shearer at Stonehenge on one occasion:

> At shearing time 12 shearers were engaged and the shearing until 1920 was done by hand shears and when one of the men was shearing his sheep it kicked and knocked the blade into his left arm, making a severe gash. Blood squirted everywhere and when Mother was called she applied a tourniquet to stop the bleeding and later on inserted several stitches into the man's arm.

Stonehenge's remote location and the lack of a school meant governesses were hired to provide education although owing to isolation they rarely stayed more than a few months. By 1916, five Darling children were at boarding school in Hobart at the same time and it was not until the following year that a Government subsidised school was organised. Even then Joe Darling paid half the teacher's salary and provided board and residence while the Education Department provided the other half.

Douglas Darling also recalled the lack of medical services at Stonehenge with some of his brothers and sisters being born without medical assistance. Fortunately, they avoided sickness with a dose of castor oil and being sent to bed, the 'cure all' at the time. Of Joe's personality he wrote of a 'strict disciplinarian, a non-smoker and a teetotaller but scrupulously fair', disliking flattery and never over-indulging in praise unless someone deserved it – perhaps a typical Scottish reserve. He was also physically fit and after passing Stonehenge to his oldest son, purchasing Claremont, and entering parliament, he continued to chop wood each day, usually for an hour after breakfast:

> From 1919 to 1935, a wood fuel stove was used at Claremont House and in the winter time, two and sometimes three rooms had wood fires burning at the one time … The firewood was sent to Claremont by rail in eight foot lengths in seven-ton trucks. A truck load did not last long, so one can well imagine the chopping which had to be done. He always insisted he did the chopping as this was his daily exercise.[5]

Joe and Alice Darling were almost 50 years of age when they took over the 32-acre property at Claremont and had a number of servants working for them. They made few alterations to the house but demolished the stables at the back and converted the coach house into a garage for up to six cars. The most significant change was to install electricity and purchase an electric stove. Alice

---

4   Darling family tree.
5   Darling, *Test Tussles*, p. 70

Claremont. Photo by Graeme Ryan

held monthly meetings at the house when guests would arrive by train and a wedding breakfast for a friend was held in 1920 with guests invited to pick roses from the extensive garden.

In a description of the house the main front door was on the right in the enclosed part of a verandah and to the left of that was a drawing room with double cedar doors leading into a sitting room. The sitting room included a pianola, picture rails and blue tiles around the fireplace. The verandah alongside the sitting room was enclosed. Behind the sitting room the dining room contained burgundy coloured furniture and led to a scullery with a kitchen and pantry next to that. On the other side of the building was a sunroom behind the enclosed verandah and this served as the tradesman's entrance. A billiard room was located to the rear of that but was rarely used. A hall led to the blackwood staircase and a door at the top opened to Joe and Alice's bedroom with an adjacent dressing room and bathroom opposite. The front two rooms were bedrooms divided by a passageway while the northern end of the balcony was enclosed and used as a nursery. Behind that was a large bedroom above the billiard room with a small bathroom opposite under the stairs leading to the tower.[6]

One occasion when Joe did play host to an important party was on 8 February 1939 when Prime Minister Joe Lyons and his Federal Cabinet left Hobart on the first stage of a three-day trip up the West Coast of Tasmania. Accompanying Lyons was Attorney-General Robert Menzies and Minister for Defence Geoffrey Street. Claremont was the first stopping place with Menzies keen to talk cricket, while both Lyons who had played grade cricket in Tasmania, and Street, a former member of the Melbourne Cricket Club's first eleven, were also willing parties to discussion. Prominent in Darling's home was a photograph of Victor Trumper jumping out to drive which caused Darling to wonder aloud 'what he would do to O'Reilly'. The ministers were also shown one of Darling's most prized possessions – the bat with which Trumper scored 300 not out against Sussex in 1899 and found its way into Darling's cricket bag by mistake but was never relinquished.[7]

---

6   Claremont House Conservation Plan, pp. 14-15.
7   *Advertiser* 9 February 1939, p. 20.

POLITICIAN

Joe Darling followed his father, John, and elder brother, John, in seeking parliamentary office. The Hon. John Darling was a prominent member of both the House of Assembly and Legislative Council in South Australia for many years and also served in the SA House of Assembly. When Joe stood as an independent candidate in the Cambridge district for the Tasmanian Legislative Council election in 1921 the electorate covered a rural area from Campbell Town in the north to Bridgewater in the south of the state.

Usually only a lethargic interest was taken in such elections but in opening his campaign at Bridgewater, Darling's first meeting was unusually well attended, and it is worth examining the policies for which he stood.

In his address he stated that he had been requested by members of the Farmers and Stockowners Association to stand as a candidate in the interests of farmers and nationalism. Primary producers had not had a fair deal in the past and Darling recognised that rural production was vital to national solvency. The man on the land brought the wealth out of the land and with increasing production purchasing power was increased and it would become cheaper for people to live.

Publicity photo of a younger Joe Darling at the time he entered the Tasmanian parliament in 1920.

The financial position was one of the most important questions of the day. The public debt of Australia – Commonwealth and states – in 1920 was nearly £800 million and more than £40 million had to be raised by federal and state taxation. In Tasmania the public debt was £16 million and with an estimated population of 216,000 the amount per head of state debt was £76 14s 6d and taking the Commonwealth as a whole it exceeded £150 a head.

Economists agreed that the only remedies were economy and increased production but wasteful expenditure in government led to an inflated paper currency, private extravagance and increased taxation which were all factors in raising living costs and in turn led to industrial unrest and strikes.

Darling agreed with the Government in joining the wheat pool and said that but for that action Tasmania would have been a dumping ground for Australian wheat. His only objection to the pool was that the farmers had to finance the millers. He had spent many years on the land and the prospects of Tasmanian wheat growers were poor where the cost of production was higher than the mainland.

He opposed the construction of the Huon railway and the bridge across the Derwent River even though these were urgent needs simply because of the financial position of the state. The hydro-electric scheme should encourage the establishment of factories in the south, but a water scheme should accompany it. He suggested that councils affected should ask Parliament for a bill to authorise such a scheme from the River Styx and if elected Darling would support such a bill. The Cadbury's factory which was a major industrial undertaking would require 5000 gallons of milk per week and that needed a plentiful supply of water.

The shearer's strike had cost Tasmania £400,000 and the price of wool had fallen by 50 per cent. In many cases farmers got less than nothing for their wool and yet in that morning's *Mercury*, Hobart's main newspaper, it was reported that shearers wanted big pay increases. He regarded the demands of the Australian Workers Union as absurd.

The economy was sometimes falsely presented, and he stated that the extravagance and waste in government spending resulted in the dissipation of money that should be available for public works and education, for railway construction and the payment of adequate salaries to efficient public servants who spent money wisely. The huge increases in salaries granted to government employees in recent years showed that tax payers were anxious that civil servants should be rewarded but the desire for a contented service was defeated by the rapidity with which it had expanded.

Darling commented that Commonwealth and state civil servants now numbered one in ten of the population, there was duplication in electoral departments, taxation departments, accounts branches, construction departments and the Commonwealth and the states maintained their own separate representation in London. The waste was staggering.

Education was controlled by the state and was free, compulsory and secular. During the last financial year Tasmania spent £175,240 on education or less than £1 per head of population. There were four high schools 431 primary schools and 62 subsidised schools making 497 schools with 1075 teachers and an attendance of 38, 239 scholars. The state should do all in their power to promote the knowledge of the rising generations, Darling suggested, but agricultural education was essential for those who wanted to settle on the land.

Railways were essential to the progress of the state, but the mountainous country meant that construction costs were high and made them a risky undertaking. Good roads were just as important and with the great developments in motor vehicles great attention should be given to the construction of good roads to enable producers to get goods to markets.

If he was returned to Parliament Darling would give these matters his attention as well as the plight of returned soldiers many of whom were receiving pensions, had been placed on the land, and provided other forms of vocational training. He would endeavour to see that the best treatment was given to the returned men.

In conclusion he added that while he would always consider all measures brought forward in Parliament in an impartial manner, he would vote in the best interests of the primary producers because in protecting their interests he was protecting those of the whole community. Finally, in referring to the question of strikes and arbitration Darling said that the repeal of the *Conciliation and Arbitration Act* was of such importance to rural industries that the Farmers and Stock Owners Association suggested that each should control their own disputes as this would be cheaper and more effective than going to the Federal Arbitration Court, an ironical point considering his earlier remarks about state and Commonwealth duplication. Darling's listeners must have been impressed by the fact and figures presented to them and they would certainly know the interests he represented and the approach he would take to government.[1]

Parliament House, Hobart where Joe Darling served for 25 years in the Legislative Council. State Library of Tasmania Collection.

Given his constituency it was no surprise that he won the election convincingly and held the seat continuously until his death in 1946. What is of interest is that he remained an independent rather than joining the Australian Country Party which had been formed on 20 January 1920 and which he was rumoured to be joining as a Senate candidate in 1922.[2] He would explain his reasons publicly a dozen years later.

Douglas Darling has stated, 'Father was a forceful and hard-hitting speaker and spared neither friend nor foe, in fact he hit as hard in his political career if occasion warranted it, as he did on the cricket ground' and an early indication of this was evident in a report from debate in the Legislative Council which appeared in the Hobart Labour daily newspaper *The World* beneath the following extraordinary heading:

TORIES WAX WILD ON PUBLIC SERVANTS.
EXTRAORDINARY DEBATE IN LEG. COUNCIL.
WHY TASMANIAN GIRLS DON'T MARRY.'
TOO WELL PAID, SAYS THE SQUATTOCRACY
AN ATTACK ON MR. E. W. TURNER, P.M.

---

1 *Mercury* 6 April 1921, p. 5
2 *Zeehan and Dundas Herald* 12 April 1922, p. 3.

Tasmania has had some extraordinary things inflicted on it in the past, but nothing can compare with last night's debate in the Legislative Council on the Public Service Bill. It would be well, perhaps, if it could be preserved for future generations to peruse, and it would make an excellent answer to any examination paper as to why the House of Tories was abolished. Its abolition must come and come quickly if such views as those put forward last night by Mr John Hope and Mr Joe Darling are to be allowed to be repeated on any future question. The debate speaks for itself.

When the debate on the second reading to 'consolidate and amend the Public Service Bill' was continued in the Council, Mr John Hope said he was not opposed to the Bill in any shape or form, and what had induced him to vote for it was the attitude of the civil servants themselves to the Bill. If he had the opportunity he would move certain amendments to the Bill. The time had come when a Bill such as they had should be passed. The sooner the civil servants were put in their place the better it would be for the State. He, however, was a representative of a district which was not troubled about civil servants, and he could snap his fingers at all the civil servants, in the State. The action of some of those at the head of affairs was very questionable. There was, for instance, the Police Magistrate, Mr E. W. Turner.

Mr. Darling said he had much pleasure in supporting the Bill. Unless they were careful they would have the civil servants controlling the Government, instead of the Government controlling them. He agreed with the remarks of Mr. Hope about the chief magistrate (Mr. E. W. Turner), thought that Mr. Turner's remarks should be put a stop to, because he was only asking the civil servants to be dissatisfied with their work, and would add to insubordination in the service. For these reasons he was pleased that the Government had brought in the Bill so as to give the Government more control over the service. Mr Darling criticised the Government's allowance of two shillings and sixpence of married men's income tax … Their greatest asset today was their children. He wanted to see a White Australia but unless they encouraged the married men they would not. He rejected reducing the salaries of the railways. Mr Darling said they had reduced in all classes while the salaries of the higher-paid offices had been increased. *They were forcing the married people not to have children and were therefore killing their greatest asset. Before any married man was retrenched in the Public Service they 'should dismiss every girl' in the service. The married men should be the last to go. Some of the girls in the service were receiving more money than some of the married men. This was a vital matter for the whole of the Commonwealth. The Government should set a good example to all business men. The mere fact of paying a girl a high salary prevented her from getting married.* The Government should tax all single people, male or female, over 21 years of age.[3]

Read with today's eyes the speech above (especially that in my italics) would see Darling branded as a macho misogynist but there would have been nothing exceptional about his views at the time. In the early twentieth century there was a deep-rooted belief that women were the feeble sex and inferior to men by law of nature. Society might fall apart if women were employed

---

3   *The World* 15 March 1923, p. 6.

on the same terms as men. There were even public service reports which said things like: 'Men command higher salaries than women because they are worth more, being stronger and more capable of getting through more work in a day.'

Three years later Darling recommended cutting expenses on education, a reversal of his position when he had stood for parliamentary office. Speaking in the Legislative Council he advocated curtailing education instead of closing non-paying railway lines. Thinking of his prime constituents he argued that by closing the railways the Government was penalising primary producers. Instead, they should cut free education at high schools the cost of which should be met by their parents.[4]

Darling had been elected in the conservative interest, but he found himself the subject of a somewhat mischievous headline 'Captain of Aust XI with Lang' which appeared in the Hobart *Labor Daily* in June 1932. Speaking on the Income Tax Bill in the Legislative Council, Darling said 'in view of the prevailing conditions he considered it impossible for Australia to pay its huge overseas interest bill', a statement which threw him into a similar economic camp as the recently-sacked firebrand Labor Premier of New South Wales, Jack Lang. As the paper argued 'there was a certain amount of the Lang Plan about it with a necessity for a compromise being reached with creditors and extended time given to pay interest. But Darling was quick to check himself. 'God forbid', he added 'that Australia should ever repudiate the capital, but they had to have a reduction of interest'.[5]

In his 25-year political career Darling never attained ministerial office but there are two reasons for that: either it was not something he sought, or he was regarded as a political maverick. For many years he was on the committee of the Farmers and Stockowners Association and very active on the committee of the Royal Hobart Show Council. He was a staunch supporter for the primary producers and battled for years to abolish the payment of land tax by farmers on their holdings. In the mid-1930s during the Labor Government of Albert Ogilvie he was successful in obtaining an exemption from land tax for small farmers. However, when national Country Party leader and founder Dr Earle Page was due to speak in the Hobart Town Hall to announce his candidates for the 1934 Federal election his tour and the candidates cut little ice with Darling. Speaking out in his usual bold style he stated:

> I have been pressed on more occasions than once to stand for the Senate in the Country Party's interests, but I'll have nothing to do with it while Dr Page is leader. Dr Page's sympathies have not been with the party and he has used it as a stepping stone to further his own political ends. Our primary producers realise what Mr Lyons has done for Tasmania. Some people may have expected more from him, but his job is like that of the cricket selectors. The selectors used to meet and pick 14 players. They weren't all unanimous. But the choice was always given out to the

---

4   *Herald* 15 April 1926, p. 26.
5   *Labor Daily* 16 June 1932, p. 6.

public as the official decision. Joe Lyons is like that. He has got to be loyal to his Cabinet, whether it always agrees with what he wants for Tasmania or not. I am sure he will win.[6]

He was a member of the Parliamentary Standing Committee on Public Works for many years and in the King's New Year's Honours of 1938 was made a Commander of the Civil Division of the Most Excellent Order of the British Empire (CBE).

Darling's independence has been noted and another example of that was the parliamentary speech he gave in January 1940 exposing the methods adopted by banks in applying interest squeezes to customers wherein he stated that steps should be taken to expose abuses practised by bodies such as the associated banks, shipping combine, secondary industries and the sugar combine. The aims of these organisations were big profits by way of excessive interest, freights, tariffs and profits.[7]

But Darling was best known politically as one of the main opponents to passing the Commonwealth Government Powers Bill in 1942-43. The Drafting Committee of the Constitutional Convention held in Canberra in December 1942, and comprising Attorney-General Dr Bert Evatt, Deputy Leader of the Opposition Billy Hughes and the six state Premiers, reached unanimous agreement on the powers which should be 'referred' to the Commonwealth by the states to overcome post-war reconstruction. Prime Minister John Curtin stated that it was proposed to submit a draft of a bill transferring the powers and this would later be considered by the state legislatures.

The likely fields of Federal control were to be:
- The reinstatement and 'advancement of those who have been members of the Commonwealth's fighting forces during the war.
- Company legislation for all Australia and control over trusts, combines, and monopolies.
- Employment and unemployment.
- Orderly marketing of commodities – a provision which meets the chief object the Government had in seeking extension of its trade and commerce powers.
- Production (except primary production) and distribution of goods, with a proviso that, with the consent of the state or states concerned, the Commonwealth can exercise a measure of control over primary production.
- Air transport.
- Uniformity of railway gauges with safeguards concerning the financial requirements that can be made of a state.
- Profiteering and prices.
- Family allowances.
- Welfare of Aborigines.

---

6 *Richmond River Herald* 6 July 1943, p. 3.
7 *Australian Worker* 17 January 1940, p. 10.

Under the Drafting Committee's report to the Convention the Premiers would undertake to put the bill through their Parliaments within a couple of months. While the Premiers could not guarantee acceptance of the Bill it was assumed the unanimity achieved by the committee would weigh heavily with the states and that those Legislative Councils considered the most likely obstacles to its passage would hesitate to bring about a rejection which would have a referendum as its natural consequence. Holding a referendum was impractical when the war was still being fought.

Political observers regarded the Committee's decisions as satisfactory from the point of view of both the Commonwealth and the states. The Commonwealth would receive virtually all the powers that it considered essential for after the war. The states were granted modifications of the Commonwealth's original proposals and these met most of the pre-conceived objections that the Premiers took with them to Canberra.

Dr Evatt's skill as a round-table negotiator was largely responsible for unanimity that on several occasions seemed unachievable. Victorian and South Australian premiers Albert Dunstan and Thomas Playford fought hard for their respective points of view but saw the necessity of making a reasonable compromise. Deputy Leader of the Opposition Hughes fought strongly for the substantial extension of Commonwealth powers.[8]

Tasmania was represented by Premier Robert Cosgrove and Leader of the Opposition HS Baker. Legislation for the transfer of the powers was introduced into the six state Parliaments. The larger states accepted the proposals, but the Legislative Councils of Western Australia and Tasmania rejected them. The Tasmanian House of Assembly accepted the case for the transfer and accepted the Bill with one dissentient.

On this matter Douglas Darling has written:

> When the Bill was sent to the Legislative Council, its consideration was postponed. Certain members of the Council were not going to be stampeded into making a hurried decision without ascertaining further information. The House of Assembly then immediately proposed a Select Committee of both Houses to consider the Bill. However, the Legislative Council rejected the proposal by 10 votes to 7.
>
> During the debate, Joe Darling was its most vocal opponent. His case against it was based mainly on the argument that during the operation of the control by Commonwealth of the proposed powers, the states would suffer permanent damage. He also claimed that only the people had the right to amend the Constitution, and that it was not the right of Parliament to do so. Later on, the Bill was re-introduced by the Tasmanian Government and it was finally defeated by the Legislative Council by 8 votes to 6, Father being one of the 8, and his old friend and former fellow member of the Australian Eleven of 1896, C.J. Eady, voted with him.
>
> Prior to the Bill being re-introduced Father received a letter from Dr Evatt, the main mover

---

8 *Sydney Morning Herald* 2 December 1942, p. 6.

for obtaining the power for the Commonwealth, which read: 'Dear Mr Darling ... When a boy I saw you play cricket and was a great admirer of yours. Your name as a sportsman was well known throughout Australia, so continue to be a good sport and vote for the Bill.'

This letter was like 'red rag to a bull' as Father disliked flattery. When he received the letter, he showed it to me remarking that he thought Dr Evatt's aim was to become the Prime Minister and a dictator. The final rejection of the Bill by the Legislative Council on 26 May 1943 made headlines in the local press and I quote from the Hobart *Mercury* of the following day.

'Powers Bill Killed. Darling's Insult by Federal Minister'[9]

Australian Attorney-General Dr HV Evatt whose flattery of Joe in order to win his support for the Commonwealth Government Powers Bill in 1942-43 got him nowhere.

What is one man (or one family's badge of pride), however, can be interpreted more widely. When the Bill was being delayed in the Tasmanian Legislative Council the *Canberra Times* reported as follows:

The rejection by the Legislative Council of Tasmania of the Commonwealth Powers Bill confronts the Commonwealth with the most serious setback that has been given to this legislation since it was launched forth on its perilous career by the Constitutional Convention at Canberra in December last. It is true that the last word has not necessarily been heard on this Bill in the Tasmanian Legislature but is equally true that in Tasmania and some other states a change of outlook has developed on the part of the elements of both the Government and Opposition parties regarding the Bill.

Since the representatives of the State Governments included in the Canberra convention gave an undertaking that the Commonwealth Powers Bill would be passed by their respective Parliaments without delay, the Bill has passed in only two states. In Victoria, the passage of the Bill has been subject to the proviso that it shall not become law until a similar Bill has been passed by all the other states. Should the Parliament of Western Australia and South Australia or either of them insert a similar provision in their Bill, the Commonwealth Powers Bill will be a dead letter while every one of the six state Parliaments has failed to carry the measure. The failure of the Tasmanian Parliament to pass the Bill into law acquires added significance from the fact that it was the Tasmanian Premier supported by the Tasmanian Leader of the Opposition, who propounded the idea that the post-war powers desired by the Commonwealth should be referred to the Commonwealth Parliament by state legislation. That decision, which was made unanimously by the Convention, implied a recognition that in the face of state opposition, a referendum for the transfer of the powers to the Commonwealth Parliament might not have been carried even if the Convention had been able to agree on the matters to be submitted by the referendum to the

---

9 Darling, *Test Tussles*, p. 73.

electors. It is now apparent that in Tasmania and some other states, considerable doubt has arisen since the Canberra Convention, and that their public statements have revealed that these doubts are entertained also by the Tasmanian delegates to the Convention. These doubts represent something more than the characteristic failure of the states in the past to honour pledges given at Premiers' Conferences. There has developed in all states a very considerable hostility to the Commonwealth Government for the manner in which it has used the powers which it has taken under the war emergency and in particular the abuse of power in the making of regulations, some of which are known by the Commonwealth authorities to be neither justifiable as war-time measures nor valid exercises of war-time powers.[10]

On the one hand the Tasmanian Legislative Council's delaying tactics might be seen as simple bloody-mindedness in a conservative chamber and thus understand the need for Evatt's attempt to flatter Darling. Since Evatt had won over as difficult a figure as Hughes in the negotiations at the Constitutional Convention, and another tough-minded negotiator in Playford, he could surely be forgiven for attempting to influence Darling's vote.

Three months later the confluence of cricket and politics in a satirical column headed 'Stonewall Joe' in the Melbourne *Herald* provided some wit:

That free hitting, left-handed batsman Joe Darling MLC seems to have developed into a stonewaller in his latter years, for his tactics in having the Commonwealth Powers Bill shelved by the Tasmanian Legislative Council are more like those of his contemporary Alex Bannerman, whose name was synonymous with batsmanship that was slow and defensive.

Anyway, bowler Evatt could make no impression on batsman Joe. His enticing googlies and out-swingers could not shift the man who held the top batting average for Australia four years running, and whose partnerships with the famous Jack Lyons provided the merriest cricket of his day. The mighty-hitting Jack used to say: 'I tap them, and they go to the boundary.'

Since Joe secured the postponement of the Bill for six months, one of my cricketing friends suggests that he has hit Dr Evatt for six so perhaps the stonewalling accusation may be out of place.[11]

However, it also overlooked the fact that as a cricketer Joe Darling could play two types of game. It is also likely that Evatt's boyhood appreciation of Darling as a player was genuine as Evatt maintained a lifelong passion for cricket as an administrator, as an author of several articles in *Wisden*, and as the Australian Board of Control's representative to the International Cricket Conference. Conversely Douglas Darling is correct in his contention that the eight members

---

10 *Canberra Times*, 4 February 1943, p. 2.
11 *Herald* 27 May 1943, p. 4.

who voted against the Bill were vindicated later when the Australian people in a referendum overwhelmingly defeated the transfer of particular powers to the Commonwealth Government.[12]

In 1944 the Curtin Government's Australian Post-War Reconstruction and Democratic Rights referendum, which asked for similar powers to those as sought in the Constitutional Convention, was defeated. Subsequently the Chifley Government's 1946 referendum did have success in gaining power over social services but failed in efforts to control the marketing of primary products and industrial employment. A further Chifley Government referendum in 1948 failed to obtain the power to make laws controlling rents and prices.[13]

Election pamphlet of 1945 when Joe Darling stood (successfully) for the Tasmanian Legislative Council for the last time.

There seems little doubt that Joe Darling also embraced his role as a Tasmanian Government watchdog as the following report in the Launceston *Examiner* from 1944 indicates:

DARLING dares! There it was, the old fighting spirit. I remember when Joe and George Giffen were practically the kings of Australian cricket, and there was a certain dour quality about J.D. even then. He has shown the same spirit more than once since he gave up cricket for politics but has seldom had the opening that the Legislative Council debate on the D'Alton expenses gave

---

12 Darling, *Test Tussles*, p. 74.
13 https://en.wikipedia.org/wiki/Referendums_in_Australia

him. He absolutely laid his ears back and spoke his mind. He objected to Mr. Tyler chipping in and laid about him right and left. He hit the Government to leg, cover drove it and finished with a shot that looked like going over the fence. Then he put himself on to bowl. It was a great day for the old timer.[14]

Darling was in the political news for the last time in November 1945 when he brought charges of corruption against Tasmanian Premier Cosgrove and other ministers relating to the administration of the Forestry Department. It was a sweeping indictment and it was originally thought that Darling might claim Parliamentary privilege and decline to give evidence. However, the seriousness of the charges which alleged that timber leases had been improperly granted; that the Minister for Forests (Mr Taylor) had improperly received money said to have been paid for a win at the races; and that the timber interests has improperly paid funds to the Labor Party and former Minister of Forests Thomas D'Alton and then Australian High Commissioner in New Zealand, seemed to demand that he appear in the witness box.[15] Whether the prospect of doing so had an adverse effect on his health is uncertain but Darling died on 2 January 1946 before any inquiry began.

The Tasmanian government was obliged to appoint a royal commission to inquire into the allegations and appointed Justice Kirby of the New South Wales District Court to head it. The outcome was mixed. While some counts failed, Judge Kirby found in May 1946 that D'Alton had accepted two bribes from representatives of timber companies for 'services improperly rendered' and that two officers of the department had also accepted bribes.[16] It might have been expected that there would be a major political fallout from this, but six months later Cosgrove won the next Tasmanian election with an increased majority. Furthermore, he continued as premier until 1958, serving a record 19 years in office.[17] Even more remarkably D'Alton re-entered Tasmanian politics as a member of the Legislative Council in 1947 and remained in that chamber until his death in 1968.[18]

14 *Examiner* 7 July 1944, p. 4.
15 *News* 23 November 1945, p. 4.
16 Melbourne *Argus* 28 May 1946, p. 3.
17 www.adb.anu.edu/biography/cosgrove-sir-robert-9832
18 www.adb.anu.edu/biography/d'alton-thomas

LEGEND AND LEGACY

Joe Darling died in hospital following an operation for a ruptured gall bladder and was buried in Cornelian Bay Cemetery, Hobart on 4 January 1946. He was survived by his wife Alice, eight sons (Gordon, Victor and Roy of Stonehenge; Ronald, Douglas and Kenneth of Hobart; and Stanley and Maxwell of Claremont) and four daughters (Mrs K Madden of Hamilton, Mrs W Colliver of Melbourne, and Kathleen and Joyce Darling of Claremont).

Joe Darling's grave. Photographed by Graeme Ryan.

As a cricketer Joe produced many remarkable achievements:
- In 1885, his score of 252 for Prince Alfred College against St Peter's College passed George Giffen's 209 as the highest individual innings scored in South Australia. It was subsequently overtaken by Giffen again in 1892 and then by Clem Hill in the intercollegiate match of 1893.
- In his initial first-class season of 1893-94, Darling was a member of South Australia's first Sheffield Shield winning team.
- In the 1897-98 series against England he was the first left-handed batsman to score a century when he made 101 in the second innings of the first Test match at Sydney.
- In the third Test of the same series at his home ground on the Adelaide Oval Darling raised a second century (178) by lofting left-arm spin bowler Johnny Briggs out of the ground to record the first six awarded in Test matches.
- In the fifth Test of the same series in Sydney he blasted an amazing innings of 160, bringing up his century in 91 minutes which remains the fastest Ashes hundred as measured by time.
- At the end of the 1897-98 series he became the first player to record three centuries and more than 500 runs.
- Darling's captaincy of three Australian teams to tour England in 1899, 1902 and 1905 is second only to Billy Murdoch who led the teams of 1880, 1882, 1884 and 1890 and is a record shared with Allan Border who led the 1985, 1989 and 1993 sides.
- His 1941 runs and five centuries on the 1899 tour of England was the highest by an Australian player during the 19th century.
- He became the first cricketer modelled in wax at Madame Tussaud's in London.
- His record of leading Australia in 18 Test matches was the most by an Australian captain until overtaken by Don Bradman with 24.
- His total of 15 children was second only to that of Australia's first Test captain Dave Gregory who had 16 offspring.

To reflect on the nature of Darling's cricket it is worthwhile following the example of his son, Douglas, who opened his book, *Test Tussles On and Off the Field*, with an extensive quote from an article in the *Northampton Herald* of 17 May 1902, and an extract from Johnny Moyes' book, *A Century of Cricketers* which was published in 1950. They bear repeating because they offer a summary of the main cricket narrative. Joe was 31-years-old and captaining Australia for the second time on an English tour at the time of the first piece and had been dead four years when the second appeared.

The newspaper article, 'The Captain of the Australians', ran as follows:

Joseph Darling, the Captain of the Australian team now playing in England, is a strong personality and a man quite worth knowing apart from his association of the virile pastime which is so popular throughout the British Empire. There is a force of character in his face. He strikes the observer at once as a man necessary to know, for there is a clear keen eye and a rather hard cast of countenance, a forbidding expression and a square-set jaw and the firm mouth of a man born to command. At once it is apparent that he was born to be a leader in whatever society Fate placed him for there is a dominant presence about Darling which keeps even his intimates at a respectful distance. As I have suggested, he wants knowing, but he is capable of strong affection once he is on familiar terms and deems a person worthy of his friendship.

Although he is of medium size, five feet eight inches, he is compactly but firmly built. He is as strong as his strong face and there is immense power in his broad shoulders and muscular arms. There is something about Darling which attracts and magnetises, of strong opinions, yet he is a man of few words. If I were asked to sum Darling up in a word or two, I should say that he is the embodiment of luck. No man can be a great cricketer without courage, without patience, and without the brains of a strategist. Rightly or wrongly, I believe Darling to possess all these attributes and yet one other invaluable quality in a cricket captain — the stimulating impulse, the gift, unconscious it may be, of making every man fighting under him strain every nerve for the general wealth of the combination.

He despises the common means to court popularity, and I do not think he cares one snap of his fingers what a journalist has to say about him. He thinks Australia the fairest and finest land in the world and his one great ambition is to win the rubber of Test matches in the Mother Country. The members of his team respect him so much that his slightest wish is law. I hold no brief for Darling, but I cannot help admiring him both as a man and as a cricketer. He leads a good life, and is a plain blunt man, despising finery and effeminacy while his cricket is like himself — solid to the point, stubborn, hard-hitting and resolute to the end. He says what he thinks and he plays for his side — not for himself.[1]

Moyes' judgement, offered nearly half a century later, placed his contribution to Australian cricket within a historical context:

This talented left-hander was one of cricket's personalities, a born leader, a man of robust fibre, a fighter, full of courage, and with a high measure of skill. Contemporaries tell of his generous outlook, his contemptuous refusal to 'take points,' and his humour. His colleagues admired the man and the captain and were proud to play under him. Darling led Australia 18 times against England, a record that stood until eclipsed by Bradman in 1948. In 1897-98 in Australia he reached heights of grandeur, hitting three centuries in that series and driving Richardson's fastest deliveries with a ferocity that has rarely been equalled and never excelled. Joe Darling could hit, and he loved fast bowling. At the same time, he could go to the other extreme and be the last word in watchfulness.

On his four trips to England, that in 1899 was his most successful, for he scored 1941 runs at an average of 41.29. Altogether he made 6305 runs in England, his highest score being 194

---

1   *Northampton Herald* 17 May 1902 cited in Darling, *Test Tussles*, p. 1.

against Leicester; he hit 12 centuries in the four visits. On the softer wickets Darling could either defend or hit, but it was his powerful and determined batting that made him feared. On the worst of wickets, he would move into attack, declining to leave the initiative to the bowler. Style didn't interest him as such, but he could appreciate it in others. For himself he was content to use to the full the tremendous power that was his by nature.[2]

Moyes (born in 1892) has written elsewhere that he was too young to appreciate Darling at his best, but this did not prevent him from offering another superb pen picture to complement it a few years later:

> With his brown moustached face tanned by the hot sun, he looked an older man than he was, but that illusion disappeared when he began to bat. Here was a man with all the vision and audacity of youth, one of the great left-handers of history, tough and rugged, exceptionally competent, able to defend for hours on end, and then suddenly turn and rend the bowlers.[3]

Further evidence might also be presented such as that from team-mate Frank Iredale who stated,

> Darling was a brave, fearless cricketer, and no danger was too terrible for him. He delighted in tight corners and was a big man in a crisis. He could, when in the mood, hit as hard as any man I know of. He had a wonderful knowledge of the game and the rules bearing on it. He was not the possessor of many strokes yet could cut and drive with wonderful facility. He was splendidly loyal to his friends but had a decided aversion to any player who was foppish and inclined to be showy![4]

and from Ray Robinson (born in 1905, the year Darling retired from Test cricket) who revealed that he had read Iredale and cricket literature closely:

> Every contour of Darling's face reveals strength of character. It fits the qualities described by people who knew him well: strong personality ... independent outlook ... unwavering determination ... purposeful concentration ... one who would countenance no frivolity ... and a good judge of his fellows ... destined to be a leader in whatever he undertook.[5]

---

2 AG 'Johnny' Moyes, *A Century of Cricketers*, Angus and Robertson, Sydney, 1950, p. 15 cited in Darling, *Test Tussles*, p. 2..
3 AG 'Johnny' Moyes, *Australian Batsmen from Charles Bannerman to Neil Harvey*, Angus and Robertson, Sydney, 1954, pp. 43-4.
4 Frank Iredale, *33 Years in Cricket*, Beatty, Richardson & Co., Sydney, 1920, p. 89.
5 Robinson and Haigh, *On Top Down Under*, p. 76.

Reference to Darling's football has already been made and he holds a couple of special records in that sport:
- He was aged just 15 years and 210 days when he made his senior association debut for the Adelaide Football Club on 19 June 1886.
- In the 1894 calendar year he achieved a unique sporting honour in South Australia of appearing in both a Sheffield Shield winning team and an Australian Rules football premiership with the Norwood Football Club.

To gain a fuller picture of the man it would have been useful to uncover correspondence between Joe and his father, John, to shed light on their relationship. Cricket and even family lore portray John snr in a harsh light through his insistence that Joe embark on a farming life after leaving school thus delaying his first-class cricket career; and then practically forcing him to abandon his Test career mid-term to establish a pastoral property in Tasmania. Unfortunately, only one letter is extant, and that courtesy of being published in the *Express & Telegraph* newspaper on 4 September 1902 in which Joe describes the excitement of winning the thrilling Old Trafford Test. In the absence of such correspondence one must surmise that John snr's ambitions for Joe were partly based on the success of his eldest son, John jnr, who proved an adept business partner in establishing and expanding John Darling & Co as a thriving concern, and of Joe's elder brothers Robert and Charles, who had taken up agricultural pursuits. In a contest of wills between father and son it seems there was gradual compromise leading to rapprochement.

As a final summation it can fairly be said that Joe Darling went a long way to restoring Australian cricket's pride after successive defeats in the Ashes series of 1893, 1894-95 and 1896.

Darling became Australian captain in 1899 but it is wrong to credit him with the inspirational selection of Victor Trumper for the last place on that tour. As he explained himself neither he nor Hugh Trumble had been impressed by Trumper's performances and it took the strong instigation of Syd Gregory to influence them plus Trumper's fine innings of 75 in Adelaide in the last of three end-of-season matches between the Rest of Australia and the Australian Eleven which won him the final tour berth. Trumper made a duck in the second innings of that same game and had the scores been reversed cricket history could well have been different. In the event, however, Trumper played a match-winning role in the series and Darling would come to idolise him above all other players.

Darling showed great flair as captain and particularly in the second Test of the 1901-02 Ashes series which began at the Melbourne Cricket Ground on New Year's Day. On a treacherous sticky pitch, 25 wickets tumbled for 221 runs on the first day but holding back Clem Hill, Trumper, Monty Noble and debutants Reg Duff and Warwick Armstrong to positions seven to eleven in the batting order enabled his side to add 252 runs in easing conditions for the loss of just four wickets on the second day and put his side in an impregnable position.

In the famous match at Old Trafford in 1902, he held his nerve twice when England looked certain to seize victory. Australia held a modest first innings lead but quickly crumbled in the second innings for 86 despite his own contribution of 37 runs in topping the score. Chasing 124,

England looked well in control at 0-37 at lunch and later at 3-92. However, Darling maintained his trust in his main bowlers, Trumble and Jack Saunders, as seven wickets crashed for 28 runs and Australia gained a sensational win by 3 runs.

Joe Darling was a strong leader who exercised discipline when necessary yet was also a cricket democrat. When it came to decision making he was willing to receive counsel from team members if he thought his side would benefit. In retirement he was greatly concerned for the welfare of past players and did much in both words and deeds to alleviate their financial distress.

Late in life Joe Darling observed that although he had made his living as a farmer and served a long term in politics he was sure that he would be remembered as a cricketer. He was right in that and it is to his credit that he played such a distinguished role in the game.

STATISTICS

TEST

		M	I	NO	HS	Runs	Ave	100
1894-95	v England	5	9	-	74	258	28.66	
1896	v England	3	6	-	47	112	18.66	
1897-98	v England	5	8	-	178	537	67.12	3
1899	v England	5	10	1	71	232	25.77	
1901-02	v England	3	6	-	69	144	24.00	
1902	v England	5	7	-	51	109	15.57	
1902-03	v South Africa	3	5	-	14	25	5.00	
1905	v England	5	9	1	73	230	28.75	
		34	**60**	**2**	**178**	**1657**	**28.76**	**3**

First-class

		M	I	NO	HS	Runs	Ave	100
1893-94	Australia	4	8	1	87	216	30.85	
1894-95	Australia	11	20	2	117	709	39.38	1
1895-96	Australia	5	9	-	121	327	36.33	1
1896	England	32	53	1	194	1555	29.90	3
1896	America	3	5	-	77	167	33.40	
1896-97	Australia	4	7	-	75	212	30.29	
1897-98	Australia	11	19	-	178	978	51.47	3
1898-99	Australia	7	12	-	210	675	56.25	2
1899	England	35	56	9	167	1941	41.29	5
1899-00	Australia	5	9	-	72	252	28.00	
1901-02	Australia	3	6	-	69	154	25.66	
1902	England	35	50	5	128	1112	24.71	2
1902-03	South Africa	4	7	-	61	91	13.00	
1904-05	Australia	4	7	-	67	159	22.71	
1905	England	31	49	7	117*	1644	39.14	2
1905	Scotland	1	2	-	49	52	26.00	

1905-06	Australia	5	10	-	73	287	28.70	
1906-07	Australia	1	2	-	77	91	45.50	
1907-08	Australia	1	2	-	11	13	6.50	
		202	**333**	**25**	**210**	**10635**	**34.52**	**19**

Centuries (19)

117	South Australia v AE Stoddart's England XI, 1894-95
121	South Australia v New South Wales, 1895-96
115	Australians v Eleven of the South, 1896
194	Australians v Leicestershire, 1896
105	Australians v Warwickshire, 1896
101	Australia v England, 1897-98
178	Australia v England, 1897-98
160	Australia v England, 1897-98
210	South Australia v Queensland, 1898-99
104	Australian XI v The Rest, 1898-99
106*	Australians v Oxford University, 1899
134*	Australians v Derbyshire, 1899
128	Australians v Marylebone Cricket Club, 1899
111	Australians v Middlesex, 1899
167	Australians v South of England, 1899
128	Australians v Nottinghamshire, 1902
116	Australians v Hampshire, 1902
117*	Australians v Gentleman of England, 1905
114	Australians v Kent, 1905

Club

		M	I	NO	HS	Runs	Ave	100
1887-88	Adelaide	1	1	-	0	0	0.00	
1890-91	North Adelaide	2	2	-	61	61	30.50	
1893-94	North Adelaide	8	8	1	106	294	42.00	1
1894-95	Adelaide	5	5	1	95*	190	47.50	
1895-96	Adelaide	6	6	-	120	216	36.00	1
1896-97	Adelaide	4	4	1	235*	290	96.66	1
1897-98	East Torrens	2	2	-	68	79	39.50	
1898-99	East Torrens	4	6	1	158	349	69.80	1
1899-00	East Torrens	7	7	2	259*	722	144.40	3
1904-05	Sturt	7	6	1	137*	431	86.20	2
1905-06	Sturt	6	6	1	83	228	45.60	

1906-07	Sturt	9	10	-	109	508	50.80	1
1907-08	Sturt	8	8	-	85	386	48.25	
1921-22	Break O'Day	4	4	-	13	23	5.75	
		73	74	8	259*	3777	57.23	10
Adelaide		16	16	2	235*	696	49.71	2
North Adelaide		10	10	1	106	355	39.44	1
East Torrens		13	15	3	259*	1150	95.83	4
Sturt		30	30	2	137*	1553	55.46	3
Break O'Day		4	4	-	13	23	5.75	

Centuries (10)

106	North Adelaide v Port Adelaide, 1893-94
120	Adelaide v Norwood, 1895-96
235*	Adelaide v Port Austral, 1896-97
158	East Torrens v Sturt, 1898-99
259*	East Torrens v Port Adelaide, 1899-1900
150*	East Torrens v Port Adelaide, 1899-1900
103	East Torrens v West Adelaide, 1899-1900
137*	Sturt v West Adelaide, 1904-05
100	Sturt v East Torrens, 1904-05
109	Sturt v Port Adelaide, 1906-07

APPENDIX I-A

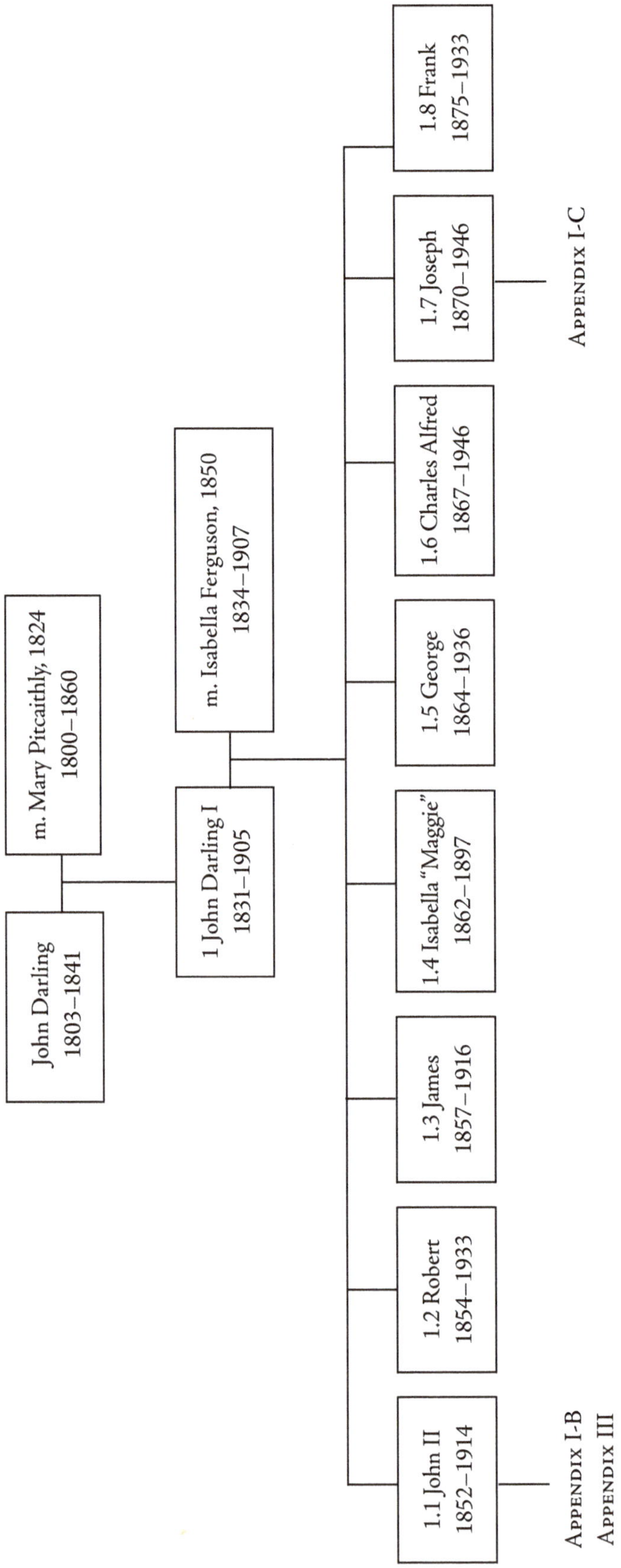

- John Darling 1803–1841
- m. Mary Pitcaithly, 1824 1800–1860
- 1 John Darling I 1831–1905
- m. Isabella Ferguson, 1850 1834–1907

Children:
- 1.1 John II 1852–1914 — Appendix I-B, Appendix III
- 1.2 Robert 1854–1933
- 1.3 James 1857–1916
- 1.4 Isabella "Maggie" 1862–1897
- 1.5 George 1864–1936
- 1.6 Charles Alfred 1867–1946
- 1.7 Joseph 1870–1946 — Appendix I-C
- 1.8 Frank 1875–1933

John Darling (1803 – 1841)

Born: 9 September 1803 in the Duns (Chirnside), Berwick, Scotland.

Parents: John (labourer) and Agnes (nee Fortune) Darling, married 15 February 1796 at Swinton and Simprim, Berwickshire, Scotland. Four children: Mary 1799, John 1803, William 1806, Abraham 1810.

Died: 4 September 1841.

Buried: New Calton Cemetery, Edinburgh, Lothian, Scotland.

Addresses: John Darling, baker, of no. 5 Hollyrood House and Mary Pitcaithly, no. 21 High Street, Canongate, daughter of John Pitcaithly, wright, Parish of Stirling gave up their names for proclamation. Certified by W.Miller Crabbie, one of the elders of this Parish.

Married: 3 January 1824 at Canongate to Mary Pitcaithly, daughter of John Pitcaithly and Margaret Henderson. Seven children: Robert 1826, Margaret 1828, John 1831, Mary 1832, Jessie 1835, James 1836, William 1839.

Born: 1799, Scots Ancestry Research wrote Major John Young in 1954.

Died: 26 February 1860, at 16 Carruber's Close, High Street, Edinburgh. Described as a baker's widow, aged 60.

Buried: New Calton Cemetery, Edinburgh, Lothian, Scotland.

1 John Darling I (1831 – 1905)

Born: 23 February 1831, Edinburgh. No record of birth in old parochial records, Scotland.

Died: 10 April 1905, Adelaide.

Buried: Family vault, Adelaide, with wife and daughter Maggie.

Addresses: 8 Paul Street, Simon Square in the parish of St Cuthbert's, Edinburgh. Arrived in Adelaide on the barque 'Achilles' in 1855 with his wife and sons John and Robert.

Occupation: Type founder.

Married: 29 December 1850 to Isabella Ferguson (1834 – 1907), third daughter of James Ferguson (printer) and Mary Ferguson (born Macmillan). Eight children.

Born: 1834, Belfast, Ireland.

Died: 1907, Adelaide.

Buried: Family vault, Adelaide, with husband and daughter Maggie.

See Appendix II for short biography.

1.1 John Darling II (1852 – 1914)

Born: 24 January 1852, Edinburgh. No record of birth in old parochial records, Scotland.

Died: 27 April 1914, Melbourne.

Buried: Family vault, Adelaide.

Addresses: Arrived in Adelaide on the barque 'Achilles' 1855 with his parents and younger brother, Robert. Bought 'Darling House' in 1886 (now 64 Fullarton Road, Norwood).

Married: 29 December 1875 to Jessie Dowie (1852 – 1915), daughter of Alexander and Jane Dowie of Adelaide. Nine children: Jessie Isabel, Alexander John, Elsie, Florence, Harold Gordon, Gertrude, Grace, Leonard, Norman.

Born: 14 July 1852, Adelaide.

Died: 23 November 1915, Adelaide.

Buried: Darling family vault at Payneham Cemetery, Adelaide.

See Appendix III for short biography.

1.2 Robert Darling (1854 - 1933)

Born: 1854, Edinburgh, Scotland.

Arrived with his parents, and older brother John, in South Australia in 1855 aged about one year. According to his death certificate he was in South Australia from 1855-1891, Western Australia 1891-1915. He was certainly in Geraldton, Western Australia, at the time of his father's death in 1905 and Victoria 1916-1933.

Died: 20 March 1933, Albert Park, Melbourne.

Buried: Brighton Cemetery, Melbourne.

Married to Mary Ann Ferguson. Ten Children: Herbert Ferguson, Fergus Drummond, Jeanie Isabel Ferguson, Isabel Ferguson, Douglas Ferguson, Annie Ferguson, Ronald Ferguson, Aileen Ferguson, Mary Ferguson, Adelaide Ferguson.

1.3 James Darling (1857 – 1916)

Born: 2 September 1857, Adelaide.

Died: 18 March 1929.

Married: 26 October 1882, to (1) Elizabeth "Bessie" Dowie (1862 – 1896), daughter of Alexander and Jane Dowie of Adelaide. Children: Arthur Garfield, Ruth Wills 'Raven', Kenneth Cleveland, James Woodville.

Married to (2) Daphne Walker. Children: Richard and Tom.

1.4 Isabella "Maggie" Darling (1862 – 1897)

Born: 17 July 1862, Mitcham, South Australia.

Died: 1897

Married to Henry Ernest Hall (tea broker) born 1860, Collingwood, Victoria. No children.

1.5 George Darling (1864 - 1936)

Born: 28 September 1864, Glen Osmond Road, Adelaide.

Died: 24 July 1936, 15 Normanby Street, Middle Brighton, Victoria.

Married to [1] Margaret HAMILTON. No children. [2] Charlotte Emily LLOYD. Six children: Dorothy May, George Colin, Phyllis Marguerite, Florence Edna, John Lloyd, Marjorie Isabel.

Occupation: Banker.

1.6 Charles Alfred Darling (1867 – 1946)

Born: 29 July 1867, Milford, South Australia.

Died: 11 March 1946, 18 Balmoral Crescent, Surrey Hills, Melbourne.

Death certificate gives the cause of death as myocarditis. It also states that he lived in South Australia for 28 years and the remaining 50 years of his life in Victoria. There is no mention of the time that he worked for the firm in London.

Buried: Springvale Crematorium, Melbourne.

Married: to Ethel Maud Carlin. Three children: Frederick Brooke, Mary 'Mollie' Ethel Carlin, Bessie Pitcaithley.

Occupation: Grain Merchant (John Darling & Co.), Farmer.

1.7 Joseph Darling (1870 – 1946)

Born: 21 November 1870, Glen Osmond, South Australia.

Died: 2 January 1946, Hobart, Tasmania.

Buried: Darling family vault at Cornelian Bay Cemetery, Hobart.

Married: 3 May 1893, Mundoora, South Australia, to Alice Minna Blanche Francis (1873 – 1952). Fifteen children: Gordon Joseph Francis, Ernest Sydney, Ethel Kathleen, Eileen Isabella, Joseph Ronald, Lillian Jean, Victor Stafford, Douglas Keith, Stanley Lawrence, Kenneth Charles, Roy Ashby, Kathleen Alice, Joyce Minna, Maxwell, Phyllis.

Born: 1 December 1873, Tungkillo, South Australia.

Died: 16 April 1952, Claremont, Tasmania.

Buried: Darling family vault at Cornelian Bay Cemetery, Hobart.

1.8 Frank Darling (1875 - 1933)

Born: 31 October 1875, Adelaide.

Died: 18 August 1933, Marine Avenue, Mornington, Victoria.

On 6 February 1901, a Tasmanian Justices' Order stated that he was a person of unsound mind and that he be detained under care and treatment at the New Norfolk Hospital for the Insane. On 6 July 1901, he was discharged into the custody and care of his brother Joseph Darling of Stonehenge.

A Victorian Magisterial Enquiry 24 August 1933 stated that he shot himself whilst of unsound mind. Death certificate notes that he was in South Australia for 18 years, Tasmania for 4 years and 35 years in Victoria. He was mentioned to be in Melbourne in his father's obituary published in the Adelaide Advertiser 1905.

Occupation: Farmer.

Buried: Mornington Cemetery, Victoria.

Married: to Lucy Brennan. One son: Louis Francis born 1901.

1.8.1 Louis Francis Darling (1901 – 1970)

Married (1932) ; to Dulcie Verona Thompson (1908 – 2004).

Three children: Peter, Virginia and Mary.

At the time of Dulcie's death, there were sixteen grandchildren and seventeen great grandchildren.

John Darling snr walking in Government House gardens, Adelaide with his son John Darling on his left after attending a levee in 1904.

Appendix 1-B

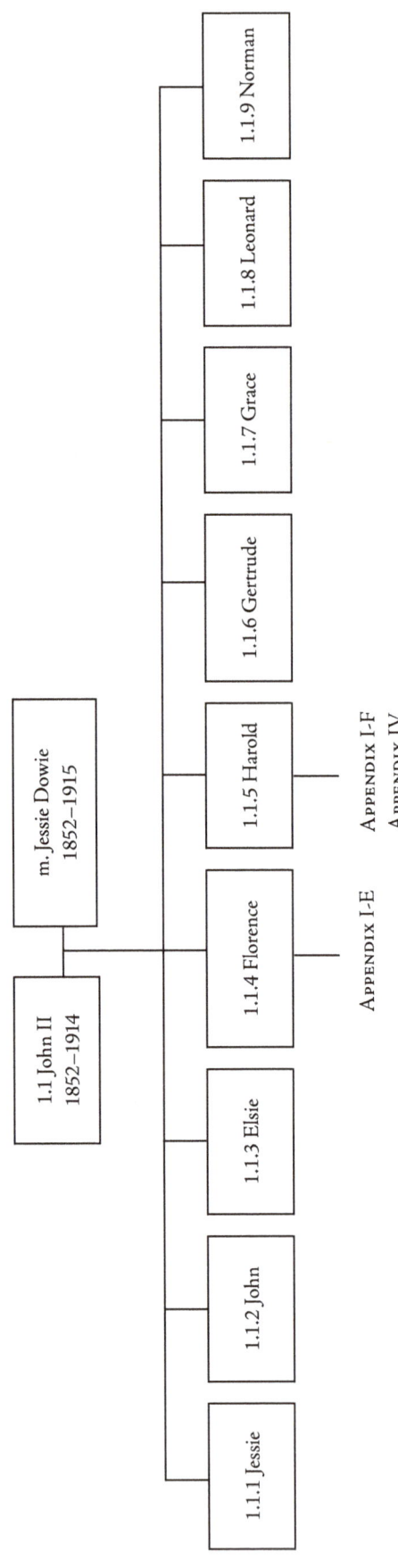

Appendixes

1.1 John Darling II (1852 – 1914)

Born: 24 January 1852, Edinburgh. No record of birth in old parochial records, Scotland.

Died: 27 April 1914, Melbourne.

Buried: Family vault, Adelaide.

Addresses: Arrived in Adelaide on the barque 'Achilles' 1855 with his parents and younger brother, Robert. Bought 'Darling House' in 1886 (now 64 Fullarton Road, Norwood).

m: 29 December 1875 to Jessie Dowie (1852 – 1915), daughter of Alexander and Jane Dowie of Adelaide. Nine children: Jessie Isabel, Alexander John, Elsie, Florence, Harold Gordon, Gertrude, Grace, Leonard, Norman.

Born: 14 July 1852, Adelaide.

Died: 23 November 1915, Adelaide.

Buried: Darling family vault at Payneham Cemetery, Adelaide.

See Appendix III for short biography.

1.1.1 Jessie Isabel (1876 – 1907)

1.1.2 Alexander John (1878 – 1896)

1.1.3 Elsie (1880 – 1891)

All born in Adelaide and buried in family vault.

1.1.4 Florence (1884 – 1947)

Born: Adelaide.

m: (Sir) Frederick Young (1876 – 1948). One son. Florence and Frederick lived in England from 1915 until their deaths.

Died: Melbourne.

Buried: Melbourne Cemetery.

1.1.5 Harold Gordon Darling (1885 – 1950)

Born: 9 June 1885, Adelaide.

m: 24 April 1913 to Dorothy Hazel Heath (1887 – 1979). Three children (Elizabeth 1918, Joan 1919, John 1923).

Died: 26 January 1950, Melbourne.

Buried: Melbourne Cemetery family grave.

See Appendix IV for short biography.

1.1.6 Gertrude Darling (1888 – 1968)

Born: 7 June 1888, Norwood, Adelaide.

Died: 1968, Adelaide. Buried in family vault.

Never married, no children. Lived in home built by herself and siblings Grace and Norman in 1929 at 19 Palmer Place, North Adelaide.

1.1.7 Grace Darling (1889 – 1964)

Born: 24 August 1889, Norwood, Adelaide.

Died: 1964, Adelaide. Buried in family vault.

Never married, no children. Lived in home built by herself and siblings Gertrude and Norman in 1929 at 19 Palmer Place, North Adelaide.

1.1.8 Leonard Darling (1891 – 1963)

Born: 28 November 1891, Norwood, Adelaide.

Died: 1963, Melbourne. Buried in family grave, Melbourne Cemetery.

m: 1920, Winifred Wilson (1896 – 1973). Two sons, Leonard Gordon and David Ian.

Chairman John Darling & Son Pty Ltd, Director Commonwealth Aircraft Corporation Pty Ltd, Broken Hill Pty Co. Ltd, Australian Iron and Steel Ltd, National Bank of Australasia.

1.1.9 Norman Darling (1893–1964)

Never married, no children. Lived in home built by himself and sisters Gertrude and Grace in 1929 at 19 Palmer Place, North Adelaide.

APPENDIX I–C

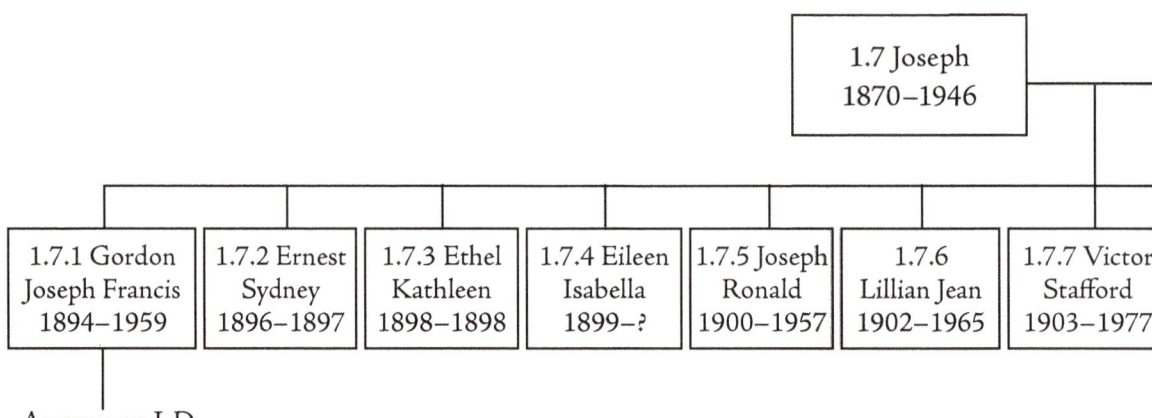

APPENDIX I-D

1.7 Joseph Darling (1870 – 1946)

Born: 21 November 1870, Glen Osmond, South Australia.

Died: 2 January 1946, Hobart, Tasmania.

Buried: Darling family vault at Cornelian Bay Cemetery, Hobart.

m: 3 May 1893, Mundoora, South Australia, to Alice Minna Blanche Francis (1873 – 1952). Fifteen children. Born: 1 December 1873, Tungkillo, South Australia.

Died: 16 April 1952, Claremont, Tasmania.

Buried: Darling family vault at Cornelian Bay Cemetery, Hobart.

1.7.1 Gordon Joseph Francis Darling (1894 – 1959)

Born: 15 April 1894, Unley, South Australia.

Died: 14 March 1959, Campbell Town, Tasmania.

Buried: Uniting Church, Oatlands, Tasmania.

m: [1] 26 Feb 1920 to Doris Kreutzner Burbury at St Peters Church, Oatlands, Tasmania.

Four children (Doris Joan, Gwenda Burbury, Harry Joseph, David Charles).

Born: 20 July 1895.

Died: 3 December 1928. Accidentally killed when horse riding at Dalmeney Park, Tasmania.

[2] to Reta Phyllis Harbach. Five children (twins Ian and Margaret, Roderick, Beth, Stuart).

1.7.2 Ernest Sydney Darling (1896 – 1897)

Born: 12 March 1896, Norwood, South Australia.

Died: 29 March 1897, Mundoora, South Australia.

1.7.3 Ethel Kathleen Darling

Born: 20 February 1898, Norwood, South Australia.

Died: 13 November 1898, Henley Beach, South Australia.

1.7.4 Eileen Isabella Darling (1899 – ?)

Born: 13 August 1899, Norwood, South Australia.

Died: Hobart.

m: to [1] Raymond Keith Madden. Five children (Thomas Joseph, Douglas Keith, Elaine Isobel, Peter John 1935, Judith Joan). [2] 26/02/1981, Horace Bertram Dalwood.

1.7.5 Joseph Ronald Darling (1900 – 1957)

Born: 12 November 1900, Stonehenge, Tasmania.

Died: 26 July 1957, Hobart.

Never married, no children.

1.7.6 Lillian Jean Darling (1902 – 1965)

Born: 8 March 1902, Stonehenge, Tasmania.

Died: 1965, Melbourne.

m: W. Colliver. No children.

1.7.7 Victor Stafford Darling (1903 – 1977)

Born: 24 October 1903, Hobart.

Died: January 1977, Lindisfarne, Tasmania.

m: 26/11/1941, Lucy Rumney. No children.

1.7.8 Douglas Keith Darling (1905 – 1981)

Born: 27 November 1905, Malvern, South Australia.

Died: 6 December 1981, Hobart.

m: 31/01/1933, Florence Barnes. Three children (Two daughters, one son).

1.7.9 Stanley Lawrence Darling (1907 – 1982)

Born: 29 January 1907, Malvern, South Australia.

Died: 5 December 1982, Hobart.

m: Eleanor Darling. No children.

```
┌─────────────────────┐
│ m. Alice Minna Blanche │
│     1873–1952       │
└─────────┬───────────┘
```

| 1.7.8 Douglas Keith 1905–1981 | 1.7.9 Stanley Lawrence 1907–1982 | 1.7.10 Kenneth Charles 1909–1981 | 1.7.11 Roy Ashby 1910–1990 | 1.7.12 Kathleen Alice 1911–1991 | 1.7.13 Joyce Minna 1913–1995 | 1.7.14 Maxwell 1914–1984 | 1.7.15 Phyllis 1918–1920 |

1.7.10 Kenneth Charles Darling (1909 – 1981)

Born: 21 January 1909, Launceston, Tasmania.

Died: 1 January 1981, Hobart.

m: 8/10/1935, Eileen Cannon. Two children (Allan 1936, Judy 1941).

1.7.11 Roy Ashby Darling (1910 – 1990)

Born: 6 May 1910, Stonehenge, Tasmania.

Died: 19 June 1990, Hobart.

m: 24/07/1943, Winnie Gwen Lester. Two children (Jim and Virginia).

1.7.12 Kathleen Alice Darling (1911 – 1991)

Born: 27 July 1911, Stonehenge, Tasmania.

Died: 5 January 1991, Hobart.

m: Cyril Knight. No children.

1.7.13 Joyce Minna Darling (1913 – 1995)

Born: 17 April 1913, Hobart.

Died: 7 November 1995, Hobart.

m: 3/09/1971, Donald Nutting. No children.

1.7.14 Maxwell Darling (1914 – 1984)

Born: 17 November 1914, Stonehenge, Tasmania.

Died: 26 July 1984, Hobart.

Never married. No children. Had Down Syndrome.

1.7.15 Phyllis Darling (1918 – 1920)

Born: 8 March 1918, Stonehenge, Tasmania.

Died: 15 December 1920, Claremont, Tasmania.

Family photograph taken 1908. L to R: Eileen, Ronald, Douglas, Gordon (back), Joe, Alice (holding Stanley Lawrence), Victor, Lillian Jean.

APPENDIX 1–D

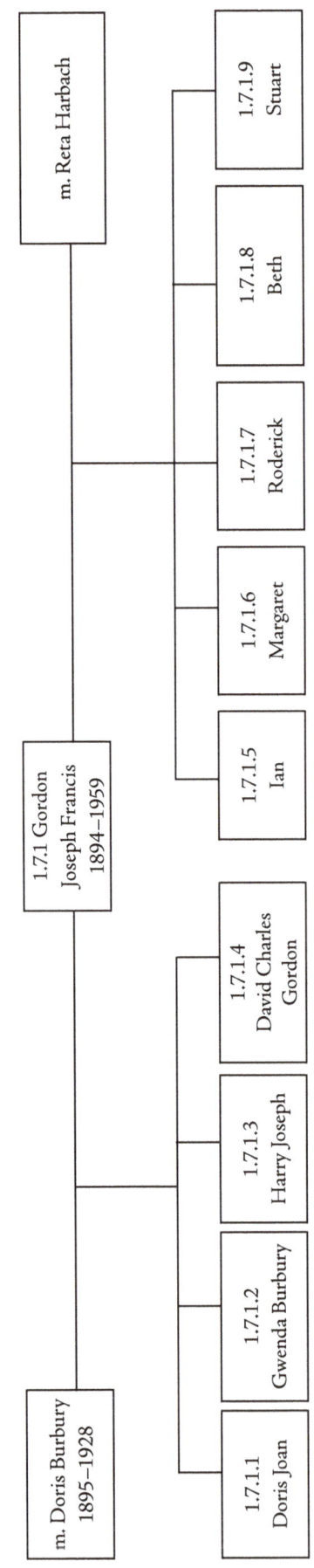

1.7.1 Gordon Joseph Francis Darling (1894 – 1959)
Born: 15 April 1894, Unley, South Australia.
Died: 14 March 1959, Campbell Town, Tasmania.
Buried: Uniting Church, Oatlands, Tasmania.
m: [1] 26 Feb 1920 to Doris Kreutzner Burbury at St Peters Church, Oatlands, Tasmania.
Four children (Doris Joan, Gwenda Burbury, Harry Joseph, David Charles).
Born: 20 July 1895.
Died: 3 December 1928. Accidentally killed when horse riding at Dalmeney Park, Tasmania.
[2] to Reta Phyllis Harbach. Five children (twins Ian and Margaret, Roderick, Beth, Stuart).

APPENDIX 1-E

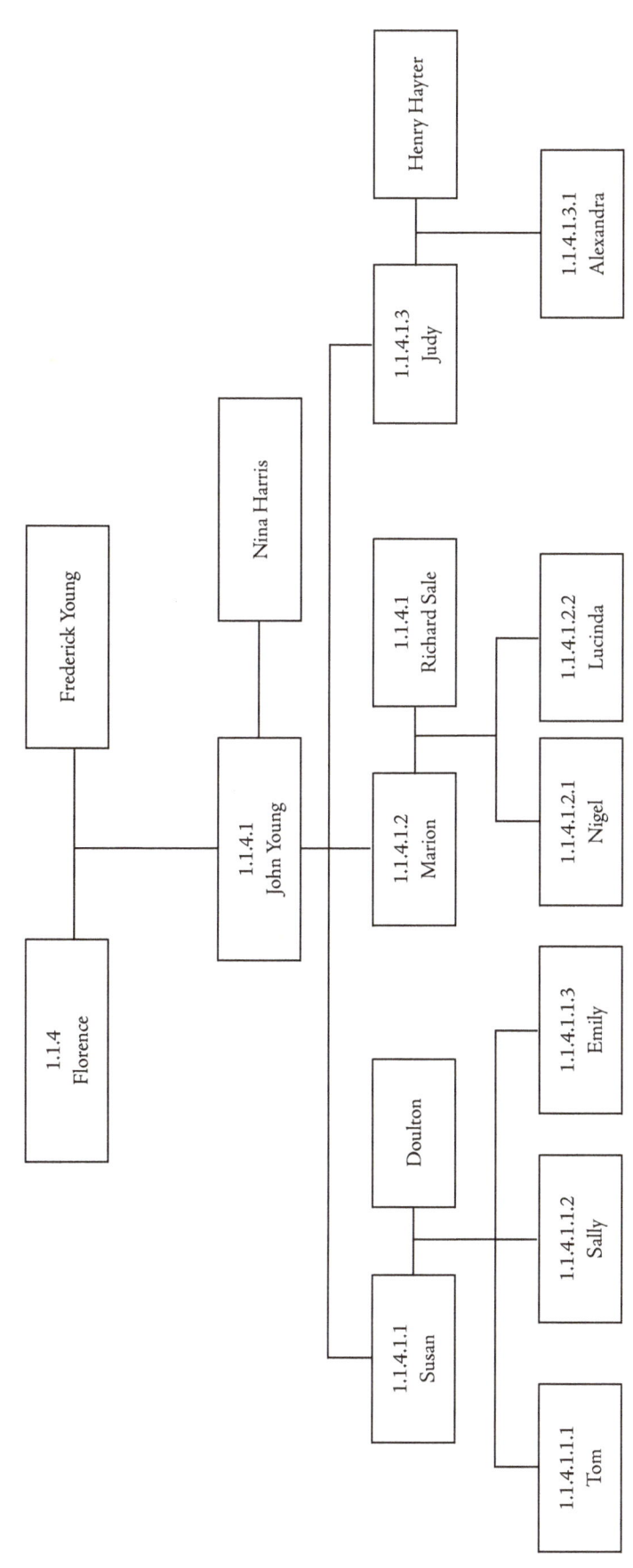

1.1.4 Florence (1884 – 1947)
Born: Adelaide.
m: (Sir) Frederick Young (1876 – 1948). One son.
Florence and Frederick lived in England from 1915 until their deaths.
Died: Melbourne.
Buried: Melbourne Cemetery.

1.1.4.1 (Major) John Young (1910 – 1989)
m: Nina Harris (1908 – 1974). Three children.

1.1.4.1.1 Susan Young (1935 –
m: D. Doulton. Three children.

1.1.4.1.1.1 Tom Doulton (1962 –
1.1.4.1.1.2 Sally Doulton (1965 –
1.1.4.1.1.3 Emily Doulton (1969 –

1.1.4.1.2 Marian Young (1938-
m: Richard Sale. Two children.

1.1.4.1.2.1 Nigel Sale (1962-
1.1.4.1.2.2 Lucinda Sale (1965-

1.1.4.1.3 Judy Young (1940-
m: Henry Hayter. One daughter.

1.1.4.1.3.1 Alexandra Hayter (1971-

Florence's wedding group, 7 December 1904.
L to R: Gertrude, Jessie, John Darling jnr, Florence (bride), Frederick Young (groom), Elsie, unknown (best man), Grace.

Family group at Florence's wedding, 7 December 1904.
Standing (L to R): unknown, Elsie, unknown, Jessie, Joe Darling, unknown, Grace, unknown.
Seated (L to R): Mrs John Darling snr, Mr John Darling snr, Mrs John Darling jnr, Mr John Darling jnr, Mr A. Dowie, Mrs A. Dowie, Gertrude.
Seated front (L to R): Norman, Leonard.

APPENDIX 1-F

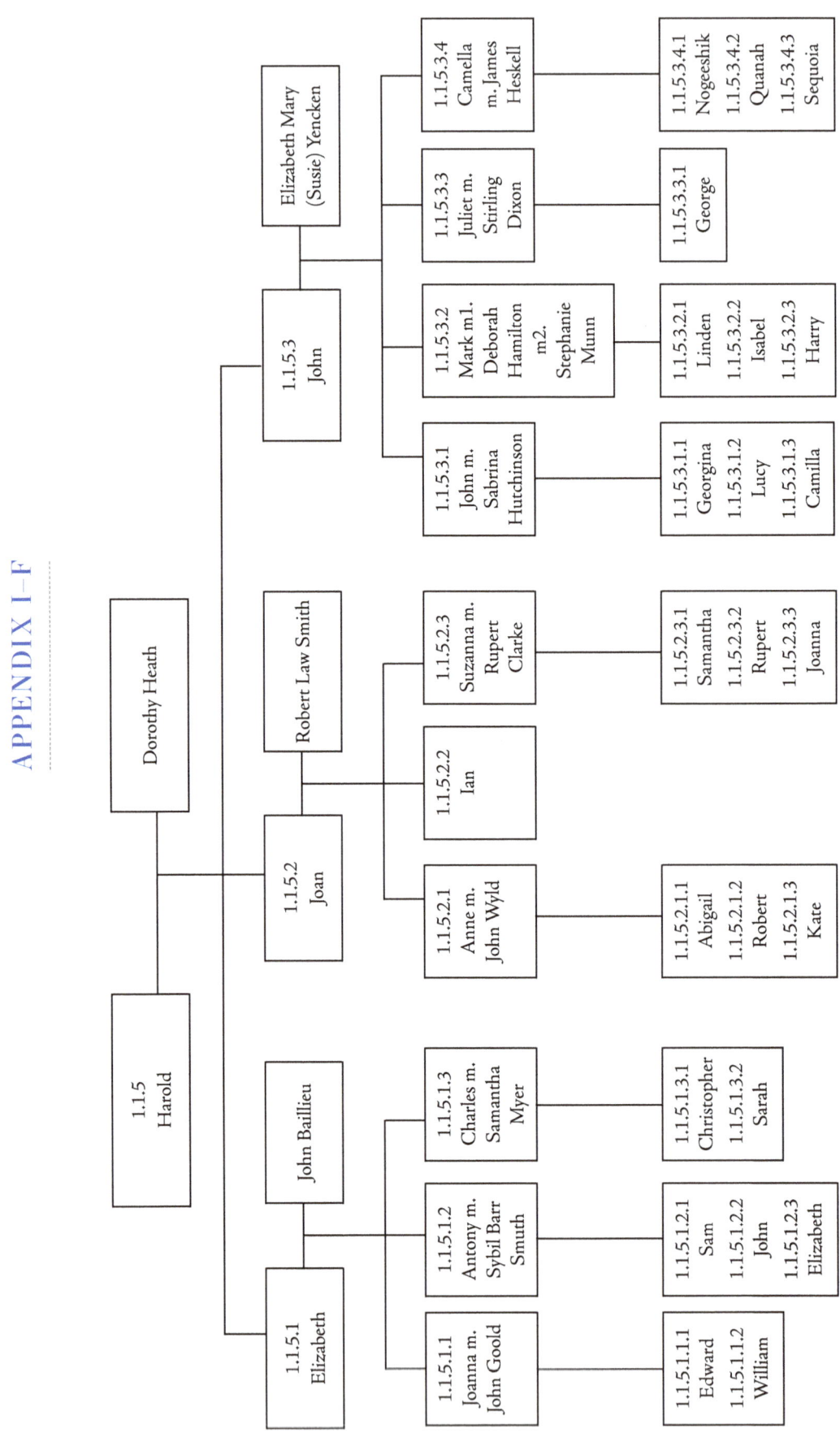

1.1.5 Harold Gordon Darling (1885 – 1950)

Born: 9 June 1885, Adelaide.

m: 24 April 1913 to Dorothy Hazel Heath (1887 – 1979). Three children (Elizabeth 1918, Joan 1919, John 1923).

Died: 26 January 1950, Melbourne.

Buried: Melbourne Cemetery family grave.

See Appendix IV for short biography.

1.1.5.1 Elizabeth Darling (1918 –

m: 1938, John Baillieu (1912 –

1.1.5.1.1 Joanna Baillieu (1947 –

m: John Goold (champion Australian footballer and polo player).

1.1.5.1.1.1 Edward Goold (1976 –

1.1.5.1.1.2 William Goold (1978 –

1.1.5.1.2 Antony Baillieu (1949 –

m: Sybil Barr Smith

1.1.5.1.2.1 Sam Baillieu (1974 -

1.1.5.1.2.2 John Baillieu (1977 -

1.1.5.1.2.3 Elizabeth Baillieu (1978 -

1.1.5.1.3 Charles Baillieu (1953 –

m. Samantha Myer

1.1.5.1.3.1 Christopher Baillieu (1991 -

1.1.5.1.3.2 Sarah Baillieu (1992 –

1.1.5.2 Joan Darling (1919 –

m: (Sir) Robert Law Smith (1914 –

1.1.5.2.1 Anne Law Smith (1947 –

m. John Wyld

1.1.5.2.1.1 Abigail (1970 –

1.1.5.2.1.2 Robert (1972 –

1.1.5.2.1.3 Kate (1978 –

1.1.5.2.2 Ian Law Smith (1949 – 1969)

1.1.5.2.3 Suzannah Law Smith (1951 –

m. Rupert Clarke

1.1.5.2.3.1 Samantha Clarke (1980 –

1.1.5.2.3.2 Rupert Clarke (1981 –

1.1.5.2.3.3 Joanna Clarke (1983 -

1.1.5.3 John Darling (1923 – 2015)

Born: 7 December 1923, Melbourne.

m. [1] Elizabeth Mary 'Susie' Yencken b. 1928. Four children: John, Mark, Juliet, Camilla.

[2] Phillis Angela Dale.

Died: 21 October 2015

Chairman Darling Collett Group, Founder Schroder, Darling and Company Limited. Director John Darling & Son Pty Ltd 1953, Perpetual Trustee Co. 1956, Goldsborough Mort 1956, Mercantile and General Reinsurance Co. 1956, BP Aust. Ltd. 1958. Night fighter pilot 1942-45, 456 Squadron.

Founder of the Lord's Taverners Australia in 1982.

1.1.5.3.1 John Darling (1952 -

m. Sabrina Hutchison. Three daughters: Georgina, twins Lucy and Camilla.

1.1.5.3.1.1 Georgina Darling (1985-

1.1.5.3.1.2 Lucy Darling (1988-

1.1.5.3.1.3 Camilla Darling (1988-

1.1.5.3.2 Mark Darling (1953 –

m; [1] Deborah Hamilton. Two children. [2] 1990, Stephanie Munn. One son.

1.1.5.3.2.1 Linden Darling (1979-

1.1.5.3.2.2 Isabel Darling (1982-

1.1.5.3.2.3 Harry Darling (1992-

1.1.5.3.3 Juliet Darling (1956 –

m: Stirling Dixon. One child.

1.1.5.3.3.1 George Dixon (1988-

1.1.5.3.4 Camilla Darling (1958 –

m: James Heskell. Three children.

1.1.5.3.4.1 Nogeeshik Heskell (1985-

1.1.5.3.4.2 Quanah Heskell (1988-

1.1.5.3.4.3 Sequoia Heskell (1992-

APPENDIX 1–G

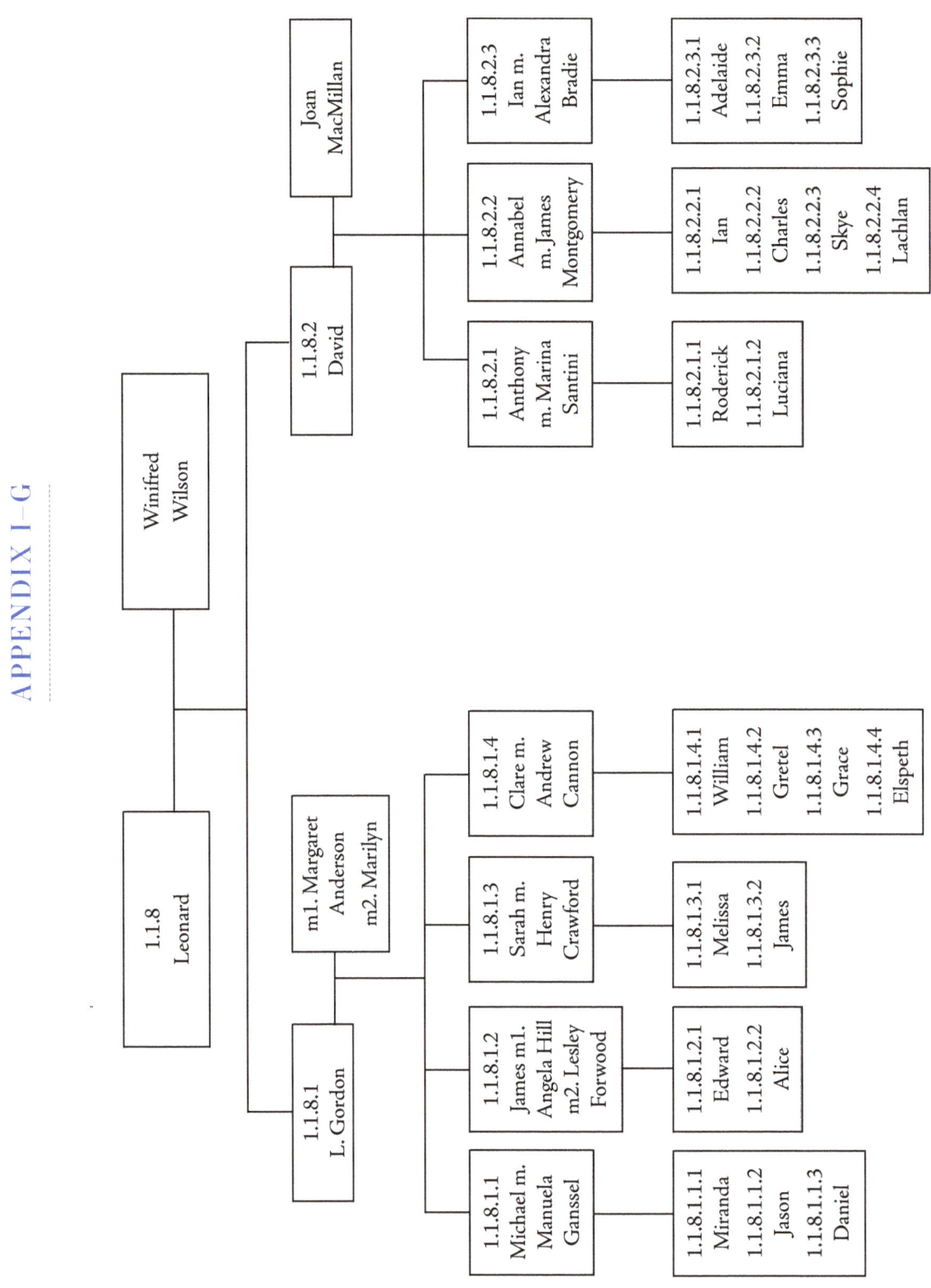

1.1.8 Leonard Darling (1891 – 1963)
Born: 28 November 1891, Norwood, Adelaide.
Died: 1963, Melbourne. Buried in family grave, Melbourne Cemetery.
m: 1920, Winifred Wilson (1896 – 1973). Two sons, Leonard Gordon and David Ian.
Chairman John Darling & Son Pty Ltd, Director Commonwealth Aircraft Corporation Pty Ltd, Broken Hill Pty Co. Ltd, Australian Iron and Steel Ltd, National Bank of Australasia.

1.1.8.1 L. Gordon Darling (1921 – 2015)
Born: 4 March 1921, London, England.
Died: 31 August 2015, Melbourne.
m: [1] Margaret Anderson (1923-2010), [2] Marilyn Shue (1943-
AO 1989, CMG 1980.
See Appendix V for short biography.

1.1.8.1.1 Michael Darling (1945 –
Born: 3 December 1945.
m: Manuela Gansser. Three children.

1.1.8.1.1.1 Miranda Darling (1975-
1.1.8.1.1.2 Jason Darling (1978-
1.1.8.1.1.3 Daniel Darling (1985-

1.1.8.1.2 James Darling (1946 –
m: [1] Angela Hill. One son. [2] Lesley Forwood. One daughter.

1.1.8.1.2.1 Edward Darling (1975-
1.1.8.1.2.2 Alice Darling (1985-
Partner: Damien Harrison. One son.
1.1.8.1.2.2.1 Raphael Harrison Darling (2017-

1.1.8.1.3 Sarah Darling (1950-
m: Henry Crawford. Two children.

1.1.8.1.3.1 Melissa Crawford (1979-
m: Nicholas Peter Kutcher. Three children.
1.1.8.1.3.1.1 Leo Kutcher (2009-
1.1.8.1.3.1.2 Sunday Kutcher (2012-
1.1.8.1.3.1.3 Florence Kutcher (2016-
1.1.8.1.3.2 James Crawford (1980 – 2014)

1.1.8.1.4 Clare Darling (1960-
m: Andrew Cannon. Four children. One son, twin daughters, one daughter.

1.1.8.1.4.1 William Robert Cannon (1991-
1.1.8.1.4.2 Gretel Rose Cannon (1994-
1.1.8.1.4.3 Grace Mathilda Cannon (1994-
1.1.8.1.4.4 Elspeth Florence Cannon (2001-

1.1.8.2 David Ian Darling (1925 – 2012)
Born: 26 August 1925.
Died: 12 April 2012
m: 1955, Joan MacMillan (1927-). Three children.

1.1.8.2.1 Anthony Darling (1956-
m: Marina Santini. Two children.
1.1.8.2.1.1 Roderick Darling (1990-
1.1.8.2.1.2 Luciana Darling (1994-

1.1.8.2.2 Annabel Darling (1959-
m: James Montgomery. Four children.
1.1.8.2.2.1 Ian James Montgomery (1990-
1.1.8.2.2.2 Charles Richard Montgomery (1992-
1.1.8.2.2.3 Skye Annabel Montgomery (1994-
1.1.8.2.2.4 Lachlan David Montgomery (1997-

1.1.8.2.3 Ian Darling (1962-
m: Alexandra Jane Brodie (1965-). Three daughters.
1.1.8.2.3.1 Adelaide Brodie Darling (1995-
1.1.8.2.3.2 Emma Georgia Brodie Darling (1997-
1.1.8.2.3.3 Sophie Brodie Darling (2000-

Appendix II

John Darling senior

Born in Edinburgh (1831) and educated at the George Heriot School until his father died, he was from 11 years of age employed by several printers and type founders. In 1854, he decided to emigrate to South Australia with his wife (Isabella) and sons (John and Robert) following several of his friends including Alexander Dowie and Joseph Ferguson who had emigrated in earlier years.

They sailed from Leith on the morning of 25 October 1854 and, after a journey lasting 151 days, dropped anchor and came ashore on sailors' backs at Semaphore beach near Adelaide. Four days later he was employed at 36 shillings a week unpacking crockery, but as business was poor, he was discharged.

He then worked for a Mr Robert Birrell at 50 shillings a week and after a month was left in full management of the business while his employer took a holiday. Birrell was a baker who had all the Government contracts and had to deliver 1750 loaves of bread every day. It was there that John Darling began to appreciate the value of flour. Also, at about this time, he established a general store in Adelaide which his wife managed.

A few months after leaving that position, a fellow member of the old Freeman Street Congregational Church offered him a position at 45 shillings a week as storeman with Giles & Smith where he learnt the wheat trade and managed the steam and wind mills for five years. After resigning from Giles & Smith, he took over the management of Bowen's wheat and grain stores, remained there for a few years, then started his own business as a grain and flour merchant.

Despite a slow start, and keen competition from other traders in the industry, John Darling used his Scottish shrewdness and commercial knowledge to acquire a substantial market share. Profits steadily increased, and export trade grew to such proportions that Australian wheat and flour became well known throughout the world. The foundations of the Darling family fortune were laid.

Many years later, in a lecture to the Caledonian Society in Adelaide, he stated, "I had carried grain and flour on my back for 12 years. I have since then carried grain and flour on my brain for over 35 years."

John Darling's parliamentary career lasted more than 25 years despite a few breaks. He represented the districts of West Adelaide, Yatala, and Stanley, in the House of Assembly, and the Northern District in the Legislative Council. In both chambers he was respected for his sound judgment, solid principles and keen awareness of community needs. He served on various Select Committees and Royal Commissions, but business commitments prevented him from taking official positions. However, for six months he was Commissioner of Public Works in the Ministry of Sir John Downer.

At about this time he travelled to America to visit his brother in New York, meet Brigham Young in Salt Lake City and see Chicago in ruins after the great fire of October 1871. His brother went with him to Scotland where he returned to the old foundry which he had left 17 years before. Standing at their same work places were many of his old mates, doing the same work, yet with type now being cast by machinery instead of hand moulds.

Another reason for the journey was to secure export contracts with buyers in Great Britain and Ireland, the colonies, France, Spain and several Mediterranean countries. On his return to Adelaide in 1872, he took his eldest son John into partnership, changed the firm's name to John Darling & Son and subsequently the entire business passed into his son's capable hands.

By 1890, the firm had built extensive interests in flour milling, trading and shipping with a large London office managed by his son Charles.

Throughout his life in Adelaide, John Darling commanded profound respect and appreciation for generous philanthropy. He was elected 'Chief' of the Caledonian Society which he had supported for many years and was active in establishing the Adelaide Oval where his son Joe Darling launched an outstanding cricket career.

Following retirement from business in 1897, he lived in Melbourne for several years before returning to Adelaide and his residence at Norwood. He died there on 10 April 1905 from heart failure leaving a widow, seven sons and one daughter. He was buried in the family vault at Payneham Cemetery.

Appendix III

John Darling junior

After arriving in Adelaide on the barque "Achilles" in 1855 with his parents and younger brother Robert, he received his education at Pulteney Street (now Grammar) School, entered his father's business in 1866 and was taken into partnership in 1872 of John Darling & Son. A few years later he became widely known as 'The Wheat King'.

Managing the firm alongside his father, it grew rapidly by acquisitions while its export trade became the most extensive in Australasia. The Darling Company grain and general merchants owned and operated grain mills and shipping in South Australia, NSW, Victoria, Tasmania and London. They also introduced a new industry to South Australia by erecting at Gawler a factory for the compression of fodder and many thousands of tons were shipped annually around Australia and overseas.

John Darling jnr

Two years after the discovery of the 'line of lode' at Broken Hill in 1883, the original syndicate of seven men decided to float a company by issuing parcels of 500 shares to buyers in Adelaide, Melbourne, Sydney and Silverton. John Darling was one of those buyers and as a result became owner of 25% of the Broken Hill Proprietary Company. He became a director in 1892 and was chairman of directors from 1907 to 1914. This created the tradition of a 'Darling Seat' on the BHP board which was occupied by members of the Darling family continuously until 1986.

Also, he was President of Employers Union SA, Shipowners Association SA, the Chamber of Commerce, Director of Port Adelaide Dock Co, Great Boulder Mining Co, Burra Burra Mining Co, The National Mutual Life Assurance and the Wallaroo Phosphate Works.

In 1896 he was elected Member for East Torrens, and later Torrens, in the House of Assembly until 1905. He served his party (the Australasian National League) as 11th Leader of the Opposition from 1902 to 1904. His wisdom, business knowledge and industrial experience were of immense value to the South Australian Parliament and, although in opposition, co-operated with the Government in their initiatives when he believed them to be in the best interests of the people.

John Darling junior inherited many of his father's characteristics and those of his Scottish ancestry. He was an important member of the Caledonian Society, of which he was Chief in 1904, and generously supported many charitable causes. Through his official positions in connection with the Flinders Street Baptist Church, and as Governor of the St Peters Union Parliament, he encouraged young people to take intelligent interest in all levels of politics.

At the age of 62 he died suddenly at a private hospital in Melbourne after arriving that morning to chair a BHP board meeting. His death was certified as heart failure and his body was sent to Adelaide for burial at Payneham Cemetery.

He left a widow, Jessie (eldest daughter of Alexander Dowie), three sons (Harold, Leonard and Norman) and three daughters (Florence, Gertrude and Grace).

Appendix IV

Harold Darling

The son of John Darling junior, Harold was educated at Prince Alfred College in Adelaide and joined the family's milling and grain business in 1903 at the age of 18. When his father died in 1914, Harold became principal of John Darling & Son, moved the head office to Melbourne and made his home there. In the same year, at the outbreak of World War I, he volunteered for military service but agreed to serve on the advisory council of the Australian Wheat Board at the request of Prime Minister Billy Hughes.

In 1914, he joined the board of Broken Hill Proprietary Co. Ltd to fill the vacancy caused by his father's death. Eight years later he was elected chairman, despite being the board's youngest member, and occupied that position until his death in 1950.

He worked closely with Essington Lewis, general manager and later managing director of BHP, and in 1920 they took a world tour visiting many steel works and iron mines in the United States. For the next 30 years, their working relationship strengthened and grew. Harold's understanding of technical details, combined with his financial expertise, enabled him to advise the board of Lewis's projects and bring them to fruition.

Due to trading losses, and a lengthy closure of the steelworks, no dividends were paid between 1921 and 1925. Yet, during those difficult years, BHP expanded into coal mining, built up a shipping fleet and established its first subsidiaries. In 1930, there was a coal stoppage and another year of no dividends, yet by 1935 profitability had returned, the takeover of rival Australian Iron & Steel Ltd had begun, and a record profit was recorded.

Portrait of Harold Darling by William Dargie, 1951. Gift of BHP Billiton in 2003 to the National Portrait Gallery, Canberra.

As a keen observer of Australian and international politics, along with the rearmament programs of Germany and Japan, Harold expressed concern about the defence of Australia and, in particular, the industrial city of Newcastle in New South Wales. He was successful in establishing closer ties between government and business for the building of ships and aircraft which, in 1936, led to the formation of a syndicate to manufacture aircraft. In October that year, he became the first chairman of the Commonwealth Aircraft Corporation.

Although he was doubtful that ship building could be commercially successful in Australia, Harold's concerns about the international situation encouraged him to prepare BHP for ship building at Whyalla in 1939 at the beginning World War II. Progress was rapid, and the first order was received in June 1940 for the corvette *HMAS Whyalla*. Three more corvettes were built for the Australian Navy and launched in 1941, after which BHP began building ships for its own needs.

As chairman of BHP, he was chairman of AIS, Wellington Alluvials, Stewarts & Lloyds, Rylands Bros and BHP By Products. Also, he was director of BHP Collieries, Tubemakers of Australia, Imperial Chemical Industries ANZ and the National Bank.

He strongly believed that only private enterprise could create prosperity and a stable economy. As a private citizen he contributed time, energy and money to conservative politicians, and in 1942 was a founder of the Institute of Public Affairs. At the end of 1944 he voiced alarm at the Labor government's plan to nationalise airways, banks and insurance companies by saying, "we must … face this crowd with an undivided section of the community that is opposed to socialism and chaos".

Harold died on 26 January 1950 of cancer. He was survived by his wife Dorothy (nee Heath), three children Elizabeth, Joan and John.

First Wirraway with some of the first CAC directors—Essington Lewis, L. J. Wackett, H. G. Darling, Sir Colin Fraser

Appendix V

Gordon Darling

Born on 4 March 1921 in a grand house near Hyde Park Gate in London, where his father Leonard represented the family's flour milling and wheat trading business, Gordon later joked that he was born at the No. 74 bus stop. Named after his mother's brother who was killed in World War I, he was educated at two distinguished English public schools, Highfield and Stowe, where he excelled at cricket. At the start of World War II he left for Australia.

He served overseas as a Captain in the AIF from 1941 to 1945 and suffered hearing damage in a poorly pressurised aircraft when flying to join the allied war room for the southern Mediterranean campaign. His wartime experiences included service on the personal staff of Australian commander Syd Rowell before being sent to the Middle East as an intelligence officer.

Following the War, Gordon married Margaret Anderson who had served with distinction in signals intelligence with the WRANS. They had four children and Margaret was honoured for her work in heritage building conservation when she became a Member of the Order of Australia (AM) in 1991.

Margaret Darling (nee Anderson) in WRANS uniform.

In the long tradition of the Darling family, Gordon enjoyed a successful business career as director of John Darling & Son, Australian Iron & Steel, Austral Bakeries, Rheem Australia and Koitaki Ltd. Due to his hearing impairment, he retired from the BHP board in 1986 after 32 years as occupant of the hereditary 'Darling Seat'. During that time, he had seen it develop into a major conglomerate with mining, mineral processing and manufacturing activities worldwide.

As one of Australia's most significant philanthropists, he greatly influenced the development of some of the country's important artistic institutions. He was the first chairman of the National Gallery of Australia from 1982 to 1986 and, with his second wife Marilyn, inspired the creation of the National Portrait Gallery. Among the earliest acquisitions of the NPG were gifts from Gordon Darling, who accepted the inaugural Board's invitation to become the Founding Patron of the Gallery in 1998. Since then he has enabled the acquisition of many key works for the collection, and his support carried the Gallery to the opening of its new, dedicated home in December 2008.

Gordon and Margaret's youngest child, daughter Clare, fondly remembers her father's passion for art, travel, cricket and farming which he shared with her and her siblings. She also remembers his willingness to empower women and encourage them to take positions of responsibility and influence.

At the age of 89, Gordon had a Cochlear 'bionic ear' implant which restored his hearing and enabled him to converse freely for the remaining years of his life. He died at 94 leaving his wife, four children and ten grandchildren.

Gordon Darling handing over a portrait of Sir Donald Bradman AC to Andrew Sayers, Director of the National Portrait Gallery, in 2008

Appendix VI

David Darling

David Darling

David Darling's father Leonard represented the family's business in London, where, as an active member of the Baltic Exchange, he chartered ships to freight wheat and flour to Britain. He pioneered this trade which was later run by the Australian Wheat Board.

Leonard served in the Royal Artillery during World War I and met Winifred Wilson, a Voluntary Aid Detachment nurse, while both were at the Western Front. Married in 1920, they had two sons: Gordon in London in 1921 and David in Melbourne, 1925.

David spent his childhood in London and boarded at Selwyn House preparatory school at Broadstairs in Kent until the family returned to Australia shortly before the outbreak of World War II. From September 1939 until 1943 he boarded at Geelong Grammar School where became school captain, captain of Perry House and captain of cricket. An outstanding sportsman, he was awarded colours for cricket and Australian football.

On leaving school, headmaster (James Darling, no relation) wrote to his father thanking him for entrusting "so good a boy" who had given him the greatest help he had known from a senior prefect. The headmaster recognised a loyalty and integrity in David which formed the basis of his character. History master and cricket coach, Manning Clark, wrote that he had the "soul of a poet".

David joined the RAAF, was discharged in late 1945 as a leading aircraftman, then spent three years at Brasenose College at Oxford studying philosophy, politics and economics, and playing cricket. Then, through the 1950s, he worked with John Darling & Son, selling flour to bakeries across the Pacific and, in 1955, married Joan Macmillan from Dalby in Queensland. They had three children.

David Darling (seated far right, wearing blazer) in the Geelong Grammar XI, 1941. Cricket coach (and history master) Manning Clark is seated centre.

A gentle, self-effacing man, courteous and correct in manner, he was an achiever and giver who won wide respect and affection. With a reputation as a sound investor and good judge of character, he would only do business with those he thoroughly trusted. He was chairman of the Koitaki/Clayton Robard Investment Group in the 1980s, director of Carlton and United Breweries (1969-84), EZ Industries (1973-82), Elders IXL and Foster's Brewing (1981-92) and Caledonia Investments (1992-2009).

A keen pastoralist, David managed a family property in southern New South Wales with an original and innovative approach. On one occasion he received the district's 'Farmer of the Year' award.

He served on the Council of International House (1966-69), Geelong Grammar School Council (1970-74), was a member of the Old Geelong Grammarians committee (1967-73) and Chairman of the Glamorgan (Toorak Campus) Advisory Committee. Members of his family have been major donors to Geelong Grammar's School for Performing Arts and Creative Education with his son Ian as a driving force. The 800-seat theatre is named The David Darling Playhouse.

David Darling died at his home in Melbourne on 12 April 2012, aged 86. He is survived by his wife Joan, children Anthony, Annabel and Ian and nine grandchildren.

Appendix VI

Stonehenge

On an east facing hillside overlooking extensive farmland, originally swamplands reclaimed by the Page family, Stonehenge is a substantial two-storey Victorian Italianate house about 30km east of Oatlands in the Southern Midlands of Tasmania.

Built of locally quarried sandstone with a Welsh slate roof and a two-storey verandah facing north and east, the property includes several outbuildings and a substantial two-storey stable. The property is permanently registered by the Tasmanian Heritage Council for its cultural significance and ability to demonstrate the evolution of State pastoral and agricultural history.

Stonehenge c.1940.

Samuel Page (born in England in 1810) was an Oatlands publican who launched a coach service in 1847 between Hobart, Oatlands and Launceston. His wife, Grace (nee Harris) was actively involved in running the business until the opening of the Main Line Railway in 1876 which consigned the stage coach to history.

At the time of his death in 1878, Samuel Page owned many large grazing properties in Tasmania. His total stock holding reportedly included 63,000 head of sheep which was the largest ever held by one person in the history of Tasmania. He also bred racehorses and helped to found the Tasmanian Racing Club in Hobart.

The house was designed by prominent Tasmanian architect Henry Hunter and built by Joseph Hawkes during the late 1870s, probably at the request of Samuel and Grace Page's youngest son Sydney Page, who inherited the property in 1883.

In 1884, Sydney Page ran horses on 613 acres and leased the remaining 17,500 acres of pasture to Erskine Parker who grazed about 700 cattle and 12,000 sheep. In later years, Stonehenge became well known for its horses and Parker, a farmer, wool merchant and horse trainer, later supplied horses to the army during the Boer War.

View across grazing pastures (reclaimed swamp lands) from beside the house.
Photograph by Graeme Ryan.

Following the sale of Stonehenge to Erskine Parker in 1888, the acreage was extended to 30,000 and the brothers John and Frederick Roe worked the property in partnership during the 1890s until it was sold, sight unseen, to John Darling snr who gifted it to his son Joe in 1900.

When Joe arrived, the property was seriously run down, and his first task was to eradicate the infestation of rabbits by fencing 10,000 acres. He also introduced subterranean clover which, although a European native and despite vehement condemnation by the Tasmanian Department of Agriculture, became a valuable fodder crop in Australia and elsewhere that revolutionised farming practice and converted many struggling farms into profitable livestock holdings.

Joe Darling was a successful farmer who achieved high wool prices, became a leading member of the Tasmanian Farmers, Stockholders and Orchardists Association as well as a long-term committee member of the Royal Hobart Show Council. In 1920, he purchased Claremont House near Hobart and moved there before being elected as an independent Member of the Legislative Council for Cambridge in 1921.

Dining room at Stonehenge which still contains Joe and Alice's furniture with seating for 14 people at the table. Photograph by Graeme Ryan.

Stonehenge was sold to Walter Rodda and Joe's sons, Gordon and Victor, continued farming an adjoining property, Dalmeny Park.

During the 1920s, Stonehenge changed owners several times and was reclaimed by Joe on behalf of his sons, Victor and Roy, in 1930. They continued to farm the property until it was purchased by James McShane in 1948, passed on to son Robert in 1973, then to his son Eliot in 2013.

Eliot McShane is the current owner and manager of Stonehenge. He, his brother Marcus, and their wives, Felicia and Dianna, are highly respected in local and Tasmanian farming communities and frequently called upon to comment on important issues. The tradition established by Joe Darling and his family is being continued.

Appendix VII

Claremont House

A recent promotional photograph of Claremont House with Mount Wellington far left in the background.

The first known inhabitants of the Claremont area were the Mouheneener people, a band of the South East Aboriginal tribe, who exploited coastal resources down the D'Entrecasteaux Channel and across to Bruny Island. A number of prehistoric middens in Claremont date back 6000 years and it is believed that Aboriginal people occupied the area many thousands of years earlier.

John Pascoe Fawkner, one of the founders of the city of Melbourne, was in 1813 granted 93 acres of land on which Claremont House stands, then offered it for sale in 1819. The *Hobart Town Gazette* of 4 December 1819 described it as:

> That most valuable farm … conveniently situated near the New Road leading to New Norfolk from Hobart Town … in the district of Glenorchy. It consists of 93 acres of land; 5 of which are

cleared and have been in Cultivation. This farm is well worth the Attention of Persons settling in the Colony, being convenient to land and water carriage and near a run of good water.

There is no evidence that Fawkner erected any buildings on the property which was acquired by Henry Bilton in 1826.

Born in England in 1798, Bilton at the age of 27, was sent by his doctor to Tasmania because he was not expected to live. He died many years later, aged 91. During that time, he had been a Magistrate, Councillor and well-respected member of the Glenorchy community.

Bilton lived on the property from the late 1840s, built many structures and, it is understood, named it Claremont after Princess Charlotte's residence in Surrey, England. In the 1848 census it is recorded that he lived in a rendered brick house, with a household of 14 which included three convicts and one ticket-of-leave holder.

It is believed that the original house was a two storey Georgian residence with two rooms on the ground and two rooms above with a central hallway and staircase. The present ground front windows and upstairs doors and frames are from the original fabric of the house. Within the roof cavity, areas of the original shingles remain where they have been roofed over with iron. The external fabric is a rendered struck joint brick to resemble stone.

By 1858, Bilton had increased the land holding of Claremont House to 350 acres, making it one of the most significant and valuable properties in the municipality. Over the next 30 years, this increased to 734 acres.

When Bilton died in 1889, and since he had no children, the property was subdivided and auctioned. *The Mercury* of 16 December 1889 stated:

> One of the most charming spots for a gentleman's residence in and around Hobart, commanding, as it does, a magnificent and extensive view of the River Derwent, from the Elwick Racecourse to Bridgewater, and the hills from Mount Direction to the Dromedary, including the Coign, Constitution Hill and table Mountain in the distance, as also the agricultural districts of Old beach, green Point, Brighton, etc
>
> …all cedar fittings inside, exclusive of ballroom, two kitchens, pantry, storeroom, besides workshops, large barn, six stall stable, hay loft, coach house, meat house, shearing sheds, cowshed, men's hut, etc. there is also a productive garden of about two acres.

At auction, all separate lots of land were bought as one by Francis (Frank) Bond, a bank merchant and Parliamentarian. He owned the property from 1889 until 1897 and his contribution to the evolution of the house included the Italianate tower, the billiard room and the iron gates at the entrance to the driveway.

Albert Flexmore acquired the property from Bond in 1897 and lived at Claremont House from 1899 until he auctioned it, along with many items of furniture, in 1911.

Little is known about Flexmore's ownership and, if any, development of the property. He was a wealthy man who served on the committees of the Tasmanian Racing Club and Royal Agricultural Society. He also entertained the Hobart Hunt Club at Claremont House in 1902.

Flexmore reduced the property to 53 acres by sub-dividing and relinquishing pieces of land including a parcel of land he gave to the Anglican Church for the construction of St Albans Church in Claremont.

Kathleen Brock, at 21 years of age, purchased the property from Flexmore in June 1911 and lived there with her sister Dora until her marriage to Captain Otway Cottrell-Dormer, Aide-de-Camp to Governor Strickland. She introduced several structural changes which included moving the front door and external staircase, enclosing the end verandas and laying a new floor in the drawing room for dancing.

A very popular young woman, from a wealthy family background, Kathleen held many social events at Claremont House. These included afternoon teas, tennis parties and fundraising picnics. A garden party in 1912 raised money for a new church, and a 'Café Chantant' was held in 1916 for the On Active Service Fund and the Seamen's Mission. This latter event attracted over 250 people, including army officers and enlisted men from the nearby Claremont Training Camp, who enjoyed music, singing, dancing, bridge, billiards and supper in a marquee. Kathleen's husband, now a major, was away on active service at the time.

Kathleen Cottrell-Dormer did a great deal of work in the garden. She built a bush house, a shed with wooden slats to allow sunlight on to the camellias, a fountain and a cottage for the chauffeur brought out from England.

The Cottrell-Dormer's marriage was apparently not a happy one, and it appears that when the couple sold much of the property in 1919, Kathleen did not follow her husband to their other home near New Norfolk.

During the years following World War I, the Claremont area rapidly developed as a residential suburb due to sub-divisions and sales of blocks for houses, shops, garages, etc. This markedly reduced the land on which Claremont House stood, while the development of the Cadbury-Fry-Pascal chocolate factory after 1921, on a former section of the Claremont property, accelerated the changing nature of the district.

Joe and Alice Darling bought Claremont House, then on 32 acres, in 1919 and did not move in until the following year due to their concern about the influenza epidemic sweeping many populated areas.

The Darlings had a big family, although some of their children had grown up and remained at their Stonehenge property near Oatlands. Generally, they had two or three servants working for them at Claremont House. They made few changes to the house, although they did enclose the right end of the top veranda after a son had fallen from it to the sunroom roof below. They also demolished the stables and used the timber to build a shearing shed at Stonehenge. The coach house was converted to a garage for four to six cars with a pit for mechanical work and a cellar underneath. One of the most significant changes was the connection of electricity and purchase of an electric stove.

Although she did not entertain as often as Kathleen Cottrell-Dormer, Mrs Darling did have monthly meetings at the house when guests would arrive by train. Occasionally there were other functions, such as in 1920 when a wedding breakfast was held for friends, and the guests were invited to pick roses from the garden. The house was still a drawcard with its imposing presence and spectacular views. The well-known photographer JW Beattie sometimes came to take panoramic photos from the tower in the 1920s.

Joe and Alice at Claremont House, 1939.

The Red Cross bought Claremont House and the entire 32 acres in November 1940 to establish a convalescent hospital for returned soldiers. This decision was largely due to Lady Clark, wife of the Governor and patron of the Red Cross, who was greatly impressed by the attractive wisteria growing over the veranda. No doubt, convenient access to a railway station on the main line, and its connection with a long succession of distinguished owners, also influenced that decision.

Frederick Rust was put into the former chauffeur's house as caretaker of the property until renovations had been completed and the new hospital opened in 1941. Later he was employed

Norwood at 9 Pascoe Avenue, Claremont, where Joe, Alice and younger members of the family lived from 1940.

there as a gardener and, during the war years, had Italian prisoners of war barracked in a cottage and working for him in the grounds.

About 2000 war veterans were patients from 1941 until 1947, and after the war it became the Lady Clark Rehabilitation Hospital, although it still had 75% of bed places reserved for them. As the only rehabilitation centre operated by the Red Cross in Tasmania, it provided numerous services along with workshops and occupational therapy units.

Work carried out on the building at this time was extensive, with the addition of the rear north wing, dining room extension, sub-division of many of the larger rooms for hospital wards and construction of various ancillary buildings at the rear of the site.

In 1951, the Royal Hobart Hospital took over the property and continued to operate it as Hobart's major rehabilitation centre. Then after 1967, the lower and northern part of the site where the formal gardens and tennis court were located, were re-developed for hospital housing. This development comprised small detached houses arranged around the site and bordering the northern side of the entry drive.

The years of the Lady Clark Convalescent Hospital, and later Rehabilitation Hospital, saw the most profound changes to Claremont House in its history.

In 1980, the property became an Adult Education Centre, and with little funding for maintenance, it deteriorated rapidly. The rear of the property was used for the Claremont Education Park, a secondary college, which opened in 1989. By the early 1990s, the building was in crisis. The Claremont House Association was formed and they, with local volunteers, worked selflessly to save the property. A conservation plan was commissioned from an architect and professional advice on the gardens obtained. On 12 December 1995, Claremont House was listed by the National Trust and placed on the Register of National Estates.

A program was organised with unemployed youth to address some of the most urgent problems and they repainted some rooms and demolished some of the more recent buildings and additions at the rear. During its 16 years occupancy, Adult Education installed a fire alarm system and hose reels in the buildings, but apart from that only undertook minor works.

In 1996, Claremont House was offered for sale with a residential rezoning. It failed to sell at auction but was sold privately the following year. Since then, numerous owners have called Claremont House their home.

The current owner since 2007, Joel Van Sanden, has meticulously restored Claremont House to its former glory and now manages the property as boutique heritage accommodation and restaurant. In addition, tours, functions and events are held there.

Upstairs bedroom suites and the chauffeur's cottage provide premier rooms for guests along with dining, billiards and other areas for socialising and entertaining downstairs. The five acres on which Claremont House stands are being restored to create a Victorian/Edwardian botanic setting with a blend of formal, informal and productive gardens.

BIBLIOGRAPHY

Archival

<u>Prince Alfred College</u>
Photograph of 1885 Prince Alfred College cricket team, series 428
Prince Alfred College Chronicle 1884, 1885, 1886, 1887
Prince Alfred College Examinations 1884, 1885, 1886, 1887

<u>State Records</u>
GRS/12046 Admission registers – Norwood Primary School 1877 to present.

<u>University of Adelaide</u>
Correspondence with Sue Coppin, Collection Archivist, University Archives and Recordkeeping, 17 April 2018.
Roseworthy Agricultural College Annual Report, 1891
Roseworthy Agricultural College Student Register
Series 1047 – Roseworthy Agricultural College Examination Papers 1887-88

Books, reports, articles

Association of Cricket Statisticians and Historians, *First-Class Cricket Matches 1896, 1899.*

Australian Dictionary of Biography for entries on Joe Darling, John Darling, Sir Robert Cosgrove and Thomas D'Alton.

Barker, Ralph and Rosenwater, Irving 1969, *Test Cricket England v Australia*, William Heinemann, London.

Cashman, Richard et al (eds) 1996, *The Oxford Companion to Australian Cricket*, Oxford University Press, Melbourne.

Claremont House Conservation Plan. Paul Davies Pty Ltd, Heritage Consultant, 628 Darling Street, Rozelle.

Darling, DK 1970, *Test Tussles On and Off the Field*, DK Darling, Hobart.

Downer, Sidney 1972, *100 Not Out: A Century of Cricket on the Adelaide Oval*, Rigby, Adelaide.

Dundas, Ross in association with Pollard, Jack 1990, *Highest, Most and Best: Australian Cricket Statistics 1850-1990*, Angus & Robertson, Sydney.

Frindall, Bill 1979, *The Wisden Book of Test Cricket 1876-77 to 1977-78*, Queen Anne Press, London.

Gibbs, Ron 1984, *A History of Prince Alfred College*, Prince Alfred College, Adelaide.

Giffen, George 1898, *With Bat and Ball*, Ward, Lock and Co., London.

Green, Benny (ed.) 1984, *Wisden Anthology 1900-1940*, Guild Publishing, London.

Haigh, Gideon 2001, *The Big Ship, Warwick Armstrong and the Making of Modern Cricket*, Text Publishing, Melbourne.

Haigh, Gideon 2016, *Stroke of Genius: Victor Trumper and the shot that changed cricket*, Penguin, Melbourne.

Harte, Chris 1987, *The History of the Sheffield Shield*, Allen and Unwin Australia, Sydney.

Harte, Chris c1990, *SACA: The History of the South Australian Cricket Association*, South Australian Cricket Association, Adelaide.

Harte, Chris 1993, *A History of Australian Cricket*, Andre Deutsch, London.

Herbert, Peter and Sando, Geoff 2003, *Parade to Paradise: 100 seasons of East Torrens cricket and cricketers 1897-98 to 2002-93*, East Torrens District Cricket Club, Adelaide.

James, Alf, 'Giffen's Mission to the "Golden West" in 1897, *Between Wickets* Vol.7 Summer 2016/Winter 2017, pp. 92-101.

Iredale, Frank 1920, *33 Years of Cricket*, Beatty, Richardson & Co., Sydney.

Kelly, Kym, *Mundoora Centenary 1874-1974*, Mundoora Centenary Committee, 1974.

Kensington and Norwood Heritage Review 1995, conducted by Mark Butcher Architects, 48 Elizabeth Street, Norwood.

Lysikatos, John 2005, *108 not out: The history of the Sturt Cricket Club*, Sturt Cricket Club, Hawthorn, South Australia.

Moyes, AG 'Johnny' 1950, *A Century of Cricketers*, Angus & Robertson, Sydney.

Moyes, AG 'Johnny' 1954, *Australian Batsmen from Charles Bannerman to Neil Harvey*, Angus & Robertson, Sydney.

Pollard, Jack 1982, *Australian Cricket: The Game and the Players*, Hodder & Stoughton/ABC, Sydney.

Pollard, Jack 1992, *The Complete Illustrated History of Australian Cricket*, Pelham Books, Melbourne

Robinson, Ray and Gideon Haigh 1996, *On Top Down Under: Australia's Cricket Captains*, Wakefield Press, 2nd edition, Adelaide.

Sando, Geoff with Whimpress, Bernard 1997, *Grass Roots: 100 Years of Adelaide District Cricket 1897-1997*, South Australian Cricket Association, Adelaide.

Vamplew, Wray (ed.) 1987, *Australia Historical Statistics*, Fairfax, Syme & Weldon Associates, Sydney.

Webster, Ray 1991, *First-Class Cricket in Australia Vol. 1 1850-51 to 1941-42*, Ray Webster, Melbourne.

Whimpress, Bernard (ed.) 2007, *Clem Hill's Reminiscences: The 'Unwritten History of His Test Career 1896-1912*, Association of Cricket Statisticians and Historians, Cardiff.

Whimpress, Bernard 2007, *Ernie Jones: Australia's First Great Fast Bowler*, Association of Cricket Statisticians and Historians, Cardiff.

Whimpress, Bernard 2011, *On Our Selection: An alternative history of Australian Cricket*, Bernard Whimpress, Adelaide.

Whimpress, Bernard and Hart, Nigel 1984, *Adelaide Oval Test Cricket 1884-1984*, South Australian Cricket Association/Wakefield Press, Adelaide.

Whimpress, Bernard and Hart, Nigel 1994, *Test Eleven: Great Ashes Battles*, Wakefield Press, Adelaide.

Wynne-Thomas, Peter 1989, *The Complete History of Cricket Tours at Home and Abroad*, Hamlyn, London.

Newspapers, periodicals, websites

Newspapers sourced via Trove through the National Library
Advertiser (Adelaide), *Age* (Melbourne), *Argus* (Melbourne), *Australian Star* (Sydney), *Australian Worker*, *Australasian* (Melbourne), *Barrier Miner* (Broken Hill), *Bundaberg Mail & Burnett Advertiser*, *Bunyip* (Gawler), *Burra Record*, *Chronicle* (Adelaide), *Daily News* (Perth), *Daily Telegraph* (Sydney), *Evening Journal* (Adelaide), *Evening News* (Sydney), *Evening Star* (Boulder, WA), *Examiner* (Launceston), *Express & Telegraph* (Adelaide), *Herald* (Melbourne), *Inverell Times* (NSW), *Labor Daily* (Hobart), *Mercury* (Hobart), *National Advocate* (Bathurst), *News* (Adelaide), *Northern Argus* (Clare), *Observer* (Adelaide), *Quiz & Lantern* (Adelaide), *Referee* (Sydney), *Register* (Adelaide), *Sporting Globe* (Melbourne), *South Australian Register* (Adelaide), *South Australian Weekly Chronicle* (Adelaide), *Sun* (Sydney), *Sydney Morning Herald*, *The Times* (London), *Western Australian* (Perth), *The World* (Hobart)

Between Wickets (Sydney), *Cricket: A weekly record of the game* (UK), *Cricketer* (UK), *Wisden Cricketers' Almanack* (UK).

cricinfo.com, cricketarchive.com, Wikipedia-referendums in Australia

Index

Photos highlighted in **Bold**

A
Abel, Bobby, 44, 92
Achilles (ship), 3
Adelaide
  places, Light Square, 4
  streets
    Beulah Road, 8
    Gawler Place, **42**, 44
    Glen Osmond Road, 4
    Grenfell Street, **42**
    Kent Terrace (now Fullarton Road), 12
    Osmond Terrace, Norwood, 8
    Rundle Street, 4
  suburbs, Glen Osmond, 3
Adelaide and Suburban Football Association (ASFA), 157
Adelaide Cricket Club 1896-97, **41**
Adelaide Football Club, 10, 157, **159**
  premiership win, **158**
Adelaide *News*, 36
Adelaide Oval, 10, 23, 31, 42, 55, 73, 81, 98, 99, 115, 119, 157, 158, 182
  parliamentary Bill, 4
Adelaide Railway Station, 61
Adelaide Town Hall, 77
Advertiser, 23
Alberton Oval, 73, 75, 157
Alfred, Duke of Edinburgh, 7
Andrew, George, 18
Anglican Pulteney Grammar School, 7
Argall, Philip, 152, **152**
Armstrong, Warwick, 1
  Big Six member, 139
  as a cricketer, 79, 85, **85**, 87, 94, 96, 100, 101, 105, 108, 110, 113, 140, 142, 147, 148, 185
Australasian, 78, 147
Australasian Cricket Council (ACC), 137
Australia Hotel, 103
Australian Board of Control, 137–147, 152, 177
Australian Bushmen's Contingent, arranged cricket match for, 74–75
Australian Country Party, 171
Australian Cricket Council (ACC), 54, 137
Australian cricket team 1896, **33**, **39**
Australian cricket team 1899, **61**
Australian cricket team 1905, **105**
Australian Dictionary of Biography, 1
Australian Football Carnival, 164
Australian Post-War Reconstruction and Democratic Rights Convention, 178
Australian Rules Football, 23, 157
Australian team at Crystal Palace, **104**
Australian tour brochure, **32**
Australian Workers Union, 170
Avenue Cricket Club, 14
Ayres (sporting goods company), 45

B
Badcock, Jack, 149
Badger, Mr, 18
Bailey, Abe, 96
Bailey, Bert, 98
Bailey, R, **102**
Baker, H S, 175
Bannerman, Alex, 177
Bannerman, C, 28
Bardsley, Warren, 147
Barlow, Dick, 65–66
Barnes, Sydney, 79–80, 118
Bartlett, Robert, article in *Oxford Companion of Australian Cricket*, 1
Barton, King, 38
Bat and Ball, 38
Bean, Ernest, 142, 146, 149
Beldam, George, 108, 111
Big Six, 139
Blackham, Jack, 24, 26
Blackie, Don, 149
Bleechmore, A J, **54**
Blinman, Harry, **23**, **156**
Blythe, Colin, 79, 80, 81
Bodyline, 153
Bonnor, George, 64, 100
Bosanquet, Mr, 108, 109
Boucaut, James, 115
Bowen, R G, **41**
Bradman, Don, 1, 143, 149, 182, 182–183
  dispute over earnings, 144
  The Invincibles Team, 94
Bramall Lane, 89
Braund, G C, **9**
Braund, Len, 87
  as a cricketer, 69, 79, 81, 91, 92, 94, 118
Break O'Day club, 121, **122**
Brearley, Mr, 110
Bricknell's Cafe, 103, **103**
Briggs, Johnny, 24, 27, 29, 47, 48, 50, 68, 119, 182
Brisbane Courier, 58
Bristol Hotel, 62
Brockwell, William, 24, 29, 44
Brown, Johnny, 29, **29**, 67
Brownwell, A, 123
Bruce, William, **28**, 29–30, 33
Buchanan, W, **102**
Bundaberg Mail and Burnett Advertiser, 52
Burra Football Club, 161
Burra Oval, 16

C
Caledonian Society, 6
Cambridge University, 66, 86, 88, 109
Canberra Times, 176
Cardus, Neville, 90
Carlton Cricket Club, 102
Carter, Hanson, 85, **85**
  Big Six member, 139

Castine, E W, **9**
Chapman, Percy, 153
Chapple, Frederic, **9**
    3rd Headmaster of Prince Alfred College, 7
    his educational philosophies, 7
    his support of sport, 7
Checkett, Charles, 30, 31, 117
Cheltenham College Ground, 113
Chinner, H, **102**
Chipperfield, Arthur, 149
Church of England, 7
City Mission Hall, founding of, 4
Claremont House, 120, 167, **168**
    cricket matches, 121
Clark, E W, 38
Clarke, G R C, 78
Clarke, William, 65
Claxton, Norrie, 116, 117
Colliver, F, **54**
Colliver, W, 181
Commonwealth Government Powers Bill, 1942-43, 174, 176
Concilliation and Arbitration Act, 171
Coningham, Arthur, 21
Cook, A E, **9**
Cornelian Bay Cemetery Hobart, 181
Cosgrove, Robert (Premier of Tasmania), 175, 179
Cotter, Albert (Tibby), **106**
    Big Six member, 139
    as a cricketer, 100, 101, 111, 113, 128, 132, 148
court case, Darling v Watt, 18
Crawford, Jack, 118
Creswell, John, 81, 137, **137**, **156**
cricket matches
    at Crystal Palace, 87
    at Edgbaston, 87
    at Gawler, 14
    at Headlingley, 109
    at Lord's, 35, 44, 88, 113
    at Old Trafford, Manchester, 36, 40, 44, 68, 90, 113, 185
    at The Oval, 37, 48, 68, 70, 108, 111, 148
    at Roseworthy, 14
    at Trent Bridge, 65, 87
    Triangular Test Series, 139
Cricket Teams
    Adelaide and Suburban Association, 98
    Adelaide Young Men, 14–15
    Australian Eleven, 10, 54, 59, 62, 74–75, 78, **88**, 98, 132, 137, 145, 185
    Bananalanders, 57
    Barunga Braves, 17
    C J Thornton's Eleven, 65
    Coolgardie Eighteen, 43
    Eastern Districts Twenty Two, 43
    England Eleven, 90, 113
    Fifteen of Australia, 10
    Fremantle Eighteen, 43
    Gentlemen of England, 107–108
    Kalgoorlie and District Eighteen, 43
    Kent Town, 16
    Lord Sheffield's Eleven, 34
    MacLaren's Eleven, 78
    Middlesex, 16
    New South Wales Graziers, 122
    New Town District Club, 123
    New Zealand Elevens, 105
    Nottinghamshire, 107
    Prospect, 16
    The Rest, 74
    Rest of Australia, 132, 185
    South Australian Fourteen, 10
    South Hobart, 123
    South Suburban, 16
    South United, 16
    Surrey, 107
    Tasmanian Pastoralists, **122**
    Thornton's Eleven, 70
    W G Grace's Eleven, 68
    Western Australian Twenty Two, 43
    Wheatfielders, 57
Cricketer, The, 50
Crockett, Bob, 152, **152**
Crouch, G S, 143
Crystal Palace, 64, 68, 108, 127
Crystal Palace Exhibition, 115
Curtin, John, 174

D

Dalmeney Park Estate, 116
    purchase of, 115
D'Alton, Thomas, 179
Daly. 'Bos', 163, 164
Daly. 'Bunny', 163, 164
Darling, Alice Minna Blanche Francis (1873-1953), 86, 181
    marriage, 19
    mother of 15 children, 165
    purchase of Claremont House, 120
Darling, Charles (1867), 185
    his attendance at Prince Alfred College, 8
Darling, Douglas Keith, 1, 27, 123, 165, 167, 171, 175, 177, 181
    Test Tustles On and Off the Field, 182
Darling, Eileen Isabella, 166
Darling, Ernest Sydney
    died in infancy, 165–166
    headstone, **166**
Darling, Ethel Kathleen
    died in infancy, 166
    headstone, **166**
Darling, Frank (1875), **41**
    his attendance at Prince Alfred College, 8
Darling, George (1864), his attendance at Prince Alfred College, 8
Darling, Gordon, became manager of Stonehenge, 120
Darling, Gordon Joseph Francis, 166, 181
Darling, Isabella (née Ferguson) (1834-1907), 3
Darling, James (1857)
    attended Anglican Pulteney Grammar School, 7
    his attendance at Prince Alfred College, 8
Darling, John, attended Anglican

Pulteney Grammar School, 7
Darling, John I (1831-1905), 3, **25**, 52
  as a politician, 169
  became a contractor, 4
  death, 12, 31, 107
  known as the 'Grain King,' 4
  as a member and chief of the Caledonian Society, 6
  as a Member of Parliament, 5
  a philanthropist, **4**
  as a poet, *A plea for a foundling hospital*, 5–6
  as a politician, 169
  purchase of land, 13
  religion, 4–5
  religious affiliations, 5
  served as Commissioner of Public Works, 4
  served in South Australian Parliament, 4
  worked as a deacon, 4
Darling, Joseph "Joe" (1870-1946), 175, 177, **180**, 182–183, 186
  academic achievements, account, 11–12
  attended Norwood Model School, 7
  birth, 3, 4
  campaigned for players' rights, 138
  cartoon, **60**, **100**
  court case, accused of slander, 18
  as a cricket selector, 147
  as a cricketer, 1, **9**, 14, 21, **23**, 25–26, 28, **28**, 29, 35–47, **35**, **41**, 49–52, **50**, 52, **54**, 55–60, **57**, 62, 64, 65, **66**, 67–68, 70–71, **71**, 73, 78–83, **84**, 85, **85**, **87**, 88, **89**, 90–91, 93, 94, **94**, **96**, 97, **98**, 100–103, **101**, **102**, **107**, 108–109, **108**, 109, **112**, 113–114, **114**, 116, 118, 121, **122**, 123, **125**, **128**, 139, **156**
    in Burra, 16
    career ending, 115
    at college, 14
    first century in England, 34
    at Port Broughton, 17
    retirement, 119
    at school, 9–10
  critical of the status of Australian Cricket, 150
  death, 181
  education, 7
  elected as a Member of Parliament, 124
  first appearance in first class cricket, **22**
  First English Tour, 33
  first meeting with WG Grace, 127
  as a footballer, 157
    at school, 10
  his admiration of Syd Gregory, 131
  his attendance at Prince Alfred College, 8
  his interest in cricket and football, 8
  his views on a White Australia, 172
  home, **99**
  as an importer, 98
  letter, 53
  marriage, 19
  as a pastoralist, 1, 165–168
  as a politician, 1, 169, **169**
  purchase of Claremont House, 120
  purchase of Stonehenge, 76
  purchases on board ship, 95
  as a rival captain, **104**
  sketch, **25**
  as a South Australian and Tasmanian delegate on the Australasian Cricket Council (ACC), 137
  South Australian Cricket Debut, 22
  studied at Roseworthy Agricultural College, 14
  supporter of the Big Six, 139
  Wisden's Five Cricketers of the Year, **71**

Darling, Joseph Ronald, 166
Darling, Joyce, 181
Darling, Kathleen, 181
Darling, Lillian Jean, 166
Darling, Phyllis, 166
Darling, Robert (1854), 185
  attended Anglican Pulteney Grammar School, 7
Darling, Ronald, 181
Darling, Roy, 181
Darling, Victor Stafford, 167, 181
Darling House, **11**, 12
Derwent River, Tasmania, 170
Donnan, Harry, 33, 34, 38, 56, 74
Douglas, Johnny, 121, 142
Dowie, Alexander, 3
Drafting Committee of the Constitutional Convention, 174, 175, 177
Duff, Reg, as a cricketer, 79–80, 85, **85**, 87–88, **89**, 90–92, 94, 100, 109–111, 113–114, 151, 185
Dunn & Co, 18
Dunstan, Albert, 175
Durston, Mr, 18

E
Eady, Charles, 33, 85, 124, 175
East Torrens Electorate Cricket Club, 77
East Torrens premiership team 1897-98, **54**
Election pamphlet, **178**
Ellis, Jack, 148
Evan, D G, **9**
Evan, Mostyn, 43, 55, **55**
Evans, A E H, **54**
Evans, Edwin, 10
Evans, R, **54**
Evatt, Herbert V (Attorney-General), 174, 175, **176**, 177
Expres & Telegraph, 185

F
Farewell dinner menu, 1899, **59**
Farmers and Stockowners Association, 169, 171, 173

Fawcett, R W, **9**
Federal Arbitration Court, 171
Ferguson, James, 3
Ferguson, Joseph, 3
Fleetwood-Smith, L O 'Chuck,' 149
Flinders Street Baptist Church, 4
Football teams
   Adelaide, SAFA premiership win, 157
   ASFA Twent-Fours, 157
   ASFA Twenty-Threes, 157
   Carlton, 159
   Gawler, 160
   Gawler Centrals, 160
   Geelong, 159
   Hotham, 157
   North Park, 159
   North Parks, 157
   Norwood, 157
   Port Adelaide, 157, 160
   South Adelaide, 157
   South Ballarat, 159
   South Darling, 163
   South Melbourne, 157
   St Kilda, 159
   Tasmania, 159
Ford, W J, 64
Forestry Department, 179
Fry, A S J, **9**, 10
Fry, Charles, 65, 88, 94, 111

G

Garrett, Tom, 10, 29–30, 33
Gawler Association, 14
Gehrs, Algy, 100
   cartoon, **100**
George V, King, 81
Giffen, George
   account, 129–131
   as a cricketer, 10, 21, **23**, 24–29, 33–35, 37–38, **39**, 40, 43, 44, 46, 51–53, 56–59, **57**, 61–62, 73, 77–78, 124, **129**, 182
   as a footballer, 157
   retirement, 146
Giffen, Walter F, **23**, **102**, 129, 129–130
Gilligan, Arthur, 151
Glenleg Grammar School, 10
Goodfellow, J, **9**
Grace W G
   account, 127–128
   characteristics, 127
   as a cricketer, 34, 36–37, 64, 65, 108, 118, **128**, 129, 130, 151
   health issues, 133
Graham, Harry, 25, 27, **28**, 29, 33–34, 35, 43
Grand Oriental Hotel, 62
Grandsden, Albert, 18
Grayson, Alf, as a footballer, 161
Great Australian Bight, 62
Great Central Railway, 68
Green, Alby, 43
Gregory, Dave, 105, 182
Gregory, Ned (Syd's father), 27
Gregory, Syd
   account, 131–132
   as a cricketer, 25, **26**, 27, **28**, 29, 33, 35–36, 38, 43, 48, 56, 59, 64, 68, 70–71, 73, 78–79, 79, 82, 85–86, **85**, 90–91, 100, 110, 117, 127, **131**, 132, 135, 148, 185
Grimmett, Clarrie, 151
Grimmett, Mr, 148, 149, 150
Gunn, W J, **41**, **54**
Gunn, William J, 65

H

Hack, Fred, 74, **102**, 116
Haldane, H, **23**
Hardstaff, Joe, 118
Harris, Lord, 151
Hay, D F, **41**
Hay, H, **41**, **102**
Hayward, Tom, 44, 48, 70, 79, 81, 82, 108, 110, 111
Hearne, Alec, 69
Hearne, J T (Jack), 35, 38, 47, 49, 65, 68
Heath, P, **9**
Hendren, Patsy, 151
Hendry, Hunter, 148
Herald, 69
Hewer, W, **102**
Hill, Clem
   Big Six member, 139
   cartoon, **100**
   as a cricketer, 29–31, **31**, 33–34, 36, 38, 40, 43–45, 47–49, 51–52, 56, 57–58, 62, **63**, 64, 67–68, 70–71, 75, 78–79, 81–83, **85**, 89, **89**, 91, 93–94, 98, 103, 105, **106**, 108, 110–111, 113, 116–117, 120, **120**, 125, 129, 141, 146–147, 182, 185
   as a footballer, 157
   letter, 53
   Wisden's Five Cricketers of the Year, **71**
Hill, P, **9**
Hill, R J, **41**
Hindmarsh Square Congregational Church, 4
Hines, J N, **41**
Hirst, George, as a cricketer, 48, 67, 87, 88, 93, 94
HMS *China*, 113
Hobart Town Hall, 139, 173
Hobbs, Jack, 148, **148**, 151, 152
Homburg, R, **54**
Hope, John, 172
Hopkins, Bert, 74, 85, **85**, 88, 94, 100
Horan, Tom ('Felix'), 27, 78
Hornby, 'Monkey,' 68
House of Assembly, South Australia, 4, 169
House of Assembly, Tasmania, 175
Hove, Mr, 94
Howell, Bill
   as a cricketer, 41, 59, 62, 64, **64**, **71**, 79, 85, **85**, 87, 88, 89, 100, 101, 124, 147, 151
   purchases on board ship, 95
Hughes, Billy, 174, 175
Hutton, G, **102**
Hutton, P, **102**

I

Independents, 7
Inns of Court Hotel, **68**
International Cricket Conference, 177
Iredale, Frank, as a cricketer, 25, **28**, 33, 36, 38, 39, 46, 47–48, 48, 59, 62, 64, 65, 69, 71, 74, 127
Ironmonger, Bert, 149

J

Jackson, Archie, 144, 149
Jackson, J, as a cricketer, **28**, 34, 44, 70
    as scorer, 28
Jackson, Stanley
    as a cricketer, 34, 44, 65, 70, 87, 89, 91, 92, 93, 94, 97, 108, 109, 110, 151
    as a rival captain, **104**
Jardine, Douglas, 153
Jarvis, A H, **23**, **28**, 52
Jarvis, Fred, **23**, 74
Jennings, Claude, 117
Jessop, Gilbert, 80, 82, 93, **93**, 94, 136
Joe Darling's Cricket and Sports Depot, **42**, 44
John Darling & Son, 14, 185
    also known as Giles & Smith, 4
    also known as RG Bowen's wheat and grain store, 4
    establishment of a Melbourne office, 12
Johns, Alf, 33, 59, 64
Jones, Arthur, 117
Jones, Ernie
    also known as Jonah, 135–136
    as a cricketer, 21–22, **23**, 25, 27, 33, 36, 38, **39**, 40, 41, 43, 45, 47, 52, 56, 57, 64, 67, **67**, 70, **71**, 73, 79, 81, **85**, 89, **89**, 94, 118, 127, 128, 129, 148, 163
    as a footballer, 157
    letter, 53

K

Keating, Senator, 101
Kekwick, Ernie, 73
Kelleway, Charles, 148
Kelly, Jim
    benefit match, 115
    as a cricketer, 33, 36–37, 43, 64, 66, 78, 85–86, **85**, **89**, 100, **114**, 136, 145, **145**
Kennington Oval, 93
Kilner, Roy, 151
Kippax, Mr, 143, 149
Kirby, Justice, 179

L

Labor Daily, 173
Lancaster Park, 105
Lang, Jack
    Lang plan, 173
    NSW Premier, 173
Larwood, Harold, 148, 153
Larwood, Mr, 135–136
Launceston Courier, 153
Launceston Examiner, 178
Laver, Frank, 59, 64, 66, 79, 98, 100, 113, **114**, 142, **142**
Leak, P, **102**
Legislative Council, South Australia, 4, 169
Legislative Council, Tasmania, 171, 173, 175, 176, 177
    Cambridge district, 169
    Public Service Bill, 172
Legislative Council, Western Australia, 175
Life, 36
Lilley, Mr, 92, 94
Lipscombe, J T, 55
Llewellyn, Charles, 96
Lockwood, William, 24, 69, 87, 90, 91, 92, 94
Lohmann, George, 35
Love, Hammy, 148
Lowrie, William (Professor), principal of Roseworthy Agricultural College, 14
Lyons, Jack J, as a cricketer, 10, 21–22, **23**, 25–26, 42–43, 52–53, **54**, 56, 64, 73, 77, 100, 151
Lyons, Joe (Premier of Tasmania), 124, 168, 173

M

McAlister, Peter, 143
McDonald, Ted, 148
McDonnell, Percy, 107
McElhone, William, 138, **138**, 139, 142, 146
McGann, Terrence, 21
McKechnie, A, **41**
McKenzie, Aleck, 163
Mackenzie, Alex, 74
McKibbin, Tom, 29, 33, 41, 43
MacLaren, Archie, as a cricketer, 45, 46, 47, **47**, 48, 49, 50, 51, 77, 79, 80, 81, 82, 83, 89, 92, 94, 97, 108, 135, 141
McLeod, Bob, 100
McLeod, Charles, as a cricketer, 25–26, **28**, 46–49, 70–71, **71**, 78–79, 81, 100, 109
Madden, K, 181
Magarey Medal, 43
Mailer, R, 143
Manauka, 102
Marsh, Jack, 83
Mary, Queen, 81
Marylebone Cricket Club (MCC), 35, 66, 71, 109, 137, 141, 143, 153
Mason, Jack, 34
Massie, Hugh, 64, 100
Melbourne Cricket Club, 45, 53, 55, 61, 77, 137, 140, 141, 143, 168
    delegates to Australian Board of Control, 142
Melbourne Cricket Ground (MCG), 22, 41, 57, 78, 100, 125, 159, 161, 185
Melbourne Cup, 45
Menzies, Robert, Attorney-General, 168
Mercury, 76, 170

Metropolitan Cricket Association, 14
Mildren, H, 18
Monfries, Elliot, *Not Test Cricket*, 21
Moody, Clarence, 51
Moore, 45
Moore, Robert, 18
Moses, Henry, 21, **28**
Moyes, Johnny, *A Century of Cricketers*, 182
Mundoora Centenary History, 13
Mundoora Football Club, **163**
Murdoch, William, 21, 48
Musgrove, Harry, team manager, 33

N
National Party *see* Australian Country Party
Neill, R G, **41**
New South Wales Cricket Association (NSWCA), 75, 77, 103, 138, 140, 141, 143, 147
    delegates to Australian Board of Control, 142
New South Wales Patriotic Funds for the Boer War, arranged cricket match for, 74
New Town B Grade Team, **124**
New Town District Club, 122
Newland, Philip M, **54**, 100
    cartoon, **100**
Noble, Monty, 185
    as a cricketer, 41, 47–48, 56, 64–65, 68, 70–71, 71, **71**, 80, 85, **85**, 87, 88, 90, 93–94, **96**, 100–103, **106**, 107–108, 113, **114**, 129–131, 140, **140**, 147, 151
    Wisden's Five Cricketers of the Year, **71**
North Adelaide (Cricket Club), 16
Northampton Herald, 182
Northern Argus, 17
Northern Extension Railway, opening, 3
Norwood Baptist College, 5
Norwood Football Club, 10, 19, 161
    Premiership team, **162**
Norwood Model School, 7
Norwood Oval, 103
Norwood Town Hall, 77

O
Observer, 44, 161
O'Donoghue, P, **41**
Ogilvie, Albert, 173
Old Wanderer's Ground, 96
O'Reilly, Mr, 149, 168
Orient, 43
Ormuz, 61, 62, **62**
Oxenham, Rox, 149
Oxford Companion of Australian Cricket, The, 1
Oxford University, 87

P
Page, Earle, 173
Palmer, George, 10
Palmer, O, 18
Parkin, G T, **23**
Parliament House, Hobart, **171**
Parliamentary Standing Committee on Public Works, 174
Parr, George, 65
Peel, Bobby, 24, 27, 29, 38
    as a left-arm spinner, 25
Percy, Mr, 38
Perth *Morning Herald*, 106
Peters, E A, **54**
    as a footballer, 161
Pettit, A W, **41**
Phillips, Jim, 44, 47, 152
Playford, Thomas, 175
Poidevin, Leslie, 78, 86
Ponsford, Bill, 149, 151
Pope, Rowley, 86
Port Adelaide Football Club, establishment of, 3
Port Said 1905, **114**
Post and Telegraph Department, 146
Pougher, Dick, 35
Presbyterianism, 5
Prince Alfred College, 7, **8**, 10, 14, 157, 182
    cricket match, 73, 119
    cricket matches, with schools, clubs and community groups, 8–9
    cricket team, **9**
Prince Alfred College Chronicle, 9
Prince Alfred College Old Collegians Association, 103
Pye, Leslie, 74

Q
Quaife, Billy, 81
Quakers, 5
Queensland Cricket Association, delegates to Australian Board of Control, 142
Quiz and Lantern, 45

R
Ranjitsinhji, K S, as a cricketer, 34, 37, 44, 46, 48, 51, 65–66, 88, 89, 92, 94, 97, 134–135, **134**
Ransford, Vernon, 140, 147
    Big Six member, 139
Reedman, Jack C
    as a cricketer, 21, **23**, 25, 27, 74, 100, 162
    as a footballer, 157
Referee, **29**, 74, 79, 100, 120
Register, 97, 146
Rhodes, Mr, 87, 88, 90, 91, 93, 94, 110
Richardson, Arthur, 148
Richardson, Tom
    as a cricketer, 24, 27, 29–30, 35, 37, 45, 47, 48, 49–50, 51, **51**, 65, 69
    as a fast bowler, 25
Rischbieth, H W, **9**
Robinson, Ray, 68
Rofe, P, **102**
Roseworthy Agricultural College, **15**, 160
    college cricket teams, 14
    student register, **16**

Rosman, A V H, **41**
Royal Hobart Show Council, 173
Ryder, Jack, 148, 149

S
Sands & McDougall, 98
Saunders, Jack, as a cricketer, 83, **85**, 88, 92, 93, 94, 96, 102, 186
Scotland, cities, Edinburgh, 3
Scrymgour, Bernard V, **41**, 55
shearer's strike, 170
Sheffield Park, 34, 127
Sheffield Shield, 41, 55, 56, 74, 80, 132, 182
    matches, 40
    South Australia v New South Wales, 21
    South Australia v Victoria, 24
    South Australia's 1st win, 23
Sheffield Shield winning team, **23**
Sinclair, Jimmy, 96
Slazenger, 45
Smith, Edwin, 23, **54**
Smith, J, **102**
Smith, Sydney Talbot, 77
South Australia
    cities, Adelaide, 1
    places
        Clare, 16
        County of Daly, 13
        Mundoora, 13
South Australian Advertiser, 158
South Australian Cricket Association (SACA), 4, 52, 56, 77, 80, 117, 124, 137, 146, 160
    delegates to Australian Board of Control, 142
    Ground and Finance Committee, 120
South Australian Football Association, premiership, 10
South Australian Football Association (SAFA), 157
South Australian High School, 7
    became the Adelaide Educational Institution, 7

South Australian Register (newspaper), 3, 51, 76
Spofforth, Frederick, 86
Spooner, Mr, 110
Sporting Globe, 153
ss *Cuzco* (steamer), 33
SS *Dunvegan Castle*, 95, 96
SS *Mariposa*, 39, **40**
SS *Marmora*, 106, **107**
SS *Omrah*, 85, **86**
St Peter's College, 14, 157, 182
    also known as the Church of England Collegiate School of St Peter, 7
    cricket match, 73, 119
    religious rivalry, 7
Stag Inn, 4
statistics, 187–189
Stephens, Dick, 163
Stewart, Percy, 163
Stoddart, Andrew, as a cricketer, 24, 26, 29, **29**, 36, 44, 45, 50, 119, 134
Stonehenge (estate), **76**, 97, 116, 119, 165
    account, 76
    rabbit plague, 76
Storer, William, 48
Strangway, Henry (Premier), 13
Street, Geoffrey, Minister for Defence, 168
Stuart, P W, **54**, **102**
Stuckey, Mr, 75
Sturt Cricket Club Premiership team, **102**
Sun, 138
Sutcliffe, Herbert, 148, 151
Sydney Cricket Ground (SCG), 23, 25, 45, 74–75, **78**, 83, 117, 119, 141, 145
    Ladies' and Members' Pavilions, **46**
Sydney Trustees, 53

T
Tasman Sea, 103
Tasmanian Cricket Association (TCA), 122, 123
    delegates to Australian Board of Control, 142
    Ground, 124
Tasmanian Midlands, 76
Tate, 45
Tate, Fred, 90, 91, **91**
Tate, Maurice, 148
Taylor, H L, 136
Taylor, Mr, 179
Test cricket, Ashes series 1901-1902, 1
Thoms, Bob, 152
Thompson, Francis, 66
Thompson, Jim, as a footballer, 161
Thurgood, Albert, 163
Touchell, Dan, 18
Townsend, Charlie, 136
Townsend, Mr, 70
Travers, Joe, 81, 85
Travers, J F, as a footballer, 161
Trott, Albert, 27, 28, **28**
Trott, Harry, as a cricketer, 10, 25, **28**, 29, 33, 35, 36, 37, 38, 43, 59, 98, 131
Trumble, Hugh
    barred from the Victorian Cricket Association, 140
    as a cricketer, 33, 36, 37, 38, 46, 48, 49, 55, 59, 65, 69, **71**, 78, 79, 80, 83, **85**, 86, 89, **89**, 90, 92, 93, 96, 119, 132, 135, 151, 185, 186
Trumper, Victor, 143, 147, 151, 167, 168, 185
    account, 132–133
    amazing century, **91**
    Big Six member, 139
    as a cricketer, 60, **63**, 67, **69**, 71, 73, 74–75, 78, 80, 81, 82, 85, **85**, 87, 88, **89**, 90, 91, 93, 94, **96**, 100, 108, 109, 110, 111, **112**, 113, 117, 120, **132**, 134
Turner, Charles, as a cricketer, 21, 24, 25, **28**, 29–30, 33
Turner, E W, 171–172
Tyldesley, Johnny, as a cricketer,

82, 87, 94, 111

U
Unley Oval, 73, 98, 116

V
Victorian Cricket Association (VCA), 140, 141, 143
   delegates to Australian Board of Control, 142
Victorian Football Association, 157

W
Wainright, Edward, 49, 50
Waldron, Alfred 'Topsy,' 19, **19**
Wall, Tim, 149
Ward, Albert, 29
Wardill, Ben, 85, **85**
   as a cricketer, 61, 62, **62**, 69, 77
Wardill, Thomas, 166
Warner, Pelham, 97
Waste Land Amendments Act 1869, 13
Waterloo Station, 95
Watt, Thomas, 18
Waugh, Steve, 1, 94
Wesleyan Methodists, 7
Western Australian Cricket Association, not admitted to Australian Board of Control, 142
What Ho Joe? (poem), 45
Whinham College, 10, 157
White Australia Policy, 139
Whitridge, William O, **54**, 55, 56
Wilkinson, F M, **9**
Williams, Mr, 73
Wilson, J C, 57
Windsor, Edward, 75
Winnall, C H, **41**
Wisden, 45
Wisden, 108, 113, 177
Wisden Crawford Exceller bats, 44
Wisden's Special Crown cricket balls, 44
Woodfull, Bill, 125, 153
Woods, Charlie, 163

Woolley, Frank, 151
World, The, 171
World War II, 124

Worrall, Jack
   as a cricketer, 49, 50, 51, 55, 71
   as a footballer, 157

Y
Young, H I 'Sailor,' 64, 68

www.ingramcontent.com/pod-product-compliance
Lightning Source LLC
Chambersburg PA
CBHW041410300426
44114CB00028B/2971